developing with web standards

john allsopp

New Riders

1249 Eighth Street, Berkeley, California 94710
An Imprint of Pearson Education

Developing with Web Standards

John Allsopp

New Riders
1249 Eighth Street
Berkeley, CA 94710
510/524-2178
510/524-2221 (fax)

Find us on the Web at: www.newriders.com
To report errors, please send a note to errata@peachpit.com
New Riders is an imprint of Peachpit, a division of Pearson Education
Copyright © 2010 by John Allsopp

Project Editor: Michael J. Nolan
Development Editor: Erin Kissane
Production Editor: Rebecca Winter
Copyeditor: Rose Weisburd
Proofreader: Darren Meiss
Indexer: Rebecca Plunkett
Cover designer: Aren Howell & Mimi Heft
Compositor: Danielle Foster

ISBN 13: 978-0-321-64692-7

ISBN 10:   0-321-64692-4

9 8 7 6 5 4 3 2 1

Printed and bound in the United States of America

Developing with Web Standards *is dedicated to*
Scarlett Bess, and to the one not quite yet here, whom we'll know soon enough.

Thank You

Not only I, but all of us who work with the web, owe Jeffrey Zeldman a huge debt of gratitude for his groundbreaking book, *Designing with Web Standards*, and his tireless efforts to improve the web for developers, designers, and all its users. Over the last several months, I've had many sleepless moments in which I wanted to curse Jeffrey for having suggested that I write this companion to *Designing with Web Standards* but in truth it was very humbling to be asked to write this book, and I hope I have at least gone some way to living up to his recommendation.

To Erin Kissane—who has worked tirelessly and put up with an erratic schedule caused in equal measure by my far too many commitments and a sequence of personal challenges that were almost comic in their number, though serious in nature—thank you. All's well that ends well.

To Brian Suda, who from his fortress in Iceland has been the technical editor of both of my books—and whom I've yet to meet in person—many thanks for spotting my myriad inaccuracies and suggesting many an improvement.

To Sharon Lee, thank you for very generously giving of your expertise to provide this book's beautiful illustrations. They are a vast improvement over anything I might have managed, and their presence has saved our readers' eyes from the crimes against color and form I might have committed in their absence.

To Michael Nolan, who commissioned the book, I hope that it will repay your faith, and that the hair you've torn out over the months of development will grow back.

To the editorial and production crew at New Riders, who spent sleepless nights dealing with page overruns and myriad other causes of frustration, thanks for your professionalism and diligence.

To our editorial interns, Henry Li and Nicole Ramsey, who crunched through a larger number of Word files and import glitches than anyone should have to deal with, and who did it all cheerfully and at high speed, thank you.

To the countless web designers and developers, who share their experience and expertise via blogs, meetups, presentations, articles, and more, thanks for making the web a wonderful place, and a great industry to be in. This is a remarkable profession filled with extraordinary generosity—one I feel genuinely privileged to participate in.

I could easily fill a book naming the contributors to our knowledge and still leave many out. Quite a few are named throughout the book, but many more aren't: thank you to all of you.

And by no means least, to my wife Sara and darling girls ZK and Scarlie, thanks for putting up with yet one more "Daddy's got to finish his book." It's finished now, so hopefully we'll have a bit more time to play.

About John Allsopp, Author

 John Allsopp had been working with, on, for, and against the web since the first half of the 1990s. He's a co-founder of **westciv.com** and developer of Style Master, the web world's most venerable cross-platform CSS development tool. He's also the author of numerous courses, tutorials, tools, resources, and articles for web designers and developers, including the influential *A List Apart* article "The Dao of Web Design."

John is the co-founder of the web conference series Web Directions (**webdirections.org**), which is held in Australia, North America, Japan, and the UK. Most recently of all, John co-founded *Scroll Magazine* (**scrollmagazine.com**), a print, PDF, and online magazine that explores the big ideas around designing and developing for the web. He is the co-chair of a new W3C Incubator Group that focuses on educating the next generation of web professionals (**www.w3.org/2005/Incubator/owea**).

John is the father of two darling daughters, who are the light of his life, with another child on the way. In his copious spare time, he does as much mountain biking, surfing, and snowboarding as all these other activities allow, which is to say, very little.

John's personal site is **johnfallsopp.com**. Follow him on Twitter, **@johnallsopp**.

About Brian Suda, Technical Editor

Brian Suda is an informatician currently residing in Reykjavík, Iceland. He has spent a good portion of each day connected to Internet after discovering it back in the mid-1990s. Most recently, he has been focusing more on the mobile space and future predictions: how smaller devices will augment our every day life and what that means to the way we live, work and are entertained.

Brian is the author of *Using Microformats* (O'Reilly, 2006) and a stack of articles about microformats, the mobile web, and informatics. He was the technical reviewer for John's previous book, *Microformats: Empowering Your Markup for Web 2.0* (friends of ED, 2007).

His own little patch of Internet can be found at **suda.co.uk**, where many of his past projects and crazy ideas reside.

About Sharon Lee, Illustrator

The seed was sown when Sharon Lee found a box of recipe cards in an op-shop. Ham in aspic. Prawn stuffed apples. Fricassee of rabbit. Oh, the culinary delights!

Inspired, she created a food-themed website and named it after one of the recipes. Her criteria for design success? When it made her laugh. Word of the website spread, making others laugh too. Prospective clients, even.

"Are you based in Sydney? Are you available for work?"

And so, in 2001, Richapplefool the business began.

Over the years, she developed her philosophy and practice to create more effective work, fusing branding with user experience architecture and design so clients could speak with true conviction. She calls the result Human Experience Design.

The *Developing with Web Standards* Site

Developing with Web Standards has its own community online at **devwws.com**. Here you can find more resources and addenda, contact John, and much more. Come by and say hi.

Table of Contents

Part I

Foundations

Before You Begin

Like many who have been developing for the web for a decade or more, I came to it by accident—in my case, in 1994. At the time, I was a software developer; now I'm a software developer, web developer, conference organizer, and author. A background in programming isn't as common among people who build websites as you might think. Many web developers—or web designers, front-end engineers, or whatever else you want to call us—came to the web from print and graphic design. As a consequence, web design and development has been heavily influenced by the tools and techniques of these design disciplines, in many ways more even than it's been shaped by the principles of software engineering.

Some influences from print and graphic design have been good for the web; others less so. Many of the techniques developed for web page layout and typography were created in an attempt to mimic the printed page, despite the fact that the web is a screen-based medium, and screens are very different from paper. Websites can adapt to serve users with varying needs (those with better and worse eyesight, for instance), or to the wide range of screen sizes and resolutions—from tiny mobile phone screens to super high resolution 30" monitors—that are now used to access the web. As we'll discuss further in Chapter 2, the changeability at the core of the web is not a bug—it's a feature.

Since the birth of the web, many designers have written and spoken passionately about the web's unique qualities and challenges, and one of those designers is Jeffrey Zeldman. There's no better place to begin a study of web design and development than with Zeldman's *Designing with Web Standards*, to which this book is intended to serve as a companion. In the book you're holding now, I have attempted to complement *Designing with Web Standards* by diving deeply into the development side of building for the web.

Whether you've never looked at the markup for a single web page or have been developing websites for years, I hope you'll find new and useful information and ideas in the pages that follow. To this end, I have both attempted to catalogue in considerable detail the web's core technologies—HTML, CSS, and the DOM—and to explore current best practices in all of these areas, including ways in which we can build websites that are accessible, usable, search-engine friendly, and easy to maintain.

Above all, I hope to convey a sense of the best approaches to solving our industry's genuinely complex problem—how to develop media-rich, interactive websites that are:

- accessible to as many people as possible, including those with disabilities,
- functional—and even attractive—on a broad range of web-enabled devices and in all modern browsers,
- a pleasure to use, and
- easy to maintain over long periods of time and despite changes in technology.

In fifteen years of web development experience, even someone as blockheaded as me acquires a collection of tips, techniques, and "gotchas," as well as far more information about the intricacies of browser bugs than is entirely healthy. I've put as much of this know-how into this book as I could, in the hope that more of you can spend more of your time actually building great websites. More importantly, I've also included as much of the combined knowledge of the web's innovative and generous designers and developers as I could possibly squeeze between these covers. The body of web development knowledge that has been built in the last fifteen years comes almost entirely from my fellow web developers, who have openly shared their lessons, skills, and expertise in a way that is both inspiring and, outside our industry, quite rare. We'll meet some of these designers and developers by name in this book, but hundreds or thousands of other contributors to the web's current state will go sadly unnamed.

Who Is This Book For?

The book is for anyone who wants to learn to build websites. It's also for experienced developers who seek a deeper understanding of the industry's core technologies and practices. Most web developers, myself included, are self-taught. Most new developers still find their way to the profession by teaching themselves, and as a profession, we teach each other: via blogs, books, articles, wikis, workshops, conferences, screencasts, and more.

One characteristic of the self-taught is that our knowledge is often "a mile wide and an inch deep." There are good reasons for this: developing for the web is a highly practical endeavor, and knowledge "a mile deep and an inch wide" is of little use in our field. But it does mean that we often lack an inside-out understanding of even our core technologies: the DOM `element` object, for example, or CSS attribute selectors. And all too often, once we've figured out one way to accomplish a particular task, we tend to use that method over and over again instead of seeking out possibly better alternatives (after all, we've all got deadlines, and if we can solve the problem at all, that's usually good enough).

So this book is also for practicing web developers who want to deepen their understanding of their practice, and of the technologies they use, to go beyond the methods and models they already know.

Finally, this book is for an emerging audience: the generation of web developers, who formally study web development in colleges and universities around the world. If you're one of this new breed of developers, it's my hope that you'll be able to enter the profession with a solid understanding of the web's underlying architecture instead of picking it all up on the fly as first-generation web developers have done. There will, of course, be new technologies and better practices to learn (and entirely new browser bugs to deal with), but with the foundations you'll gain from this book, I hope and trust you'll find it much easier to adapt to developments as they occur.

So Who Isn't This Book For?

This book is not about learning cool tips and tricks or building your first website in an hour. There's a place for these books, but this book is different. It does include plenty of tips and tricks, but its central goal is to help you build a systematic understanding of the practice of web development.

What Will I Get from This Book?

Albert Einstein is quoted as having said "Never memorize what you can look up in books." The quote is probably apocryphal, but the lesson is a useful one. Even if the notoriously absentminded Einstein forgot the exact speed of light, he understood its context so thoroughly that it didn't matter—he could simply look it up if he needed the actual number.

Few web developers, no matter how knowledgeable or proficient they are, remember each aspect of every feature of the DOM, HTML, CSS, and so on. I certainly don't. But if you understand the core technologies of web development—how they work and don't work, why they work the way they do—you can always "look up the speed of light," because you know what to look for. Can't remember how to make a checkbox checked by default? Can't remember whether a list item is a block or inline element? Can't remember whether it's `text-align` or `text-alignment`? That's OK, because you'll know what question to ask and where to go to get the answer. Really skilled developers know a great deal, but just as importantly, they know what they don't know and where to find answers, because they have a systematic understanding of their craft.

Here's what we'll cover:

- Part I—All the core technologies of front-end development—HTML and XHTML, CSS, and the DOM—as well as recommended practices for creating accessible websites
- Part II—"Real world" development: semantic markup, techniques for dealing with browser inconsistencies and bugs, CSS-based page layouts, and the field of CSS frameworks
- Part III—Emerging technologies: cutting-edge tools you can start using today, including HTML5, CSS3, web fonts, SVG, and the Canvas

What You Won't Get from This Book

This book focuses squarely on front-end, or "client-side" development, so if you're looking for information about what happens on the server, this is not the book for you. We do cover a handful of server-related issues with direct bearing on front-end work, but anything more than that is outside the scope of the book. There's also little information that's specifically about mobile web development, though there's little throughout the book that *isn't* relevant to mobile development, either. Similarly, performance-improving techniques get little space; I'd like to have covered them as well, but we had to draw a line somewhere.

Finally, although we cover the DOM in detail, there's very little JavaScript in the chapters that follow—it's a complex enough subject to deserve its own book, several of which I recommend in the Resources section in the back of this book.

Above all, please don't expect that you can read the book and be instantly transformed, Cinderella-style, into a full-fledged development expert (and only partly because I resemble an ugly stepsister more than a fairy godmother). Web development requires a body of knowledge and skills acquired and improved over time and through practice and use. I hope the book will help you build (or shore up) the foundations of your body of knowledge, but it can't replace rolling your sleeves up and diving into the messy realities of CSS, HTML, and the DOM.

How to Use This Book

The book isn't written as a tutorial, so although there are plenty of examples, there aren't any set exercises to follow as you go. It's designed to be read sequentially; each chapter is largely self-contained, but each builds on what has come before. Experienced developers should have little trouble jumping into any section, but if you are new to web development, your best course of action is to read from start to finish. Rather than reading everything and then firing up your text editor, however, try practicing what you learn as you go. For example, during Chapter 3, try developing a simple page as you follow through the chapter, adding each component as I introduce it.

Joining the Community

The book has an accompanying website (**www.devwws.com**) that will include many more resources and links than we could fit into these pages, so make sure you check it out.

Next Up

In Chapter 2, we'll look at some of the most important philosophies and principles of standards-based web development, before diving straight into HTML in Chapter 3.

chapter two

Philosophies and Techniques

The web is a mere 5,000 days old. By comparison, the first 5,000 days of television are almost unrecognizable as what we consider "television" today. Similarly, twenty years after its introduction, cinema was still a novelty. Not so the web, which is now used by roughly a quarter of the world's population. But for all its impact on news, business, politics, and culture, the web is still in its infancy, and we're still only beginning to understand how it works as a medium. On the surface, the fundamental ways in which users interact with websites—via pages, links, and forms—haven't changed much in over a decade. But despite this seeming stasis, a great deal has happened to the practice of web development in these 5,000 days, and much of it has happened in the last five years.

The Browser Wars

In the 1990s, three major browsers—Mosaic, Netscape, and Internet Explorer—alternately dominated the web and essentially dictated what the web's technologies would be. Browser makers created their own extensions to HTML, introducing such features as fonts, colors, tables, and frames, without the involvement of any standardizing organization. As these features were introduced, makers of competing browsers reverse-engineered these new, usually poorly-documented features and countered with their own. As the decade progressed, features like JavaScript and the DOM were implemented and released to the world still without the involvement of any standards body. Web developers, meanwhile, scrambled madly to keep up, and were constantly forced to decide whether a new feature was likely to take off before investing the time required to learn and use it.

The accelerating browser wars threatened to fragment the web into its own kind of tower of Babel, where everyone spoke a different language. Into this chaos stepped the World Wide Web Consortium (W3C), an organization made up of member companies and institutions with significant interests in the web and founded by Tim Berners-Lee, the inventor of the World Wide Web.

The Dawn of Standards

Just as the UN brokers ceasefires and peace agreements, the W3C and other standards bodies and organizations, such as the ISO, the IETF, and Ecma International, brought together competing companies to agree on common web standards, like HTML and CSS, that would underpin the web.

But the standards-based web is not only a consequence of the existence of the W3C and these other bodies. Standards only work if they are adopted.

As key W3C standards emerged and began to be widely implemented in browsers like Netscape 4 and Internet Explorer 4 (often called the "version 4 browsers"), a small but influential group of web developers exemplified by The Web Standards Project (WaSP) used the medium of the web itself to promote the concept of a standards-based web to their fellow developers—and to encourage browser developers to support web standards. The resulting combination of formal standards bodies, grassroots advocacy organizations, and individual *standardistas* ushered in the standards-based web we have today. Successive generations of web browsers embraced standards support, and fewer and fewer innovated outside the context of standards.

Web Standards Today

When we speak of standards today, the key technologies we are referring to are:

- HTML/XHTML from the W3C
- Cascading Style Sheets (CSS) from the W3C
- The Document Object Model (DOM) from the W3C
- JavaScript (also known as "standard EcmaScript") from Ecma International
- Image formats such as PNG and SVG from the W3C, and JPEG from the ISO
- Accessibility technologies like WAI-ARIA from the W3C

But standards-based development doesn't refer only to the use of these technologies. It also involves a philosophy of development, one that emphasizes accessibility and platform independence—an approach that lives up to the name "World Wide Web"— with a central commitment to make web content and applications available to as many people as possible.

Why Should I Care?

But why should we, as developers, care about standards? If a technique works in common browsers, that's good enough, isn't it?

For those old enough to remember CDs, imagine that you bought a CD, and put it in your car stereo, only to have your stereo inform you that the CD was best played in a SONY player—and that as you listened on your non-Sony player, tracks skipped or wouldn't play at all. (Actually, something very like this did happen several years ago, producing a collective shriek of rage from consumers who'd unknowingly purchased the non-standard CDs.) The reasons why a CD will play in any CD player, a DVD in any DVD player, why wrenches and other tools match nuts and bolts of a particular size, why you don't have to buy Ford-branded gas, is because in all these areas, standards enable interoperability. If your gas was only *mostly* compatible with your car, you'd have a problem. And in the years before web standards were established and adopted, we did.

Standards are about interoperability: they mean you can choose which tools you want to use to develop and manage content, and then change those tools if you wish, all without being locked into a particular vendor or proprietary technology. They mean you can choose different browsers depending on your need. They mean no one controls the flow of information around the web.

Standards benefit everyone: content creators, web users, tool developers, browser developers, and web developers alike.

How to Develop for the World Wide Web

The first two words in "World Wide Web" are usually overlooked. But developing for a genuinely *world wide* web means focusing on the interoperability and longevity of the content we develop. Here, I'll outline some of the most important themes to consider when developing for the web.

It Doesn't Have to Look the Same in Every Browser

Not long ago, it was still common to see "best viewed in" badges on websites. These clearly indicated that a site was "optimized" for certain web browsers, and too bad if you were using any other. Too bad if your non-optimal browser was mandated by your IT department. Too bad if you had poor eyesight and needed to use a browser that could help you access content.

These badges are largely a thing of the past, but their underlying philosophy lives on in more subtle ways. Its core principle is that we are designing and developing for *browsers*. We aren't. We are developing for *users*. A user is often a person, but can also be a piece of software, like a search engine. And the philosophy of the "World Wide" web is that we should develop our sites in ways that provide access to as many users as possible. Many developers (and marketing departments) think this means that our sites should, or even must, look the same in every browser. In fact, the opposite is true. By striving to make our sites identical across all browsers, we can quite easily exclude users. By, for example, fixing the width of a column of text to 600px, we may well exclude users of mobile devices.

And, in truth, our sites will never look identical in every browser, no matter how hard we try. Even two different screens attached to the same computer will quite probably display the same page differently. And users can resize their windows, zoom their text, and specify preferred fonts, colors, and so on that override your design choices.

So, if we can't make sites appear the same in every browser, what should we do—just give up?

In a sense, yes. Embrace the web's flexibility as one of its greatest strengths, not as a weakness. After all, the technical term for a browser is a *user agent*—a phrase you'll see quite a bit in this book. As the term reveals, it's the *user* who is intended to control his or her web experience. It's users who should be able to choose how they view and interact with the web. We have to give up the notion that designers and developers are the ones who are in control. We aren't—and we never really were, even in the days of pixel-perfect "cross-browser" site designs.

But what does this mean in practical terms?

Progressive Enhancement

One of the concepts you'll see over and over in this book is *progressive enhancement*. Progressive enhancement is a design practice based on the idea that instead of designing for the least capable browser, or mangling our code to make a site look the same in every browser, we should provide a core set of functionality and information to *all* users, and then progressively enhance the appearance and behavior of the site for users of more capable browsers. It's a very productive development practice. Instead of spending hours working out how to add drop shadows to the borders of an element in every browser, we simply use the standards-based approach (**box-shadow**, detailed in Chapter 13) for browsers that support it and don't even attempt to implement it in browsers that don't. After all, the users of older and less capable browsers won't know what they are missing.

The biggest challenge to progressive enhancement is the belief among developers and clients that websites should look the same in every browser. As a developer, you can simplify your life and dedicate your time to more interesting challenges if you let go of this outdated notion and embrace progressive enhancement. To do so, you may need to convince clients and bosses of the benefits as well, and common ways of doing so include emphasizing lower development costs, more maintainable code, and the fact that most users use only one browser and won't know the difference anyway. Another beautiful thing about this approach is that as your users upgrade browsers, their experience on your site will improve automatically, without you touching even a single line of code.

If you'd like more coaching on selling web standards and modern development practices to clients and bosses, Chapter 3 of the third edition of Jeffrey Zeldman's Designing with Web Standards *(New Riders, 2009) will be an invaluable resource.*

Separation of Content, Presentation, and Behavior

If progressive enhancement is one pillar of modern web development, the separation of your site into three layers—markup, presentation, and behavior—is another. This means that our semantically structured content goes in the markup, the code that defines the content's appearance goes in CSS, and any front-end interactivity goes in the JavaScript. We'll return to this central concept throughout this book.

Web Pages and Web Applications

For most of its history, the web—and thus web development—has emphasized the presentation of textual information supplemented by images and audio/video content. But the web is increasingly becoming an application platform as well, hosting websites that behave more like desktop applications than like "web pages"—Gmail and Google Maps, for example.

The underlying technologies we use to develop web "pages" and web applications (or "web apps") are mostly identical, and technologies like CSS and HTML (with version 5) are being extended to make them more useful in the development of web applications. Throughout this book, we'll look at web development from the perspective of both web pages and web applications.

Once More, with Meaning

It's easy for designers and developers to get caught up in the appearance of a website or web application, but much of the real beauty of the web lies beneath the skin. If we develop our sites only to please the eye and ignore the needs of software, like browsers and search engines, we miss more than half of the users of our work. Software doesn't care about font sizes or colors. It cares about the underlying structure and *meaning* of our markup. Browsers and search engines can't yet be said to really understand English (or Mandarin or

Swahili), but they *can* understand a lot about the nature of our content if we mark it up correctly. When a browser, or search engine, or other piece of software knows that *this* piece of your page is a heading, *that* is an address, *this* is navigation, and so on, that software can do all kinds of interesting things: it can automatically build tables of contents for people who can't see, for example, or detect a location and display it on a map. But to do this, it needs to understand the semantics—the meaning—of your content. Throughout the book we'll focus on how you can make your markup semantically meaningful.

For My Next Trick

Now it's time to start actually developing with web standards. We'll begin in Chapter 3 with the fundamental web standard that started it all: HTML.

chapter three

Markup

In Chapter 2, we considered the important concept of separating structured content from presentation and behavior. In this chapter, we'll look at the content layer and how content can be marked up for the web using HTML. Then, in Chapter 4, we'll look at ways of presenting this content using CSS.

The vast majority of content on the web is marked up using some flavor of "Hypertext Markup Language" or HTML. Understanding what HTML is designed to do—and not to do—will help you write better markup. In this chapter, we'll look at the technical aspects of HTML along with its underlying concepts.

A quick note about terminology: throughout this book, I use the term HTML to apply to both HTML and XHTML unless I'm specifically referring to XHTML. We'll look at the relatively minor syntactical differences between these two markup languages in just a moment.

Why "It Works in Browsers" Isn't Enough

Developers often learn a set of techniques and concepts and then use these tools whenever they can, rather than extending their knowledge as the challenges they face increase in complexity or change in nature, or as the underlying technologies they are using mature. I've certainly been guilty of this, both as a web developer and a software developer. The approach makes a certain sense: "if it's not broken, why fix it?" But just because it's not broken now doesn't mean it's working *well*, or that it won't break in the future. Browser developers work hard to handle as many markup errors as they can, but there's no guarantee they'll always work, or that different browsers will handle a given error in the same way.

Alas, the outdated techniques, invalid markup, and other mistakes that lie under the hood of many professionally developed websites reveals that this mindset is alive and well. But since you've made it this far, I'm going to assume that you're interested in using HTML intelligently, effectively, and correctly, rather than slapping together markup that works just well enough to get by.

But enough preliminaries! Let's start acutally *developing with web standards*.

HTML and XHTML

Just what is it we are attempting to achieve when we mark up content? Those familiar with word processing and desktop publishing are likely to think about presentation: that is, we are more likely to think of a piece of text as "bold," or "italicized" than we are to consider the text "emphasized," or as a structurally significant heading. But it's the second approach—identifying the meaning of each part of our content and marking it up accordingly—that we should use when we're marking up content. We'll use HTML to mark up the *semantics* of the content (as much as HTML allows), and leave presentation to CSS.

HTML started life as an almost entirely semantic markup language. Devised by Tim Berners-Lee as a simple markup language for exchanging scientific data and publications, HTML initially had no mechanism for defining fonts or text colors, or of displaying images. Right from the beginning, HTML was designed for marking up the meaning and structure of a document (its semantics).

As the web exploded in popularity in the early to mid 1990s, browser developers like Netscape and Microsoft created their own HTML elements, like the `font` element, which gave developers the ability to use HTML to control presentation. At the time, there was no custodian or standards body for HTML, so the language rapidly devolved into a number of *mostly* compatible dialects, each of which managed presentation in slightly different ways. And so the vision of HTML as a structural and semantic markup language was swamped by the reality that designers and developers needed "stylish" websites, and were happy to use presentational markup to build them (at the time there was no alternative: CSS came later).

Why was this a problem? As we saw earlier, the benefits of separating presentation from markup include easier site maintainance and redesigns, better communication with search engines, and improved accessibility. All these benefits are lost when developers use markup, rather than CSS, to control presentation.

So what does semantic markup look like?

Syntax and Semantics

Markup languages have two key components: semantics or the meaning of various parts of the language, and syntax or the rules that developers must follow in order to produce meaningful, valid markup. The `strong` element is a good example of a semantic construction: it's used for marking up words or phrases that should be strongly emphasized. The `q` element, which is used to mark up inline quotations, is another good exampple. Here's how these elements look in practice.

```
Dad said <q>you <strong>will</strong> go to your room.</q>
```

The syntax of HTML is something slightly different. In spoken languages, syntactical rules specify such things as subject-verb agreement—for example, it's syntactically incorrect to say "he are a good boy." The syntactical rules of HTML specify which elements may contain other elements, which elements must have closing tags (and which "autoclose"), and which attributes an element may, must, or must not have.

A Very Short History of HTML

Understanding the history of HTML isn't necessary for understanding the rest of this chapter. If you *are* interested, especially about the variants of HTML, please do read on. Otherwise, you can skip straight to the "Key Concepts" section later in the chapter.

After the publication of the initial HTML proposal by Tim Berners-Lee in 1991, four years passed before anything resembling a standard for HTML was published. Two significant attempts at standardizing the language, one by Berners-Lee and Dan Connolly, and another by Dave Raggett, faltered, and in 1995, the Internet Engineering Task Force (IETF) published RFC 1866, the HTML 2.0 standard.

In January 1997, the W3C published its first version of the HTML standard, HTML 3.2 (there was never a 3.0 version). At the end of that year, the W3C published HTML 4.0, which bears a strong resemblance to HTML 4.01, itself published in December 1999. HTML 4.01 is the last version of HTML (as opposed to XHTML) published to date, as HTML5 is currently still a draft specification.

HTML versus XHTML

The differences between HTML and XHTML stem from their being derived from (or more technically "applications of") two separate general markup languages, SGML (Standard, Generalized Markup Language) and XML (Extensible Markup Language). XML and SGML aren't used directly for marking up documents, but rather used for creating specific markup languages like MathML, SVG, HTML, and XHTML, which are *themselves* used to mark up documents.

SGML has been around for over twenty years, is an ISO standard, was originally designed for managing complex documentation, and in many ways was the inspiration for HTML.

XML, developed by the W3C is essentially an updated, somewhat simplified (though by no means simple) version of SGML more focused on networked information. XML and SGML have similar but not identical syntaxes, and it's these syntactical differences which account for the differences between XHTML and HTML. However, XHTML has been cleverly designed so that syntactically correct XHTML is also correct HTML (though syntactically correct HTML will most likely not be correct XHTML).

HTML 4.01

Published in 1999 as HTML 4.0 and updated slightly in 2001 as version 4.01, this is still the most-up-to-date *published* version of HTML. HTML5, which I'll detail in Chapter 11, is still in the draft stage. The current semantics and syntax of HTML—and the semantics of XHTML—are defined by HTML 4.01.

XHTML 1.0, 1.1, 2.0

After the publication of HTML 4 in 1999, the W3C turned its focus to XHTML, a very similar markup language grounded in the more modern general markup language, XML (itself a W3C standard for creating other, specialized markup languages). XHTML 1.0, published in early 2000, was designed to be entirely compatible with HTML 4.01, sharing the same semantics (the set of elements and attributes), and with a backward-compatible syntax. All XHTML 1.0 is valid HTML 4.01, though not all HTML 4.01 is valid XHTML 1.0.

Subsequent versions of XHTML moved away from direct compatibility with HTML 4.01. XHTML 1.1 removes from the language a number of elements that had been marked as "deprecated" in HTML 4.01; when a language feature is declared deprecated in a specification, this alerts us to the likelihood that it will be removed from later versions of the language. XHTML 1.1 is a purely semantic markup language, with no presentational elements or attributes like `font` or `align`.

In 2002 the W3C started work on a radical departure from HTML: XHTML 2. XHTML 2 keeps the basic syntax of XHTML, but introduces new elements and attributes without concern for compatibility with HTML 4.01 (or current browsers). As of the time of writing, the W3C announced that the XHTML 2 working group charter will not be renewed after 2009, effectively ending the development of the language.

Case Sensitivity

Another important distinction between XHTML and HTML syntax is that HTML is not case sensitive, while XHTML is. That means

`<P>`This is a paragraph element`</P>`

is valid HTML but **not** valid XHTML, while

`<p>`This is a paragraph element`</p>`

is both valid XHTML and XHTML. This issue with case sensitivity applies to element and attribute names. It's widely recommended that developers always use lowercase for element and attribute names in both HTML and XHTML.

HTML5

HTML5 began life outside the auspices of the W3C in a group of people associated with the development of the Mozilla and WebKit browser technologies, which, respectively underpin Firefox and Safari (and other browsers). In 2007, HTML5's development was brought within the W3C. This move effectively anointed HTML5 as the future direction of HTML. HTML5 is very much a work in progress, but some aspects are usable today. For developers familiar with HTML 4.01 and XHTML 1, HTML5 won't be difficult to learn, because the language's core syntax and principles remain the same (HTML5 is backwards compatible with HTML 4 and XHTML 1).

For a detailed history of HTML5 and a lot more on how to use it, see Chapter 11.

Key Concepts of HTML

Time to get down to the nuts and bolts of markup for the web. We'll begin with the core concepts and terminology, then cover all of the most significant features of the language.

What Is a Web Page?

When you visit a page in a web browser, what is going on?

A browser takes a text file, which contains text formatted according to the rules of HTML, and uses it to locate other resources like images, video, and audio to display as part of the page. The browser then fetches all these resources and renders the resultant page.

The key point is that an HTML document (with a couple of minor exceptions) contains only text, in a specific format. Any images or other resources a page needs are stored in separate files and the browser combines these files when drawing the contents of the page.

Throughout the book, I'll use three important terms for a web page:

- An *HTML file* is the text file that contains the markup for an HTML document.
- An *HTML document* is content marked up according to the HTML syntax.
- A *web page* is what a browser renders with that HTML document.

URL: Uniform Resource Locator

A URL is a Uniform Resource Locator—a standard format for describing the unique location of web resources such as HTML documents, images, and so on.

Closely related is the concept of URI, or Uniform Resource Identifier. The terms are often used interchangeably, but the difference can be understood by thinking about URIs as the name of a resource (like a person's name), which uniquely identifies that resource regardless of where it is located, while the URL is its *location* (think of this like a street address).

Terminology: Elements, Attributes, Tags and More

HTML is a language, with a set of syntactical rules describing how content should be marked up. The basic structure of an HTML document and its core components is straightforward.

- An HTML document is made up of *elements*. Elements are, for the most part, containers for content and for other elements.
- Each element may have one or more *attributes*.
- Some types of element may contain other elements.
- Other types of elements have attributes but do not contain content or other elements.

So what does an element look like? Let's begin with the two types of elements: those that may contain other elements (called, rather clumsily, *non-empty elements*), and elements that cannot contain other elements (called *empty elements*).

Non-Empty HTML Elements

At its simplest, an HTML element looks like this:

```
<p>This is a <strong>paragraph</strong> element</p>
```

Let's break it down.

- It has a start tag (`<p>`) content—which in this case contains text and another element—and an end tag (`</p>`).
- Start tags have the form of an angled bracket (`<`), the element name (in this case, `p`), and a closing angled bracket (`>`).
- End tags are similar, but they have a slash (`/`) before the name of the element.
- Non-empty elements contain text and/or one or more other elements.

Elements may also have *attributes*. Attributes contain additional information about a particular element, and are contained within the element's start tag. For example, here's our paragraph with a unique identifier

```
<p id="introduction">This is a <strong>paragraph
</strong> element</p>
```

The form of an attribute is almost invariably the attribute name, an equals sign (`=`), and a value. For most attributes, the value must be wrapped in quotation marks; this isn't always mandatory, but for the sake of consistency and simplicity, I recommend always putting quotation marks around the values of attributes. If an element has more than one attribute, these are separated by spaces.

Although in HTML 4, some non-empty elements may omit the end tag in some circumstances, this is widely considered a bad markup practice. It can make markup less readable and adds complexity to development by introducing an extra set of rules to remember and track. Few developers currently omit end tags, and I strongly recommend not doing so.

Empty HTML Elements

An empty element in HTML looks like the start tag for a non-empty element. For example, the HTML **img** (image) element is an empty element. It looks like this

```
<img src="images/portrait.png" alt="a portrait of the
artist as a middle aged developer">
```

Don't be concerned with the **src** and **alt** attributes—we'll cover those when we look at the **img** element in detail later in the chapter.

Here, we encounter the first difference between HTML and XHTML. So far, everything we've said applies to both languages, but there are a few syntactic differences between the two. Probably the most commonly encountered is that with XHTML syntax, empty elements finish with **/>**, rather than simply with **>**. So, in XHTML, our image element would look like this:

```
<img src="images/portrait.png" alt="a portrait of the
artist as a middle aged developer"/>
```

The good news is that this is also valid HTML markup (whereas if you leave off the closing slash, it's not valid XHTML).

See figure **3.1** for demonstrations of all of these concepts.

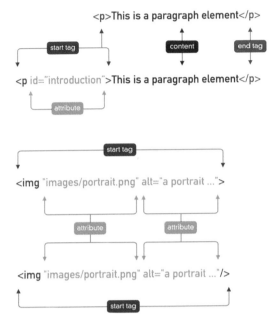

Document Types

We've seen already that there are two different "flavors" of HTML: HTML and XHTML. How does a browser know which it is dealing with? And for that matter, how will a browser know what version of HTML or XHTML a particular document is using?

Enter the *DOCTYPE*

At the very beginning of every HTML file, we provide this information via a *Document Type Declaration* or **DOCTYPE**. (The **DOCTYPE** isn't technically part of the HTML *document*, even though it's in the HTML *file*.) The **DOCTYPE** specifies the markup language and version, and also provides an additional piece of information that tells the browser how strict it should be in rendering the page. This last piece of information comes in one of the following three forms:

- Strict **DOCTYPE**—A document type that uses *only* non-presentational HTML elements and attributes. This variation is a subset of HTML 4.01/ XHTML 1.0 that does away with older presentational features of those languages. If you declare an HTML document to be strict and then go on to include such elements as **font**, the document will be invalid (more on validation later in the chapter). Strict is the recommended doctype to be used for maximum forward compatibility.

- Transitional (or loose) **DOCTYPE**—This document type indicates that the markup can include all features, both presentational and non-presentational. It can be used with legacy content that includes presentational HTML, but is not recommended for new development.

- Frameset **DOCTYPE** —This document type is for use with HTML *frames*, a now-deprecated feature of HTML that you should avoid.

Declaring a *DOCTYPE*

We declare a **DOCTYPE** with a **DOCTYPE** declaration, which comes before everything else in the file. Here's what our **DOCTYPE** will look like for HTML 4.01 strict:

```
<!DOCTYPE HTML PUBLIC "-//W3C//DTD HTML 4.01//EN"
"http://www.w3.org/TR/html4/strict.dtd">
```

You don't really need to understand this in detail, but the first part of the **DOCTYPE** declares that this is a public **DOCTYPE** with the identifier `"-//W3C//DTD HTML 4.01//EN"`— the identifier for the HTML 4.01 strict **DOCTYPE**. The URL that follows is technically optional, but has very important real-world implications. (In some browsers, if you use the transitional `doctype`, leaving off this URL makes the browser render the document in something called *Quirks mode*. We'll talk about that in Chapter 7, but in the meantime, you should just remember to always use the URL unless you're intentionally invoking Quirks mode.

Here are the most important **DOCTYPE** declarations:

```
<!DOCTYPE HTML PUBLIC "-//W3C//DTD HTML 4.01 Strict //EN"
"http://www.w3.org/TR/html4/strict.dtd">
```
HTML 4.01 strict doctype

```
<!DOCTYPE HTML PUBLIC "-//W3C//DTD HTML 4.01 Transitional//EN"
"http://www.w3.org/TR/html4/loose.dtd">
```
HTML 4.01 transitional doctype

```
<!DOCTYPE html PUBLIC "-//W3C//DTD XHTML 1.0 Strict//EN"
"http://www.w3.org/TR/1999/PR-xhtml1-19991210/DTD/xhtml1-strict.dtd">
```
XHTML 1.0 strict doctype

```
<!DOCTYPE html PUBLIC "-//W3C//DTD XHTML 1.0 Transitional//EN"
"http://www.w3.org/TR/1999/PR-xhtml1-19991210/DTD/xhtml1-
transitional.dtd">
```
XHTML 1.0 transitional doctype

The main point: once you've decided which language flavor (HTML or XHTML), version number, and document type (strict or transitional), you then add the appropriate **DOCTYPE** at the beginning of your HTML file.

For the rest of the chapter, we'll focus on features of the strict **DOCTYPE**, and will mostly use XHTML syntax. Although developers disagree on some very detailed points, these are considered to be good practices for modern markup.

The Structural Basics of HTML

An HTML document is essentially a container of containers. (Technically, this is referred to as the document's *containment hierarchy*.) Each of the containers is an HTML element, and most containers (non-empty elements) may contain other containers [**3.2**].

3.2
An HTML document as a container of containers

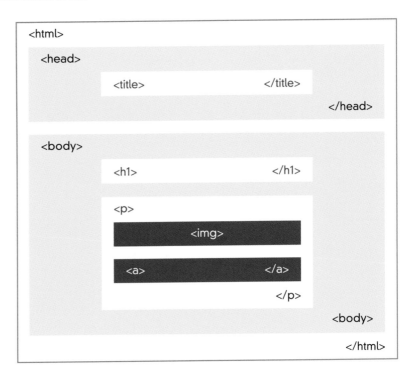

The Root *html* Element

The containment hierarchy of the document begins with the `html` element, the container that contains all of the other containers in the document. The `html` element is also known as the *root* element of the document. Every other element in the document is contained within this element, or to use the analogy of a family tree, is descended from this element. Typically, the `html` element does not have any attributes.

The `html` element contains two other elements directly: the `head` and `body` elements. By "directly," I mean that these elements are nested only inside the `html` element, not nested within other elements that are themselves contained within the `html` element. We call elements contained directly within an element the *children* of that element: the `head` and `body` elements are children of the `html` element.

The `head` element contains mostly *metadata*: data about the document, such as its title, and links to external scripts and style sheet files. This information is used by the browser, but isn't shown to actual human users. The `body` element contains the document's content, which will be rendered by the browser as a web page.

The *head* Element

The `head` element is a *required* element that contains information about the document: a `title` that is typically displayed in the browser's titlebar, `meta` elements which contain information such as keywords for the document for the benefit of search engines, as well as embedded script and CSS, and links to script and CSS files. We'll take a look at each of these types of element now.

The `head` is a required element for any HTML document

title

The `title` element provides a description of the page that is typically displayed by browsers in the browser window's titlebar. It also may be read out by screen-readers and otherwise presented to a user by a user agent.

It's a non-empty element, whose only content is the text of the page title.

```
<title>Pride and Prejudice, Chapter 1</title>
```

The `title` element is a required element of the `head`.

meta

`meta` elements are an optional mechanism for providing additional information about the page. They are empty elements and take two attributes: a `name` attribute that describes the type of data, and a `content` attribute that contains the value of the data. You might use a `meta` element to provide, for example, the name of the author of a document, the authoring tool used for the document, and keywords that are meant for search engines (although that last use is largely outdated). For example, we could add the following `meta` element for an online chapter of *Pride and Prejudice*:

```
<meta name="author" value="Jane Austen"/>
```

The use of `meta` elements for providing search engine keywords, although once recommended, is no longer supported by any major search engine. Although this practice may still be useful for internal site search, using `meta` elements provides *no benefit* for search engine optimization.

script

We'll focus on the Document Object Model, or DOM, and touch on JavaScript in Chapter 5, so here I'll just note that there are two ways of including JavaScript in a web page: the script can be embedded in the page itself, or it can live in an external file and be linked to using the `script` element. Although we've included the `script` element in the head section of this chapter, it may actually appear anywhere in the document. JavaScript is often included in the `body` of the document—usually at the end—so the script doesn't execute until after the page has fully loaded. With the rise of *unobtrusive JavaScript* as a best practice for DOM scripting, JavaScript should usually be included via a link to an external JavaScript file in the `head` of the document. (We'll look at unobtrusive JavaScript in Chapter 5.)

For completeness, here's how we'd embed JavaScript within our document:

```
<script type="text/javascript">
window.alert('hello world')
</script>
```

Alternately, we'd link to an external JavaScript file like this:

```
<script type="text/javascript" src="scripts/effects.js">
</script>
```

Although we use the `script` element for both linked and embedded JavaScript, you can't combine the two in a single element. When there is a `src` attribute on the `script` element, the browser ignores any script embedded in the element. You can, however, have as many `script` elements—with links or embedded script—as you like.

style

CSS is covered in Chapter 4, but I'll quickly touch on the two elements used to embed or link to CSS for a document. (We have to use two elements for this, unlike the single one we used for JavaScript.)

The `style` element is used to embed CSS in the `head`, and only in the `head` of the document. To link to CSS for a document, we use the `link` element in the `head`. (The `link` elements is different from the *anchor element* [a] that we use to create hyperlinks in the content of the document.)

link

The `link` element isn't only used for linking to external CSS files. It can also be used to convey information about the relationship between different documents. The use of links for this purpose is rare, and the information is hidden from the user, not being part of the content of the document.

The use of such "hidden metatdata" is increasingly considered a less-than-ideal development practice; when possible use visible data such as anchors to convey this sort of information. For example, if you want to link to the license for a document, use `a` rather than `link`.

The *body* Element

The contents of the `body` element of the HTML document is what browsers display as a web page. It is a container for structured content such as headings, paragraphs, and lists, as well as linked content such as images and video.

Headings

HTML provides six levels of heading, via heading elements **h1** to **h6**. These headings define the structure of the document, and some user agents (screen readers, in particular) use them to create a table of contents for the page.

Although it's not required by HTML, you should use headings in a logical order: headings of level three (**h3** elements) should be used one level down the document structure from **h2** elements.

Headings are non-empty elements whose content is the text of the heading. For example, in our chapter of *Pride and Prejudice*, we would mark up our chapter heading using something like this:

```
<h1>Pride and Prejudice</h1>
  <h2>Volume 1</h2>
    <h3>Chapter 1</h3>
```

Paragraphs

Paragraphs are blocks of text that typically contain thematically related content. The **p** element is used for marking up paragraphs of content. To continue with our example, we could mark up the beginning of *Pride and Prejudice* like this:

```
<p>It is a truth universally acknowledged, that a single
man in possession of a good fortune must be in want of a
wife.</p>

<p>However little known the feelings or views of such a
man may be on his first entering a neighbourhood, this
truth is so well fixed in the minds of the surrounding
families, that he is considered as the rightful property
of some one or other of their daughters.</p>
```

One thing it is important to understand is that a paragraph is a container for content, not a way of managing whitespace. Novice developers often use the **p** element as a sort of spacing instruction to the browser, but the element should never be used in that way. (CSS margins on a paragraph can easily allow us to control whitespace without misusing semantically meaningful elements for presentation.)

Breaking Lines

If we do need to break a line within a paragraph to maintain the integrity of a poem or other text in which exact line lengths are vitally important, we can use the *line break element* (**br**). This is an empty element with no content, but it isn't simply an instruction to the browser to add space between two lines. Rather, it explicitly notes that the lines are broken at this point. Here is the start of Hamlet's famous soliloquy marked up in HTML:

```
<p>To be, or not to be: that is the question:<br/>
Whether 'tis nobler in the mind to suffer<br/>
The slings and arrows of outrageous fortune, <br/>
Or to take arms against a sea of troubles, <br/>
And by opposing end them? To die: to sleep;</p>
```

If you write semantic markup, you probably won't use line breaks very frequently.

Preformatted Text

In HTML, whitespace such as spaces, tabs, and returns are not significant: they are all treated by the browser as a single space, regardless of how many you put together. In other words, four tabs, two returns, and eight spaces in a row will be treated by the browser as a single space.

There's one exception to this rule. The contents of the **pre** element are rendered with returns, tabs, and spaces as they appear in the raw HTML file itself. Here's how we might use **pre** with Hamlet's soliloquy, thus avoiding the need for **br** elements at the end of lines.

```
<pre>To be, or not to be: that is the question:
Whether 'tis nobler in the mind to suffer
The slings and arrows of outrageous fortune,
Or to take arms against a sea of troubles,
And by opposing end them? To die: to sleep;</pre>
```

Preformatted content may still contain other markup, such as links. The **pre** element is most commonly used for code examples, and you should need it only rarely.

This is probably a good place to emphasize once again that HTML is designed for structured, meaningful markup. The use of **p** as a horizontal separator, the use of **br** as a general means of achieving the same thing, and the use of **pre** to achieve a design effect are all examples of seeing HTML as a presentational markup language. As much as possible, the markup we add to our content should reflect the nature of that content. So when a block of content needs to be formatted precisely in a given way with whitespace (for example code examples in which whitespace is usually significant), or when lines must break at a specific point (as in poetry), **pre** and **br** are the correct elements. If we are simply seeking a specific visual effect, we should use CSS instead.

divs

So far, we've mostly looked at elements that contain individual pieces of content—a single paragraph, a heading, and so on. But if a page is a container of containers, how might we group together, for example, the heading and all the paragraphs of a chapter?

HTML provides the **div** element for grouping elements like paragraphs, headings, and so on. We can even make hierarchies of nested **div**s—for example, the entire book of *Pride and Prejudice* might be marked up as a **div**, then each volume as a **div** within the book's **div**, then each chapter a **div** within the volume's **div**:

```
<div>
  <h1>Pride and Prejudice</h1>
  <div>
    <h2>Volume 1</h2>
    <div>
      <h3>Chapter 1</h3>
      <p>It is a truth universally acknowledged, ...</p>
      <p>However little known the ...</p>
    </div>
  </div>
</div>
```

The **div** element is very common in modern web development. Its use can make markup much more readable, especially if whitespace is used to aid readability—since browsers ignore whitespace in HTML, we can (and should) indent our markup as in the preceding example to reflect the containment hierarchy of the document we're working on. (More on that and other techniques for creating readable markup may be found in Chapter 8.)

The `div` element can also be combined with the `class` and `id` attributes to create meaningful sections of a document and make it easier to style content with CSS. We'll get to that in just a moment. First, though, note that it's best not to indiscriminately wall all sorts of content within `div`s. Use `div`s to group sets of elements that form a *logical grouping*, such as a chapter, an article, and so on.

Commenting Markup

Software developers know that commenting code helps make much more readable, maintainable code (though they don't always use good commenting techniques as much as they should).

Commenting is far less widely used for markup, but is no less important. An HTML comment has this form:

```
<!-- this is a comment -->
```

One place they can be very useful is for noting which `div` a closing `div` tag closes. In our simple example above, we have nested `div`s, which close together further down in the file:

```
            </div>
        </div>
</div>
```

Even here, it might be difficult to determine which closes which `div` element (particularly as the opening tags can be a long way away in the markup). By adding a comment after the close of each of these elements, we can keep track of this.

```
            </div> <!-- closes the chapter div -->
        </div> <!-- closes the volume div -->
</div> <!-- closes the book div -->
```

HTML comments can be used almost anywhere in an HTML document, and are ignored by the browser when it renders a page.

Lists

HTML provides several types of list elements for marking up lists.

Ordered Lists

Ordered lists are meant for marking up lists of information in which the sequence is important, such as with steps in a recipe. The `ol` (ordered list) element contains one or more `li` (list item) elements.

```
<ol>
  <li>obtain items in shopping list</li>
  <li>put on rain jacket</li>
  <li>open Bottle of Diet Coke</li>
  <li>place 4 mentos in bottle</li>
  <li>stand back</li>
  <li>???</li>
  <li>profit</li>
</ol>
```

Unordered Lists

An unordered list is very similar, but here the sequence of the items is not significant.

```
<ul>
  <li>Diet Coke 3l Bottle</li>
  <li>Mentos (Mint Flavored)</li>
  <li>Rain Jacket</li>
</ul>
```

A very common use for unordered lists in web development is for marking up page and site navigation. The navigation for a site after all consists essentially of a list of lists.

Definition Lists

A rather different kind of list is a definition list, which is for marking up a word and the definitions for it. Definition lists comprise a `dl` element, then a `dt` element for each definition term, and one or more definition description (`dd`) elements for each dt element. Definition lists can also be used for other highly structured information, such as detailed data about an event.

```
<dl>
   <dt>When</dt>
      <dd>7pm-late, Friday 2nd October</dd>
   <dt>Where</dt>
      <dd>Pyrmont Bridge Hotel (Upstairs), </br>
      96 Union St, Pyrmont. </dd>
</dl>
```

Definition terms may be associated with more than one dd element. We'll look at this element in greater detail in Chapter 8.

Nesting Lists

It's possible to nest lists within another lists, which would be common for complex site navigation. Here's an example:

```
<li>Software</li>
<li>Hardware</li>
<li>Caffeine
<ul>
   <li>Coffee</li>
   <li>Cola</li>
</ul>
</li>
<li>T-Shirts</li>
</ul>
```

Note that the nested ul is itself inside an li element, because the nested list is *an item of the list that contains it*.

Inline Elements

With the exception of the br element, all the elements in the body that we've looked at have something in common: they're all *block elements*, which means that they can (mostly) contain other block elements and can only be contained within block elements. (The p element, which is a block element that cannot contain other block elements, is the only exception.)

There's a second kind of element called an *inline element*. Inline elements can only contain other inline elements, but may be contained by both inline and block elements.

To summarize these containment rules of HTML:

- Block elements can contain other block elements and inline elements.
- Block elements can only be contained within block elements.
- Inline elements can only contain inline elements.
- Inline elements can be contained in both block and inline elements.
- Paragraphs are block elements, but cannot contain other block elements.

Let's turn to inline elements.

There are many inline elements, but we'll focus on those used to write semantic, structured markup.

Emphasis

In English, we often make use of italics or bold text for emphasis. HTML provides two different elements for providing emphasis: the **strong** element, for strong emphasis, and the **em** element, for slightly less strong emphasis. By default, browsers render text contained in a **strong** element as bold weight text and text contained in an **em** element in italics, but it's easy to change this using CSS.

Developers have been known to use the bold (**b**) and italic (**i**) elements for the purposes of emphasis, but the semantic **strong** and **em** elements are recommended in place of these presentational elements.

Abbreviation

Another relatively commonly used semantic inline element is the abbreviation (**abbr**) element. This can be used for a term that is abbreviated, or for an acronym, and the full or expanded version can be included in the **title** attribute of the **abbr** element, thus providing additional semantic information for abbreviations. For example:

```
<abbr title="World Wide Web Consortium">W3C</abbr>
```

Extending HTML Semantics

HTML provides a number of other semantic elements, both inline and block, and we'll look at some of these, including elements for quotations and block quotations, in Chapter 8. But for all the elements HTML has, it still lacks elements that are associated with even the most common page components found in newspapers, magazines, and books. Additionally, a new set of design patterns (navigation bars and so on) made specifically for websites has evolved, but HTML doesn't have elements for these components either. And since there's no way to add elements to HTML, we must rely on the small number of elements that the language already offers.

Luckily, HTML does offer an informal but very useful way to extend its semantic capabilities via the `class` and `id` attributes.

class

The `class` attribute allows developers to describe an element in greater detail. If we think back to our example of *Pride and Prejudice*, and the three different levels of `div` (book, volume, and chapter) we might use the `class` attribute to *classify* each of these `div`s accordingly. If our document contained the whole of *Pride and Prejudice*, it would have 3 `div`s to contain the 3 volumes and a total of 61 divs to contain each of the chapters. Here is how we might mark up the first two chapters of volume two:

```
<div class="volume">
  <h2>Volume 2</h2>
  <div class="chapter">
    <h3>Chapter 1</h3>
      ...
  </div> <!-- chapter 1-->

  <div class="chapter">
    <h3>Chapter 2</h3>
      ...
  </div> <!-- chapter 2-->

  ...

</div> <!-- volume 2 -->
```

We've given related elements the same `class` values because they share a classification. Adding `class` like this makes our markup more readable and, very importantly, makes it much easier to style our documents with CSS and to use JavaScript to control behavior.

Precisely when and why an element should get a `class` attribute is something we'll turn to in Chapter 8.

Note that elements may only have a single `class` attribute, but that they can have multiple `class` values, which are separated by spaces. `class` values may include most characters other than spaces and tabs, but letters, numbers, underscores, and hyphens are the most commonly used characters.

id

Closely related to the `class` attribute is the `id` attribute. Whereas `class` describes a group (or classification) to which an element belongs, `id` is a unique *identifier* for a given element. Only one element in a particular HTML document may have a given `id` value.

How might we use `id`? Turning once more to *Pride and Prejudice*, we see that although each of the chapters belong to the `class` of `div`s called chapter, each chapter is also unique and numbered. So, we could add an `id` for each chapter:

```
<div class="volume" id="volume2">
  <h2>Volume 2</h2>
  <div class="chapter" id="volume2Chapter1">
    <h3>Chapter 1</h3>
      ...
  </div> <!-- volume2Chapter1-->

  <div class="chapter" id="volume2Chapter2">
    <h3>Chapter 2</h3>
      ...
  </div> <!-- volume2Chapter2-->

  ...

</div> <!-- volume2 -->
```

Because we have many chapters with the same number in this document (each volume has a Chapter 1, and so on), we've had to use the longer value `volume2Chapter1` to ensure that the `id` value of each chapter is unique.

There's no need to add an `id` value to every element in a document. Determining just when to add this attribute is more an art than a science, and we'll consider it in detail in Chapter 8. As a rule of thumb, when an element is unique, and plays a significant role in the document, an `id` value may be valuable.

`id` and `class` attributes are not restricted to `div` elements, but they are often used with these elements, as is the next element we'll turn to, the `span` element.

span

Almost all HTML elements have their own semantics. A paragraph, a heading, a list—all model things that make sense to us. The `div` element is different. It has no semantics of its own, and is simply a container for block and inline elements. There's also an inline element that plays a similar role: the `span` element. We can use `span` to add additional, meaningful markup to our content. Well see `span` in action in Chapter 8, where it plays an important role in microformats.

Links: The "Hyper" in "Hypertext"

One of the things that makes the web the web is the hyperlink. In HTML, we link from an anchor to another location within the same page, or to another web page.

Anchors

The anchor (`a`) element plays two roles in linking. It's the source of most outbound links, and it can also be the destination of a link.

When an anchor is the source—that is, the thing a user will click—it has an `href` attribute that points to the destination of the link.

```
<a href="http://devwws.com">Developing with web standards
home</a>
```

When an anchor is a *destination*, it has an `id` that can be used as the destination of another anchor, For example, developers who are concerned with accessibility often use a link at the beginning of the page that allows users to skip over navigation elements and go to the contents of the page. To accomplish this, we can put an anchor at the beginning of the page and make another anchor (with an `id` of `contents`) that anchor's destination.

```
<a id="contents"></a>
```

With modern browsers, it's also possible to use *any* element with an `id` as the destination for a link. So, for example, in our *Pride and Prejudice* site, if we have a table of contents with links to each of the volumes and chapters, we could link to the first volume of Chapter 2, which we marked up a little while ago like this:

```
<a href="#volume1chapter1">Volume 1 Chapter 1;</a>
```

This approach is preferable to adding extraneous empty anchor elements simply as a destination of a link.

In addition to linking within a document, we can link to:

- Other pages on the same site— that is, other pages within the same root directory on your server
- Parts of other pages on the same site
- Other pages on the web
- Parts of other pages on the web
- Other resources on the web, such as image files, resources located on ftp servers, and so on

We can also use a link to open a new email message in a mail application.

title and *rel* Attributes

Anchor elements can take two additional attributes that can add more information about the link. The first is the `title` attribute, which most HTML elements can take. According to the HTML 4 specification, the `title` attribute is designed for "advisory information about the element," and is often used with links to provide additional information about the link that some browsers display as a tooltip, and that screen readers may read out to their users.

The `rel` attribute can be used to describe the relationship between the destination of the link and this document. We'll look at this attribute in detail in Chapter 8.

Anchors and Containment

An anchor is an inline element, so it can only contain other inline elements. So if you have, say, a heading element that you want to be a link, the anchor element must be nested inside the heading element and not the other way around.

Absolute and Relative URLs

We can link to another document at the same site in one of two ways: via relative or absolute URLs. An absolute URL is a fully formed URL, with domain, directory and file names, and looks just like a link to another site. Relative URLs use only a *relative* path on the server—a path that shows the relationship between the location of the linking document and the location of the linked-to document.

Relative URLs can only be used when two files share a common root directory on a server. Most websites reside on a server within a single root directory, so it often makes sense to use relative links to link together resources at the same site.

Relative links are created using the following rules:

If a file we want to link *to* is in the same directory as the file we are linking *from*, the relative link is just the name of the destination file. For example if the **index.html** file where we are linking from and the **contact.html** file we are linking to are directly contained within the same directory, our link would look like this:

```
<a href="contact.html">Contact us</a>
```

If the file we want to link to is inside a directory that is contained directly within the directory that the file we are linking from is in, then the relative url is the name of the directory that contains the *destination* file, a slash (/), and then the name of the destination file. In this case, our link would look like this:

```
<a href="details/contact.html">Contact us</a>
```

This says that the destination file is called **contact.html**, and it's contained inside the directory called **details**, which itself is inside the same directory as the file we are linking from [**3.3**].

3.3

Relative links when a destination file is one level down in the server structure.

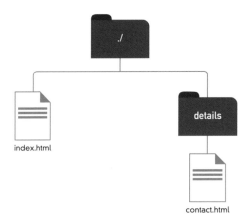

The same logic applies no matter how deeply nested in directories the destination file is. For example, if the destination file is inside a directory that is inside a directory that is in the same directory as the file we are linking from [**3.4**], our link in this instance would look something like this:

```
<a href="details/contactus/contact.html">Contact us</a>
```

The other direction we will need to make relative links is "up" the server hierarchy. To go up one step in the hierarchy, we use "../" at the beginning of the relative url. To go up two levels, we use "../../" and so on.

To link from the **contact.html** file to **index.html** in figure 3.4, we need to go up two levels, and so our URL would look like:

```
<a href="../../index.html">Home</a>
```

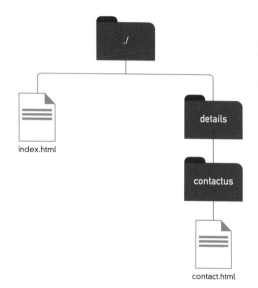

3.4
A destination file nested several directories deeper than the file we are linking to.

Lastly, we can combine these two directions, if we need to go back up the directory hierarchy and then down into another directory. For example, in figure **3.5**, we needed to link from **contact.html** to **buy.html**.

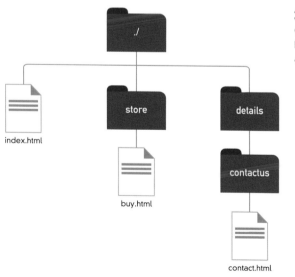

3.5
Going up the directory hierarchy and back down again

Here's the link we'd use:

```
<a href="../../store/buy.html">Buy Now</a>
```

Creating relative URLs may seem a little confusing, but the underlying logic is simple: Go down the directory hierarchy by naming the directory to go "into." Go up the hierarchy by using "../"—and at the end of it all, you identify the file you are linking to by name.

> There's another little known and underused trick to constructing a relative URL. "./" takes you directly to the root directory of the site (the directory which resolves to the domain name for the site). So, to link to the index.html file from anywhere in the site's hierarchy, simply use ./**index.html**.

If we want to link to a specific part of any document, we simply add the `id` for the element we want to be the target of our link to the end of the URL. So if we want to link to the form with the `id` contactform inside the **contact.html** document we simply add #contactform to our link:

```
<a href="details/contactus/contact.html#contactform">
```

Linking to Resources on the Web

Linking to resources, including web pages on other sites, is simpler. We just use the entire absolute URL. For example, to link to my contact details, I would use the full URL: **http://devwws.com/contact**.

```
<a href="http://devwws.com/contact/">Contact the author
(he's very nice)</a>
```

Note that the protocol (**http**://) is essential: without it, many browsers won't resolve the link to the domain.

In this example, I've linked to a directory rather than a file. This can be risky, because it relies on the server to resolve a link to a specific file inside that directory. Most servers will resolve to a file called **index.html**, but unless they've been specially configured, most servers won't resolve to files like **index.php**, which would be the default page for a PHP-driven site. If a server doesn't resolve correctly, your link will lead to a 404 error page. If that happens, you can either change your server settings so that it returns **index.php** if no file name is specified, or you can link to the file by name.

Embedded Content

As we saw earlier, HTML files don't themselves contain images, video, and other non-text content. These are contained in separate files and are linked to from the HTML document in various ways depending on the type of content. Images, video, audio, and content like Flash and Silverlight are often referred to as *embedded content*, which is a little confusing, as these aren't literally embedded in the HTML file.

Images

The most common embedded content in websites is images. The most common of image type, supported by all modern browsers, is these types of bitmap format:

- Portable Network Graphics (PNG, pronounced "ping")
- JPEG (pronounced "jay peg")
- GIF (often pronounced "giff" with a hard "g" as in "gift," but officially "jiff")

We include images in all these formats in our HTML documents the same way, using the `img` element. (There's also a standard vector graphics format for the web called SVGf which we examine in considerable detail in Chapter 16.)

On Image Formats

PNG

PNG is an open file format for bitmap images from the W3C. It supports alpha channel transparency and lossless compression. It's supported by all modern browsers and IE back to version 4, though until version 7, IE did not support transparency in PNG images. PNG is recommended for bitmap images other than photographic images, for which the JPEG format is often a better choice, due to higher compression.

JPEG

The JPEG format is ISO standard ISO 10918-1 from the Joint Photographic Experts Group, and was standardized in 1994. It is designed for compressing photographic images, and provides different levels of compression, with progressively more loss of information from the image the more you compress. Because of the low resolution of screens, typically images can be compressed heavily (as much as ten times) with little noticeable loss of image quality.

All browsers have supported the JPEG format for many years, and it is the format of choice for photographic images.

GIF

Before the advent of the PNG format, GIF was widely used. GIF is a proprietary format of Unisys, and until various patents associated with the format expired, Unisys charged a license fee for the developers of software which supported the format. Most animated images for the web which rely on the image format rather than on JavaScript for the animation use an animated variation of GIF. (There is an unofficial animated PNG extension, which is not widely supported in browsers.) Animated images on the web are increasingly developed using JavaScript and multiple images, rather than animated GIFs.

GIF transparency, unlike PNG transparency, is a single-color transparency, so it's generally useful only for creating transparent images which sit on backgrounds with a single color. It also only supports 256 colors for any particular image, unlike PNG's 24-bit color, which supports up to 16 million colors in a single image.

PNG has largely supplanted the once widely used GIF, and the GIF format is not recommended.

Embedding Images

Each of these image formats is embedded in an HTML document using the `img` element. This is an empty element that takes the URL of the image (relative or absolute) as the value of an `href` attribute. For example, to link from an HTML file to a shopping cart image in a directory called "images" in the same directory we'd use this markup:

```
<img src="images/shoppingcart.png" alt="" />
```

That's really all there is to including an image in a document. Or rather, that's almost all. HTML also requires every `img` element to have an `alt` attribute, which contains text that describes or takes the place of the image. This text is typically used by assistive devices and user agents for people with impaired vision, but most browsers also show this content when images are not available.

There's quite a bit more to be said about `img` element accessibility, and you'll find a full discussion in Chapter 6.

Content or Decoration?

Some images are purely presentational—for example, background or decorative border. These images should be added via CSS rather than being included in your HTML. Images that serve as *content*—maps, illustrations, portraits, logos, and so on—should be included in your markup.

One particularly challenging area that we'll return to in Chapter 4 is image replacement, a technique in which the text of an element is hidden and an image of that text (in a desired font) is displayed in its place. For now, I'll just say that text in a document should never be replaced by an image of that text using an HTML `img` element—this technique is inaccessible to users with disabilities and is hostile to search engines to boot.

Multimedia Content

As broadband internet connections become more common and with the rise of podcasting and of video-sharing sites like YouTube, there is an increasing use of video and audio content on the web. Rich Interactive Application (RIA) formats like Flash and Silverlight are also often part of the content of sites. These kinds of content are all embedded into HTML documents the same way. The exception, as we'll see in Chapter 11, is HTML5's new **video** and **audio** elements.

Most browsers require a plug-in of one kind or another to play audio, video, and other embedded content, whereas the image formats we've just discussed are supported "natively" by browsers, which means they don't require a plug-in.

The *object* Element

The **object** element is the sole standards-based way of embedding multimedia content. This element can get quite complicated, but I'll focus on its use for essentially embedding content that will begin playing once it has been downloaded. For a more detailed understanding of **object** and all it can do, check out the links in the Resources section at the end of this book.

The **object** element is a non-empty element, and its contents can be used to provide alternate content if the embedded object itself is not supported. An object can take a number of attributes, but the most important for our purposes are:

- **data**—A URL (relative or absolute) for the file to be embedded.
- **type**—The type of content. This is an optional attribute, but is recommended, because it allows the browser to determine whether it supports the format of the content before downloading the content.

Content Types (aka MIME Types)

When content is served by a server, it comes with a MIME (Multipurpose Internet Mail Extensions) type, which lets the browser (or other user agent) know what type of content it is. Common types you'll see in this book include "text/html," "image/png," and "video/mpeg."

Suppose we want to include a video of a local production of *Hamlet* along with the soliloquy we marked up earlier in this chapter—provided, of course, that we have the appropriate permissions and license for the content. First, we'll link to an MPEG version of the file.

```
<object data="/video/hamlet.mpeg" type="video/mpeg">
</object>
```

Here the `data` attribute is a relative URL to the video file, and the `type` lets the browser know what content to expect.

Now suppose the browser doesn't have support for MPEG. We can specify alternate content, for example a still image from the video. We can simply include an `img` element inside the `object` element.

```
<object data="/video/hamlet.mpeg" type="video/mpeg">
<img src="images/hamlet.jpg"
alt="Hamlet gives his famous soliloquy"/>
</object>
```

It's also possible to provide several different `object` elements, each linking to the same video content in different formats, as the content of the main `object` element. This way, we'd have fallbacks to cover the common formats supported by common browsers on common platforms. In Chapter 11, we'll look at this fallback mechanism in more detail in relation to the `video` element.

applet and embed?

You may have come across two other related elements, the `applet` element, and the `embed` element. `embed` was once widely used to embed content that required plug-ins to be rendered. It was never actually part of any HTML standard, and although it was once the only way to ensure cross-browser multimedia embedding, this is no longer the case.

The `applet` element is designed solely for use with Java applets, which were once quite common on the web. Since `object` can be used to embed Java, `applet`, which is deprecated in HTML 4, need not be used.

Forms

Most websites feature some type of form, whether it's a simple contact form, or a complex e-commerce interface. It's outside the scope of the book to consider how forms are integrated with server-side systems, but we will look at the ways in which forms are marked up.

HTML forms should always be contained within a **form** element. HTML provides several different *form controls*, including:

- Text fields
- Checkboxes
- Radio buttons
- Buttons
- Popup menus
- Labels for form controls

Forms can also be structured into related sets of controls using a **fieldset** element, which we'll examine in Chapter 6.

The *form* Element

The **form** element is a container for all the controls of a web form. It has the **method** attribute that specifies what happens to the data when the user submits the form, and the required **action** attribute specifies the URL of a script on a server that will receive and process the data sent, and return any results.

The *input* Element

Form controls are unlike most other HTML elements. Most elements in HTML have different names (for example **p**, **div**, and so on) but only one—**input**—handles most form controls; the difference between these controls is determined by the value of the **input** element's **type** attribute. All **input** elements must also have a **name** attribute, the value of which is sent along with the element's value when the form is submitted. Without the name, it would not be possible to make sense of the data sent to the server. Let's look at several of the most common input element types.

text and password

An **input** element with a **type** of text is a single-line text input element. **input** elements of **type** text can also take a **size** attribute, which specifies the width of the element in characters (not the maximum number of characters it may contain). While **size** is still commonly used, it's better to use CSS to specify the width of an element. The **value** attribute can optionally be used to specify an initial value for the element. Here's an example **input** element of type text:

```
<input type="text" name="company" />
```

It's possible to specify a maximum number of characters the user may enter, via the `maxlength` attribute.

When the form is submitted, the browser sends the name of the `input`, along with the text the user has entered, to the server. As mentioned above, without a `name`, the data doesn't make sense.

Closely related to inputs of `type` `text` are those of `type` `password`. The difference is that when the user types in a `password` field, a character that looks like a bullet point replaces each character, thus preventing curious onlookers from seeing the password as it's typed in—importantly, though, this input does not offer protection from malicious scripts, keyloggers, and similar attacks.

Checkboxes and Radio Buttons

Checkboxes and radio buttons are familiar controls seen in Windows, Mac OS, and other GUI-based operating systems. In web forms, radio buttons are used in a group to provide several mutually exclusive options. A checkbox, on the other hand, may be used individually or along with other checkboxes to present related, but independent options, any combination of which may be selected. Both can be set as initially checked by setting the value of the `checked` attribute to `checked` (more on that in a moment).

The `name` attribute plays an important, but different role for each of these inputs. With checkboxes, more than one may share the same name. In this case, several different values may be sent to the server when the form is submitted—that is, the browser will send a `name` and value pair for each of the checked checkboxes, though no value is sent for unchecked checkboxes.

Here's how we might mark up a checkbox, if we were trying to trick users into opting in to a mailing list by making the default state of the opt-in checkbox `checked`.

```
<input type="checkbox" name="pleasespamme"
checked="checked" />
```

Keep `checked` in mind—we'll look at something unusual about it in a moment.

When more one than radio button shares the same `name` value, the buttons are considered to be a group. The browser ensures that one—and only one—of these buttons will have a `checked` value of `checked`. When the form is submitted, the value of the checked radio button is sent along with its name. It's important to specify which of the radio buttons in a group should be initially checked, because different browsers will make different default choices if this is not set explicitly.

Here's how we might mark up a group of radio buttons:

```
<input type="radio" name="gender" value="male"
checked="checked" />
<input type="radio" name="gender" value="female" />
```

In this instance, only one of the `male` or `female` radio buttons will ever be checked. When this form is submitted, only the value of the *checked* radio button will be sent to the server, along with the name `gender`.

Push Buttons

HTML provides a number of different ways of marking up push buttons.

- With **input** of **type** submit
- With **input** of **type** reset
- With **input** of **type** button
- With **input** of **type** image
- With the **button** element

An **input** of **type** submit is a button which, when activated, will submit the form. Forms may have more than one submit button, though all the buttons will submit the form to the same location. These buttons label themselves as *Submit* but this can be changed by changing the `value` attribute to a label you want. Because the **type** is submit, the button will still function as a submit button even if relabeled.

An **input** of **type** reset is a button that, when activated, will reset all the values of the form controls to their initial values. They label themselves *Reset*, but as with submit **inputs**, this can be changed using the `value` attribute.

An **input** of **type** button is a push button with no default behavior or label. You can give it functionality using JavaScript—we'll see how we can attach an event handler for the click event in Chapter 5—and a label using the **value** attribute. For example, here's a button with the label *Calculate*.

```
<input type="button" name="calculate" value="Calculate">
```

An **input** of **type** image is a button that displays itself using the image found at the value of its **src** attribute. These are infrequently used, and are not recommended, since CSS provides much more accessible ways to style buttons.

The *button* Element

The **button** element was introduced in HTML 4, and is more consistent with the way in which HTML elements typically work. It is a non-empty element, and the content of the element, rather than its **value**, is its label. **button**s may also take a **type** attribute value, one of submit, reset, and button, and very importantly, by *default*, the **type** is submit. If you want a **button** that will have its own JavaScript-based action, then make sure the **type** is button. Here's how we'd create the Calculate button in the preceding example using **button**.

```
<button type="button" name="calculate">Calculate</button>
```

One of the strengths of the **button** element is that the **value** can be different from the label. But this is also the most serious problem with the **button** element. Internet Explorer 6 and 7 handle the **button** element very badly. When activated in IE 6 or 7, the **button** element will send the *contents* of the element, rather than the value of its **value** attribute to the server. To make matters worse, when there are multiple **button**s, *all* of their names and contents are sent to the server, even though only the activated button should have its **name** and value pair sent.

There are a number of ways of working around the problem, but none of them are perfect, and so the rough consensus of developers is that unless you don't need to support IE 6 and 7, you should use **input** elements rather than **button**s.

Menus

When you want users to choose between a small number of mutually exclusive options or a small number of related options more than one of which may be selected, the radio button and checkbox input types are appropriate. But when a large number of choices must be presented—for example, if you need users to select the country in which they live—dropdown menus are appropriate. We use the `select` element, along with the `option` and `optgroup` elements, to create dropdown menus.

The `select` element contains one or (usually) more `option` elements. Each of these is a menu item in the associated menu. If `select` contains a significant number of `option` elements, or it makes sense to group them, we can do so using the `optgroup` element, which is a container for the `option` elements. (A `select` element might have some `option` elements inside `optgoup` elements, and others directly inside the `select` element.)

For example, here's how we'd create a menu of car models, grouped by make:

```
<select name="cars">
        <option label="none" value="none">None</option>
  <optgroup label="Mazda">
                <option value="CX7">CX-7</option>
                <option value="CX9">CX-9</option>
                <option value="Tribune">Tribune</option>
    </optgroup>
    <optgroup label="Subaru">
                <option value="Forester">Forester</option>
                <option value="Legacy">Legacy</option>
                <option value="Outback">Outback</option>
    </optgroup>
    <optgroup label="Volkswagen">
                <option value="Tiguan">Tiguan</option>
                <option value="Touareg">Touareg</option>
    </optgroup>
</select>
```

It's possible to accept multiple selections from the user by setting the `multiple` attribute on the `select` element. This attribute, and others like it (such as `checked`), are a little different from most attributes we've seen. They are either true or false, and so are called Boolean attributes. We might expect them to take values of either true or false, but they don't. Rather, if the attribute is present, then the value is true, and if the attribute is absent, the value is false. But the strangeness doesn't end there. There are also two ways of including these elements in our markup. We can use the form `checked="checked"`—that is, the value of the attribute is its name in quotes—or we can simply include the attribute name without any value.

So, we could specify that multiple selections should be allowed for our `select` element in one of two ways:

```
<select name="cars" multiple="multiple">
<select name="cars" multiple>
```

Both are valid, but for consistency, some developers recommend adding the attribute value.

Text Areas

The `text` `input` is sometimes too small to accommodate the type of response you want from a user. When you want a more expansive response that requires multiple lines, use the `textarea` element instead. In addition to presenting a larger area for user input, `textarea` elements can receive "return" keystrokes thus allowing users to add line breaks, whereas `text` inputs will pass returns to the submit button for the form.

There are two optional attributes specifically for `textarea` elements—`rows` and `cols`—which specify, respectively, the width and height of the element in characters. Use CSS instead.

A `textarea` is a non-empty element, and its content (if any) will be the initial value of the element. For example a `textarea` for monkeys to try their luck at randomly typing *War and Peace* might look like this if we've given them a head start, thus immeasurably increasing the odds of any given monkey achieving the goal:

```
<textarea name="warandpeace">
Well, Prince, so Genoa and Lucca are now just family
estates of the Buonapartes
</textarea>
```

Disabling Controls

All of the form controls in an element can be initially disabled using the `disabled` attribute (like `checked` and `multiple`, this is a Boolean attribute). The only way for a disabled element to then be reenabled is via JavaScript.

Labeling Controls

If we were to take a look at almost all of our code examples in a browser, we'd notice something important: most lack labels. So there's no way for our users to know what each radio button, checkbox, text area, or text input is for. Some elements label themselves, either with the `value` attribute or the contents of the element, but to those which don't, we need to add a label.

The HTML `label` element is made to do just this. These non-empty elements may contain the elements for which they are the label (*implicit labeling*), or be associated with that element via the `for` attribute (*explicit labeling*). The `for` attribute contains the value of the `id` attribute of the element for which it is the `label` (although we've given most of the form controls a `name` attribute, we can't use the value of this attribute in the `for` attribute).

Proper labeling makes a form much more accessible because assistive devices use labels to present information about a form. It also provides a huge usability advantage by setting user expectations about the behavior of controls. When a user clicks or otherwise activates a `label`, its associated form control is activated (though in IE 6, this only works with explicit labeling). With a text input or text area, the focus is put into the field; in the case of a radio button, it's checked, and so on.

Proper use of form labels is often overlooked by developers, but it's an important part of form markup best practices.

So should you make a label implicit, explicit, or both? Where possible, it makes sense to do both, but at the least, make the labeling explicit. This requires adding an `id` to each labeled form control, and using the `for` attribute for each `label`. It's a little extra work, but has significant usability and accessibility benefits. Here's how we'd label a text input, both implicitly and explicitly:

```
<label for="warandpeace">Monkeys please type here:
<textarea name="warandpeace" id="monkeyinput">
Well, Prince, so Genoa and Lucca are now just family
estates of the Buonapartes
  </textarea>
</label>
```

Containing Controls and Labels in a Form

A common error developers make with form controls and labels is containing them directly inside the `form` element. While this sounds eminently sensible, it's not permitted in HTML. A label or form control cannot be the direct child of a `form`. Rather, it must be contained inside a block element like a `div` or paragraph.

Grouping Controls

Complex forms often consist of groups of related controls. HTML provides the `fieldset` element for grouping together form elements (it's a container for related form controls), along with a `legend` element for providing a specific caption for this group of elements. We look at these in detail in Chapter 6, where we also focus on form accessibility in more detail.

It pays to explore forms beyond the basics, because a little extra effort and understanding can pay big dividends when it comes to accessibility and overall usability. The more accessible and usable form is, the more likely it is to be completed and submitted, which means the efforts will be rewarded by more leads, sales, and other interactions.

Tables

Tables have a difficult history for web developers. Long misused for page layout (as discussed in Chapter 9), they are often treated as pariahs. In fact, tables are entirely appropriate for *tabular data*, whether it's a price list, financial data, experimental results, or one of many other possible types.

Table Structure

A table is a simple thing: it's a **table** element with a number of rows (the **tr** element). These rows can be grouped into header rows (the **thead** element) one or more table body (**tbody**) elements, and table footer (**tfoot**) element. These groups are useful for more complex and longer tables, where a browser may present the **thead** and **tfoot** as fixed, and the **tbody** as a scrolling element.

Where used, the **tfoot** element must come before the **tbody**, which seems illogical, but allows the browser to render the **tfoot** rather than waiting for a large **tbody** to load before rendering the footer. Each of these elements must contain at least one table row.

Table rows contain one or more *cells*, which can be either **th** elements (a header cell), or **td** elements (a data cell). These cells can contain content, including HTML (even block elements).

Before we continue, here's a very simple table, with a small number of rows, and no **thead**, **tfoot**, or **tbody**.

```
<table>
  <tr>
    <th>Make</th>
    <th>Model</th>
    <th>Number of Seats</th>
    <th>Engine Size</th>
    <th>Price</th>
  </tr>
  <tr>
    <td>Mazda</td>
    <td>CX-7</td>
    <td>5</td>
    <td>2.31 Turbo</td>
    <td>$$$</td>
  </tr>
  <tr>
    <td>Volkswagen</td>
    <td>Touareg</td>
    <td>5</td>
    <td>2.51 Turbo Diesel</td>
    <td>$$$$$</td>
  </tr>
</table>
```

Here, we have headers as the cells in the top row, and in each column, we have matching data. Figure **3.6** shows how a browser might render this. It's not especially pretty, but that's where CSS comes in, as we'll see in Chapter 4.

Make	Model	Number of Seats	Engine Size	Price
Mazda	CX-7	5	2.3l Turbo	$$$
Volkswagen	Touareg	5	2.5l Turbo Diesel	$$$$$

3.6
A simple table.

If we were to have a particularly large number of makes and models, we could group the first row into a **thead** element, like this:

```
<thead>
    <tr>
        <th>Make</th>
        <th>Model</th>
        <th>Number of seats</th>
        <th>Engine size</th>
        <th>Price</th>
    </tr>
</thead>
```

Spanning Columns

There are times when one cell will span several columns. For example, in a conference timetable, some time slots will have a single event (a keynote presentation for example), while others will have multiple events at the same time [**3.7**].

Here, we can specify that a **td** (or **th**) element spans a number of cells using the **colspan** attribute, and giving this a value of the number of cells it should span. As there are four columns of cells, and only two cells, the second cell spans three columns.

```
<th>7:30am - 9:00am</th>
<td colspan="3">
<div class="summary">Registration</div>
</td>
```

3.7

A timetable with some
events spanning multiple
columns of the table

TIME	DESIGN TRACK	BUSINESS TRACK	DEVELOPMENT TRACK
7:30 AM - 9:00 AM	Registration		
9:00 AM - 9:10 AM	Opening comments		
9:10 AM - 10:15 AM	Opening keynote – Matt Webb: Escalante		
10:15 AM - 10:45 AM	Morning tea		
10:45 AM - 11:40 AM	Font embedding and typography Mark Boulton	Beyond SEO Cheryl Gledhill & Scott Gledhill	Best practices for speeding up your site Mark Stanton
11:40 AM - 11:45 AM	Changeover		

It's important that the number of cells—plus the columns they span—adds up to
the number of cells there would otherwise be in the row.

For the most part, you are likely to find yourself using simple tables, with a number of rows, each containing either header or data cells. In Chapter 6 we'll return
to tables, and look at some of their more advanced features that aid accessibility.

Frames and *iframes*

The `frame` element was at one time one of the most widely used features of
HTML, but it's now quite rare. It was used to present the contents of different
HTML documents within the same browser window, but due to accessibility
and usability challenges, it has fallen almost entirely out of use. As such, we
won't spend much time on it.

However, to clarify one area of potential confusion, inline frames (the `iframe`
element) are widely used in mashup-style pages, as a way of embedding content

from other sites and communicating across different domains. (`iframe`s are a complicated topic associated with Ajax and mashup programming; you can find some resources on them at the end of this book.)

The reason `iframe`s are superior to traditional frames is that `iframe`s are part of the markup of a document, whereas frames are contained in entirely different documents, and contain within them links to the pages that display inside them. As such, `iframe`s can be styled using CSS, and placed anywhere on the page; the placement of traditional frames is determined by various attributes of the frame element itself.

Characters and Entities

HTML and other web technologies are designed to be as universal as possible. One area in which this applies is accessibility, which is discussed in detail in Chapter 6. Another is that of languages.

Those of us who read and write English and other European languages typically don't have to deal with the complexities of character sets other than those associated with Roman alphabets. The full complexities surrounding character encodings are too extensive for me to discuss here, but it is import to note how to include nonstandard characters in HTML documents. If we need to make occasional use of such characters as curly quotes(""), the copyright symbol (©), characters from other alphabets, and so on, we can often use character entities or numeric character references to do so.

Character entities have the form of an ampersand (&) followed by the name of the entity. Common entities include:

- The copyright symbol (`&copy;`)
- The ampersand (`&amp;`)
- Less than and greater than (`&lt;` and `&gt;`)
- Left and right single curly quotes (`&lsquo;` and `&rsquo;`)
- Left and right double curly quotes (`&ldquo;` and `&rdquo;`)
- The Euro sign (`&euro;`)

Numeric character references have the form of an ampersand, followed by the pound sign (#) and a number, plus a semicolon (;). The common entities above have the following numeric character references:

- The copyright symbol (`&#913;`)
- The ampersand (`&#38;`)
- Less than and greater than (`&#60;` and `&#62;`)
- Left and right single curly quotes (`&#8216;` and `&#8217;`)
- Left and right double curly quotes (`&#8220;` and `&#8222;`)
- The Euro sign (`&#8364;`)

When you use `>` and `<` and `&` characters in the text of a document, they must be included as the character entity or numeric reference, not as "raw" characters. (This is technically referred to as *escaping* these characters.) Browsers treat `<` and `>` as the beginning and end of HTML elements, but render `&lt;` and `&gt;` as the less-than and greater-than symbols. One of the most common validation errors for HTML documents is using unescaped ampersands in the text of a document. The character `&` should only appear in character entities and numeric references. At all other times—even in URLs—it should be escaped.

What's the difference between numeric entities and references? Entities were invented as a more developer friendly version of some of the more common numeric entities. Entities are typically easier to remember and understand when you see them in code. But, while only a subset of characters has an entity, there's a numeric character reference for *every* unicode character.

Quality Assurance

Browsers are usually very forgiving of markup that is incorrect (or *invalid*), which is both very good for users, and very bad for the quality of code on the web. Although browsers will work very hard to make sense of invalid markup, different browsers will handle the same invalid markup in different ways, which can make it very difficult to debug browser differences and rendering bugs. There's one very simple way of ensuring your markup is correct: use a validator. Validators check that your markup conforms to the rules of HTML, and will report in detail where errors have been found. This, along with checking to ensure your links aren't broken, are two easy to use, important quality assurance tools that should be as widely used as by developers as spell checking is for writers.

Validating Your Markup

There are commercial and free validators online and available as desktop applications. The one most widely used is that maintained by the W3C at **validator.w3.org**.

Validators take the **DOCTYPE** of a document and then check the document against the syntactical rules of the language variant you've chosen. At the W3C validator, you can check a document at a URL, via file upload, or by pasting in the HTML .

When you first validate a document, you might be surprised to see that there are several errors and warnings, when you might have thought that your document was entirely correct. Errors can creep into any code quite easily, and the forgiving nature of web browsers' HTML parsers means they can easily go unnoticed. Sometimes a single containment error (for example an unclosed anchor) can cause multiple errors, and fixing that one error will fix all the errors that flow from it. Some of the most common validation errors are

- Unescaped ampersands in URLs and elsewhere in a document. The & character should only appear in character entities and numeric references.
- With XHTML **DOCTYPE**s, failing to use the correct syntax for empty elements (that is leaving off the / before the >).
- Uppercase letters in XHTML element names and attribute names.
- Incorrectly nested HTML elements (for example `<strong><a href="index.html">`Home`</strong></a>`).
- Block elements nested inside inline elements.
- Form controls and labels contained directly inside `form` elements (they must be inside block elements inside the `form` element).
- `img` elements and other elements that require an `alt` attribute missing this attribute—it can have an empty value, but must be present.
- Deprecated elements and attributes (like `font` and `color`) in documents with strict **DOCTYPE**s.
- A **DOCTYPE** directive at the top of a document that is not in all uppercase letters.
- In XHTML, failing to quote attribute values.

Validation is an essential though often overlooked quality assurance tool for your markup. It's not difficult to include as part of your workflow, and it is something you'll benefit from if you do it as you go—particularly if you aren't quite sure about something— rather than leaving it to the end of your coding, only to find an overwhelming and hard to address cascade of errors.

Checking Links

Broken links are far too common on the web. These can be checked with many desktop and web-based tools, including the W3C's own link checker. This can ensure that pages you link to haven't moved or disappeared, and can also help you find errors where you've misentered a URL, either an internal or external one. The W3C's link checker is at **validator.w3.org/checklink**.

HTML Tidy

If you're cleaning up legacy markup, or markup generated by a word processor, such as Microsoft Word, HTML Tidy—a free, open source tool from the legendary Dave Raggett—is invaluable. While the command line versions for Unix, Linux, Windows, and Mac OS are not for the fainthearted, there are numerous desktop applications that incorporate Tidy, as well as web-based versions such as HTMLHelp's **valet.htmlhelp.com/tidy**.

Tidy can convert HTML to XHTML, fix all kinds of errors like the ones we've discussed here, and deal with some of the particularly poor HTML that Word produces with its "Save as Web Page" feature. Tidy is not a replacement for good coding practices, but it is a great tool for freshening up legacy and other less than perfect code.

HTML versus XHTML

Throughout this chapter, we've referred to XHTML and HTML as essentially the same thing. We've noted that there are some differences, particularly when it comes to syntax, but that they share identical semantics. Let's look a little closer.

Syntax Differences

We've seen that these two languages have syntactic differences. XHTML is designed so that all valid XHTML documents are also HTML documents. You should be able to validate any XHTML document you develop as HTML. The reverse is not true. Valid HTML documents, unless they contain no empty elements, cannot be valid XHTML documents.

Serving the Document

As we've touched on briefly, when a server serves any file, it does so along with a MIME type (also known as a content type). For example, PNG images are served as "image/png," style sheets as "text/css," and so on. Most of the time, we can safely ignore the type the server uses to serve the document. When it comes to XHTML, though, we can't. Keep reading just a little longer to find out why.

Error Handling

As noted earlier in this chapter, the forgiving nature of HTML parsers in all web browsers means that no matter how invalid a document's markup is, a browser will do its best to render it in a sensible manner. This is both a blessing and a curse. XHTML, on the other hand, is an application of XML, and XML has very strict parsing rules. If an XML parser encounters even the slightest error in XML markup—and XHTML is XML markup—it must report this error and stop parsing. You can imagine the impact on the web if this were the error handling rule for HTML.

Why is it then that we see little of this problem on the web? Do XHTML developers routinely create perfectly valid markup? Sadly, the answer is no: it's often extremely hard to do so, since many sites include third-party content such as advertisements, user comments that may contain HTML, mashup content, and so on. Ensuring that this third-party content is perfectly valid is often impossible.

Faced with this disparity, browser makers hit on a compromise when it comes to XHTML. If XHTML documents (those with an XHTML **DOCTYPE**) are served as "text/html," then browsers treat them as HTML, not XML. If, on the other hand, they are served with a MIME type of "application/xhtml+xml," then browsers should treat them as XML, so if there is a single error, the parsing stops and the user gets an error message. So documents should only be served as "application/xhtml+xml" when you can be absolutely sure they are and will remain valid.

There's a further complication. Internet Explorer, even as of version 8, lacks an XHTML parser. Rather than treating documents served as "application/

xhtml+xml" as HTML, it asks the user whether they want to download the document to disk, effectively treating these documents as being of an unknown type.

While the full complexities, including techniques for serving different types to different browsers, is beyond the scope of this book, unless you are particularly well versed in the issues, XHTML and HTML should both be served as "text/html."

Which Should You Use?

As mentioned right at the start of this very long chapter, for many years, XHTML was considered by most developers—and the W3C—to be the future direction of HTML. With the demise of XHTML 2 and the rise of HTML5—which can be marked up using either HTML or XHTML syntax—the situation is no longer so clearcut. Both HTML and XHTML syntax will be with us for a long time to come.

But which should you use, and why?

In many respects, it boils down to a matter of taste. As someone who has used the XHTML syntax for many years, along with many professional developers, I am sure I'll instinctively use it long into the future. Arguably, one benefit its syntax has over traditional HTML is a consistency that can make both writing and reading markup easier. All attributes are quoted, empty elements always close with the trailing slash, and all elements must close themselves.

There are arguments against using XHTML syntax, one of the best of which was written by Maciej Stachowiak (a core developer of WebKit and co-chair of the W3C HTML Working Group), can be found here: **webkit.org/blog/68/ understanding-html-xml-and-xhtml**. If you are interested in learning more, there's no better place to start.

My personal choice is for XHTML markup, along with a strict **DOCTYPE**, to simplify the language (strict versions of HTML and XHTML omit all presentational elements and attributes). Regardless of which syntax you choose, a strict **DOCTYPE** for new projects will help ensure that your markup focuses on the semantic aspects of your content, not on its presentation, which is the domain of CSS.

Which, not coincidentally, is where we'll turn next.

chapter four

Presentation

In this chapter, we'll look at the core concepts and syntax of CSS. Later on, we'll put this knowledge into practice with focused chapters on page layout (Chapter 9), CSS resets and frameworks (Chapter 10), CSS3 (Chapters 12 and 13), and web typography (Chapter 15).

A Short History of Style for the Web

The idea of separating structured content from information about how that content should be presented has been around since the 1970s. The initial proposal for HTML included the idea that presentation would be the domain of a separate style sheet language, but no such language was developed. In the mid-1990s, browser makers responded to a huge demand for control over presentation by creating such new HTML features as the `font` element, the `bgcolor` attribute for the `body` element, `vlink` and other attributes for styling links, and so on.

As a result of these changes, HTML devolved from a semantics-focused markup language to one festooned with presentational elements and attributes, few of which were part of any standard. Such HTML was difficult to write and to understand. Worse, web content marked up using these incarnations of HTML was hidden by vast swaths of purely presentational markup, making it difficult for search engines and user agents like screen readers to make sense of the content itself. Complex presentational markup is also extremely difficult to maintain: sites marked up solely with presentational HTML were so difficult to redesign that their markup often had to be abandoned and recoded from scratch.

In 1996, the W3C published the CSS1 specification, based in large part on earlier work by Bert Bos and Håkon Wium Lie. Internet Explorer 3, released in 1996, had experimental support for CSS, and both Internet Explorer 4 and Netscape 4—the "version 4" browsers that ushered in the era of modern web development—offered more complete though painfully buggy support for CSS1. With these browsers, CSS became a real option for basic styling including fonts, colors, and whitespace control. Complex CSS page layout, however, was still some way off.

Internet Explorer 5 for the Mac, released in 2000, was the first browser that could be said to have genuinely usable support for the features of CSS1 and many of the features of CSS2 (which was published in 1998, but never fully supported in any browser). IE 5 for the Mac, whose Tasman rendering engine was developed under the leadership of Tantek Çelik, showed what could be done with CSS, particularly when it came to page layout. It also made developers realize that targeting older, less capable browsers—as well as newer, more sophisticated browsers—would be an increasingly important part of their jobs. (See Chapter 7 for a much longer discussion of this issue.)

The release of Internet Explorer 6 for Windows was another important milestone for CSS-based development; though its CSS support is now seen as buggy and uneven in comparison to later browsers, IE 6 was the first browser that offered reasonably good CSS support for Windows users. Sadly, the demise of Netscape Communicator slowed updates to Netscape 4, which meant that developers had to keep coding for Netscape's version 4 well after Internet Explorer had moved on to more sophisticated (though still buggy) CSS implementations. Through the late 1990s and early 2000s, support for CSS and web standards as a whole grew among web developers. Yet the slow pace of development of CSS support in browsers—and of browser upgrades by users—also made the period one of great frustration for developers. Many experienced developers who had perfected their presentational HTML skills resisted the adoption of CSS, often with the frustrated (and not entirely unreasonable) cry of "CSS doesn't work!"

The introduction of Safari for the Mac in 2003 and Firefox in 2004 shook the world of web browsers out of its complacency. Safari, which was based on the open source KHTML—which Apple themselves later open sourced as the rendering engine WebKit—and Firefox, which was based on the Mozilla open source codebase started by the Netscape team, placed a strong emphasis on standards support. Simultaneously, Opera Software, led by CTO Håkon Wium Lie, continued to support standards in the Opera browser and promote standards-based development to the developer community.

At about this same time, Microsoft announced that they would not release new versions of Internet Explorer for their then-current OS, Windows XP, causing many developers' hearts to sink at the thought of being forced to support IE 6 for all eternity.

The rapid adoption of Firefox and Safari, however, may have prompted a change of heart at Microsoft, which later announced that Internet Explorer 7 would be available on Windows XP as well as the newer Vista operating system—and that it would include improved standards support. With the release of IE 7 and the subsequent introduction of IE 8 (also available for Windows XP), which offered even better standards support, web standards had finally become central to both web developers and all browser makers. As a result, CSS finally became the undisputed technology for controlling the presentation of web content.

Why Separate Content from Appearance?

But why is CSS so important? What are the practical benefits of separating the presentation of a page from its markup?

- When markup is decoupled from presentation, multiple developers can work on different aspects of a site's development independently.
- Site maintenance is far more efficient: a complete redesign can often be achieved with little or no changes to a site's markup.

- When we increase the ratio of content to markup, we're almost certainly improving the visibility of a page's content to search engines, which is as important as any other factor in search engine optimization.
- Clean, well structured markup is usually much easier for assistive devices like screen readers to understand, which makes sites more accessible.
- The file sizes of pages that are marked up semantically and structurally are usually considerably smaller than those marked up presentationally, which results in bandwidth savings and (usually) improved site performance.

But if you've read this far, you're probably already convinced. So let's dive into CSS.

What Is CSS?

CSS is a language for describing the presentation of elements in a document marked up in HTML (and other markup languages, in theory at least).

How Is CSS Used?

There are several ways in which style sheets can be associated with an HTML document.

Inline Style

CSS can be added to individual HTML elements as the value of the `style` attribute. This method is called *inline CSS*. For example, we can give an individual paragraph a text color of red using this code:

```
<p style="color: red">
```

This, however, isn't a good idea. Applying style like this doesn't separate presentation from markup and content, so it's really not much better than using presentational HTML. Furthermore, it's not possible to override inline styles, which makes this method even harder to work with than presentational HTML in some respects.

Embedded CSS

Embedded CSS puts the styles for an HTML document in the document's head, inside a `style` element:

```
<style type="text/css">
  p {color: red}
</style>
```

The **style** element contains a **type** attribute that tells the browser the type of contents of the element, and **must** be contained in the **head** of the element, unlike **script** elements, which may be contained anywhere in a document.

Embedding CSS is not the best possible way of adding CSS to a page, as it works only on a per page basis, and it too should be avoided in favor of the recommended approach, which we'll look at next.

Linking to External CSS

The recommended technique of adding CSS to an HTML document is to link to one or more CSS files using a **link** element in the **head** of the HTML document. This allows us to experience the full benefits of using CSS in place of presentational HTML.

```
<link rel="stylesheet" href="style/style.css"
type="text/css" />
```

This **link** element has three attributes, all of which are important:

- The first is the **rel** attribute, which we saw in Chapter 3. It specifies the relationship of the linked file to this one—in this case, that the linked file is a style sheet for this document.

- The second attribute, **href**, specifies where the style sheet file is located. We can use a relative or absolute URL (style sheets can even be located on different domains from the HTML document).

- Lastly, we must also have the **type** of text/css. This tells the browser what type of style sheet language to expect. Some browsers also support XSLT style sheets, so we want to ensure the browser is aware of what it is getting.

An external style sheet is simply a text file. It usually takes the file extension .css, which will typically ensure that the server serves the file as text/css, the MIME type the browser expects based on the **type** attribute we set.

Basic CSS Syntax

Of course, we need to have something to put into our external (or embedded) style sheet. This is CSS, a simple language, which uses just text. We'll start with the core of the CSS syntax, then dive into the major features of the language.

Selectors, Declaration Blocks, Declarations, and Properties

A style sheet, like an HTML file, is quite simple: in essence, it's just one or more statements, which are also referred to as rules.

Each statement has two parts, a *selector* and a *declaration block*. The selector specifies what elements in an HTML document the statement will style. The declaration block specifies the style that will be applied to the elements the statement selects.

The declaration block contains one or more *declarations*. A declaration is made up of a property name and a value. Here's an example statement:

```
p {
  color: red;
  font-weight: bold;
}
```

Try breaking this down in your own mind into selector, declaration block, declarations, and properties before we continue.

In the preceding example, our selector is **p**. This is one of many different types of selector we'll cover in this chapter, and throughout the book. It matches every element with the name **p**—that is, every paragraph element in the page's markup.

The declaration block is everything contained within the curly braces. It contains two declarations: one with a `color` property, and one with a `font-weight` property. Notice that the two declarations are separated by a semicolon (;). The semicolon after the second declaration is optional, as it is after the last declaration of any declaration block.

And that's **all** the syntax you need to learn to use CSS. You will need to understand the various types of selectors, their structures, and what types of elements they match in a document. In this chapter we'll cover all the major selector types in CSS1 and CSS2, and in Chapter 12, we'll look at CSS3. The other thing you'll want to learn are the various properties for styling these elements. There are several dozen, though only about two dozen are in common use. We'll cover all the most commonly used CSS1 and CSS2 properties in this chapter, and in Chapter 13, we'll look at CSS3 properties.

One note about the structure of this chapter: rather than simply cataloguing all the selector types and then all the properties of CSS, I'll begin with some of the simplest selectors and properties and then build up to progressively more sophisticated versions.

The Basics of Selectors

CSS selectors are the least understood part of the language, but a good understanding of selectors and their uses is a hallmark of a good professional developer. Here's your chance to really get to grips with the sophistication of CSS selectors.

Type Selectors

A CSS selector specifies which HTML elements a particular statement will style. The simplest kind of selector of the dozen or so is the HTML element, or *type selector*. These selectors use just the name of an HTML element (for example **p**, **h3**, or **body**), and select **every** element of that type. So **p** selects every paragraph, **h3** selects every heading of level three, and **body** selects the **body** of the document (an HTML document can have only one **body**).

Grouping Selectors Together

We can group selectors so that the same declaration block of properties applies to all of elements selected by any of the selectors in the group. A *selector group* is simply the selectors separated by commas. For example, to select all heading levels at once, we can use the selector:

```
h1, h2, h3, h4, h5, h6
```

As we'll see later, we can group together selectors of different kinds. Selector groups produce more compact, readable, and maintainable style sheets. For example, if all headings in a document use the same font, we can simply use the selector group in the preceding example rather than having to repeat the font selection property six times (and then change it six times if the style changes).

Basic Properties: Font Styles

CSS support in browsers began with simple text style properties, so it's fitting that we begin our investigation into CSS properties with these foundational properties.

color

The `color` property specifies the text color for selected elements.

The property takes a single color value. Color values, which are also used by a number of other CSS properties, come in a number of forms.

The simplest color values are color keywords, of which there are two kinds: seventeen basic color values like `red` and `blue`, and a larger number of system colors, including `ButtonFace`, `ButtonText`, and other values. In addition, all browsers have long supported a large palette of 140 color keywords from the X11 color chart, and though these are not part of CSS1 or CSS2, they are part of the draft versions of CSS3.

The seventeen common colors are `aqua`, `black`, `blue`, `fuchsia`, `gray`, `green`, `lime`, `maroon`, `navy`, `olive`, `orange`, `purple`, `red`, `silver`, `teal`, `white`, and `yellow`. A full list of the X11 colors can be found at **en.wikipedia.org/wiki/X11_color_names**.

System colors don't set text to a specific color—instead, they let developers match the style of their own elements (like buttons) to the current system colors as defined in each user's operation system preferences, thus harmonizing their interfaces with the system's.

Color in CSS can also be specified in a number of other ways, the most common of which is hexadecimal RGB colors. These have the form `#RRGGBB`, where RR is a red hexadecimal color value, GG is a green hexadecimal color value, and BB is a blue hexadecimal color value. You won't generally need to manually determine the color value, as most design tools do this part for you, but now you know what the code means. When all three colors have their two digits or letters repeated (for example, `#FF2277`), the value can be truncated using the form `#RGB` (in this case, `#F27`). Note that this truncation can occur not when the second digit is a zero, but when the digit or letter for *each* color value is repeated. One very common CSS error is leaving off the `#` at the beginning of the hex value; don't do this. The third and fourth way to specify color values is via decimal and percentage RGB colors. Both of these methods have the basic form `rgb(color value)`, with the color value inside the parentheses. In decimal RGB, a number between 0 and 255 is used for each color, with these values separated by a comma. In percentage RGB, a percentage value from 0% to 100% is used. So, orange, which is `#FFA500` in hexadecimal, would be `rgb(255, 165, 0)` in decimal RGB and `rgb(100%, 65%, 0%)` in percentage RGB.

Let's cut to the chase and give our `body` a color of orange:

```
body {
   color: orange;
}
```

We've created our first statement. Easy, right?

font-family

Next, we'll give our headings a font. In CSS, we use the `font-family` property for this. This property takes one or more font names, separated by a comma. Why specify more than one? In CSS, we can generally only use the fonts already installed on our users' systems. There are exceptions to this rule, but web typography is sufficiently complex to deserve its own chapter (Chapter 15), so we'll stick with basics for now. The fonts on users' computers will depend on their operating systems, what fonts they have installed themselves, what software (such as Microsoft Office) they have installed, and several other factors. If we could only specify a single font, we'd really be stuck with the tiny subset of fonts that all platforms have in common. Luckily, we can specify more than one, so we can take advantage of a wider range of fonts. It's usually best to use a set of fonts that are similar to each other—by which I mean not simply fonts that look alike, but that have similar metrics—so that the same characters will occupy a similar amount of space in the various fonts we select.

A common pair of fonts with very similar metrics is Helvetica and Arial. One or the other of these two fonts are found on most browsing platforms,

so specifying both together makes a lot of sense. We'd do this with the
`font-family` property like this:

```
font-family: Helvetica, Arial
```

It's also a good idea to use a fallback generic font family, of which CSS
provides five:

- `serif`
- `sans-serif`
- `monospace`
- `cursive`
- `fantasy`

Here's how this all works together. When a browser sees the `font-family`
property, it takes the list of font names (which are separated by commas) and
looks to see whether the user's system has a font that matches the first name. If
so, it uses this font. If not, it goes to the next font name, and sees whether it has
a match for this one. If so, it uses that; otherwise, it continues along the list.
You can name as many alternate fonts as you like. If none of the names match a
font on the user's system, the browser takes the generic family name and uses
either its default font for that family or the user's preferred font for that family
(most browsers let you set a preferred font for generic families).

When a font has one or more spaces in its name—like Times New Roman—
the name of the font must be wrapped in single or double quotation marks.
For example:

```
font-family: Times, "Times New Roman", serif
```

Common mistakes with the `font` property include using quotation marks with
font names that don't have spaces, using quotation marks with generic font
family names (particularly `sans-serif`), and not using quotation marks with
font names that do have spaces.

font-size

You can set the size of text with the `font-size` property. `font-size` is the first property we've seen that takes more kinds of values: length values and percentage values.

Length Values

A length value is a numeric value associated with a unit of measurement. In CSS, with very rare exceptions, when a property takes a numeric value, that value includes a unit. In HTML, unitless numeric values are assumed to be px values, but in CSS, a length value without a unit is almost always considered an error; there are one or two exceptions, which we'll discuss shortly. This is one of the most common errors CSS developers make, and it's so common in part because some browsers wrongly treat numeric values with no units as pixel values. There are several different units, the most common being pixels (px) and ems (em). Percentage values, though they're not strictly length values, are very similar to length values; the trick is that percentage values don't always refer to the same thing from property to property, as we'll see shortly.

Relative and Absolute Values

There are two types of length value—absolute values, which are most commonly length values with a px unit, and relative values, which are most commonly values with an em unit. Percentage values are effectively relative values as well.

Absolute length values are (usually) fixed, regardless of factors like the user's text zoom, window size, and so on. Relative values allow layouts, text size, and other CSS-applied styles to adapt to the user's preferences and setup, so they're generally preferred. We'll see plenty of examples of the benefits of relative units throughout this book, but some very common examples include:

- Specifying `font-size` in em units or percentages. This allows for text to grow and shrink as users increase and decrease their font size (this is less of a problem today, but older browsers typically fixed the size of text so that it couldn't be zoomed by the user if the unit for `font-size` was pixels).

- Specifying the width of an element in ems. This means that the element remains more or less the same number of characters wide regardless of how big or small the text is zoomed. This can be especially helpful for legibility, where particularly long or short lines of text can very much impact the ease of reading.

The em Unit

So just what is this thing called em? For starters, it's not related to the **em** element! In typographical terms, and in CSS, an em is the height of a font—for example, for a 12 point font, 1em is 12 points.

The em unit is particularly useful because it allows us to specify many CSS properties relative to the current font size. So, for instance, we can specify a margin that is four times the height of the font, and when users zoom their text size, the margin stays in proportion. We'll see ems used repeatedly throughout the book.

It's possible to set `font-size` in pixels, but it's much more preferable to set it in either percentages or ems. We could set our headings to have different font sizes using statements like these:

```
h1 {font-size: 2em}
h2 {font-size: 1.6em}
h3 {font-size: 1.4em}
h4 {font-size: 1.2em}
```

This means that the text of **h1** elements will be twice the size that it would otherwise be, **h2** elements 1.6 times the size it would otherwise be, and so on. We could similarly use equivalent percentages to do this:

```
h1 {font-size: 200%}
h2 {font-size: 160%}
h3 {font-size: 140%}
h4 {font-size: 120%}
```

Much less common is the use of keywords to specify font sizes. It is possible to use keywords like `xx-small`, `small`, and `large`, but it's usually best to avoid these, as there's no consensus among browsers—or in the CSS standard—as to exactly what these seven sizes should be in relation to one another.

font-weight

The `font-weight` property, which controls how bold or heavy a font should be, can be specified in two ways: we can use the keywords `bold` and `normal`, or we can use one of nine weights from `100` to `900`. It's rare that fonts have a wide range of weights, and so values of `100` to `400` map typically to the value of `normal`, and `500` and up are considered `bold`.

Keyword Values

In addition to color, length, and percentage values, the other main values we'll see are keyword values. We've seen this briefly with color keywords, and many other properties take predefined keyword values—sometimes exclusively—while other properties take either keyword or other types of values.

---

font-style

One of the challenges of becoming proficient in CSS is learning and remembering all the different possible property names, which don't always align with what we commonly call these properties outside of CSS. A perfect example is how we specify whether an element's text should be italicized. In CSS, we use the `font-style` property, with three possible keyword values—`italic` (not `italics`), `normal`, and `oblique`. We can essentially consider `italic` and `oblique` to be the same thing.

text-decoration

With the `text-decoration` property, we can add or change text strikethrough, `underline`, the far less commonly used `overline`, and the mercifully unused and largely unsupported `blink` decorations. The `text-decoration` takes one or more space-separated (not comma-separated) keyword values:

- `underline`
- `overline`
- `line-through`
- `blink`
- `none` (which removes, for example, the default underline most browsers apply to anchors)

Putting these common properties together, we might style a heading of level 1 like this:

```
h1{
    font-family: "Times New Roman", Times, serif;
    font-weight: bold;
    font-style: italic;
    text-decoration: underline;
    font-size: 2em;
}
```

Inheritance

If we were to set for example a `font-weight` on the `body` element using, say, this statement:

```
body {
font-weight: bold
}
```

then all of the text in paragraphs, headings, and other elements would be bold. But why? What's going on?

Many, though not all, CSS properties are inherited by child elements from their parent elements. For example, `font-weight` is inherited. This means that all descendants of the `body`—that is, every visible element in the document—will have a `font-weight` of `bold` as well, unless some other CSS statement specifies that its `font-weight` should be normal.

Inheritance is powerful and sometimes confusing, but without it, CSS would be much less efficient. We'd have to specify `font-size`, `font-weight`, `color`, `line-height`, and many other properties for every single type of element in a document, which would produce larger and more difficult to maintain CSS files. I won't exhaustively list the properties that are inherited and those that aren't (these are detailed in the CSS specification). The good news is that in almost every case, properties that we'd want to be inherited will be, and those that we wouldn't want to be inherited—`border` and `padding`, for example—aren't.

In addition, we can always use a special keyword `inherit` for any CSS property, which specifies that the value should be inherited from the parent element, regardless of whether the property is inherited by default.

Getting Specific: class and id Selectors

Being able to select and style every paragraph or heading of level 1 is a leap forward over presentational HTML, but it's still quite unsophisticated—after all, what happens if we only want to style specific paragraphs or other elements? Fortunately, CSS has different kinds of selectors that select HTML elements according to specific characteristics. The most commonly used (and also the most overused) of these are the class and id selectors. These selectors select any element with a given `class` value or `id` value.

class Selectors

Class selectors, as we've just seen, select every element with a given `class` value. The syntax is straightforward: just a period followed by the value of the `class` attribute we want to select. For example, in Chapter 3, we used the `class` value of `chapter` for the chapters of our book. We'd select every element with a `class` value of `chapter` like this:

```
.chapter {}
```

This will select, for example, **p** `class="chapter"`, but also **div** `class="chapter"`.

We can make class selectors more specific by adding the type of element we want to select (in addition to the `class` it must have) before the period. For example, **p.chapter** will only select paragraphs of `class` `chapter`. It won't select **div**s with that `class` value.

id Selectors

Closely related are id selectors. We saw in the last chapter that `id`s differ from `class`es mainly because whereas any number of elements may share the same `class` value, only one element in any document may have a given `id` value. We construct an id selector by using the pound (or hash) character (#) followed by the `id` name. So, if we wanted to select the **div** with the `id` volume1chapter1, we'd use this selector:

```
#volume1chapter1 {}
```

As with the class selector, we can make the id selector more specific, and only select an element of a particular type that also has a given `id` value by adding the type of element before the # character. For example, **div#volume1chapter1** will only select a **div** with the `id` value volume1chapter1.

Specificity

Now, what happens if we have the following two CSS statements?

```
div#volume1chapter1 {
    font-weight: bold;
    font-size: 1.1em
}
div {
    font-size: 1.0em;
    color: red
}
```

What **font-size** will the text of a **div** with id volume1chapter1 have? There are a few rules that, once we learn them, will allow us to easily determine which properties apply. The technical name for this is *specificity*—and in short, the more specific statement overrides less specific statements.

It's important to note that whole statements don't override one another. Rather, *specific properties* are overridden. Let's come back to this point once we've looked at the basic rules of specificity:

- Different types of selectors have different specificities. The rules are technically quite involved, but they're not difficult to remember: id selectors always trump class selectors, and class selectors trump type selectors. As we see more selector types, we'll add them to our specificity rules.

- When they have the same specificity, statements closer to the end of a style sheet have higher precedence than those closer to the top of the style sheet.

Returning to our example, `font-weight` will be `bold`, because there's no conflict with the second statement. `font-size` will be `1.1em`, because the id selector trumps the type selector. `font-color` will be `red`, as there's no `font-color` property in the first of the statements, and thus nothing to override this property.

Common Text Layout Properties

In addition to font styling properties, CSS also has a number of text layout properties for aligning text, specifying line heights, letter spacing, word spacing, and more.

text-align

Text can be aligned left, right, center, or fully justified using the `text-align` property and one of these four keywords:

- `left`
- `right`
- `center` (only the American spelling may be used)
- `justify`

Justified text on the web is usually a bad idea, because the justification algorithms in browsers are less sophisticated than those in page layout and word processing software. This leads to a much higher chance of undesirable effects like *rivers*, in which vertical rivers of whitespace occur when the spaces between words are stretched to fill the full width of the element.

line-height

In CSS, `line-height`, unsurprisingly, specifies the height of a line of text in an element.

The judicious use of `line-height` can have a noticeable effect on the appearance of a block of text. The CSS `line-height` property allows you to specify the line height as a length value, such as `1.4em`, a percentage, or (in a rare exception to the rule) a number without units. Numberless units, when used with `line-height`, specify a multiplying factor rather than a pixel height.

This unusual multiplier allows a new way for elements to inherit `line-height` values. Before looking at this method, let's consider the way inheritance works with percentage values. If a `line-height` whose value is specified with a percentage is inherited, the value of the `line-height` for the element is a percentage of the current font size of the element's parent; child elements inherit this precalculated value, not the percentage itself. Consider the following statement (in which I've used a pixel `font-size` to simplify the calculations, though this isn't a recommended in actual development):

```
dd {
    font-size: 12px;
    line-height: 120%
}
```

In this example, the `line-height` for our **div** will be 120% of 12px, which is 14.4px—which will be rounded down to 14px, the nearest whole px value. A paragraph inside this element will inherit a `line-height` of 14px, **even if** its `font-size` is, say, 16px. And any child of that paragraph will **also** inherit a 14px `line-height`—which essentially loses the whole point of using a percentage value to begin with.

The multiplier value—a unitless numeric value—is nearly identical but is inherited in a different way. Suppose we specify the very similar statement

```
div{
    font-size: 12px;
    line-height: 1.2
}
```

Here, the parent **div** will have a `line-height` of 1.2 times 12px, which is 14.4px, again rounded down to 14px. So far it's identical to a percentage `line-height`. But this time, the children of the **div** will also have a `line-height` of 1.2. So if, for example, we have paragraphs inside the **div** with a font-size of 16px, their `line-height` will be 16px times 1.2 which is, 16.8px (17px, rounding to the nearest whole pixel value).

Importantly, using a multiplier rather than a percentage means that the `line-height` of elements doesn't need to be individually specified in individual statements. Instead, the multiplying value is inherited from, for example, the **body** element. This is the recommended way of specifying `line-height`.

Incidentally, by default, most browsers use a `line-height` of 1.0 to 1.2.

Letter and Word Spacing

CSS allows developers to expand or condense the space between letters or words, using the properties `letter-spacing` and `word-spacing`. Each of these takes a length value, though not a percentage value. A positive value expands text spacing, and a negative value condenses it. Figure **4.1** shows text with no additional spacing and the same text condensed by .1em using `letter-spacing: -.1em`, and expanded by .1em using `letter-spacing: .1em`. We've used ems here, as we will do often in the book because with relative units, when a user zooms text, the proportion of letter spacing will stay the same. If we'd used a pixel-based `letter-spacing`, at some text sizes the spacing looks fine, while at others, it's unnoticeable, or negatively affects legibility.

4.1

Text with no `letter-spacing` (top), with a `letter-spacing` of .1em (middle), and with a `letter-spacing` of –.1em (bottom)

text-indent

Frequently, with blocks of text such as paragraphs, the first line of text is indented or "outdented" to distinguish it from the rest of the block. We can do this easily with the rarely used `text-indent` property. For example, we could indent the first line by 5em like this:

```
p {
    text-indent: 5em
}
```

We could also "outdent" the first line by using a negative value. Again, we've used em units so that our design will retain its proportions as the text grows and shrinks based on user preferences.

Putting all these properties together, here's the CSS for a paragraph with `text-align`, `line-height`, `letter-spacing`, and `text-indent`:

```
p {
    line-height: 1.3;
    text-align: left;
    letter-spacing: .1em;
    text-indent: 1em;
}
```

And here's what it looks like in a browser [4.2], along with some extra CSS and even CSS3 properties we'll cover later in the book, just to give you something pretty to look at.

4.2

Our styled paragraph as rendered by Safari 4

"Why, my dear, you must know, Mrs. Long says that Netherfield is taken by a young man of large fortune from the north of England; that he came down on Monday in a chaise and four to see the place, and was so much delighted with it, that he agreed with Mr. Morris immediately; that he is to take possession before Michaelmas, and some of his servants are to be in the house by the end of next week."

Combinators: Descendant and Child Selectors

So far, we've selected elements based on their individual qualities—their type and their `class` and `id` values. But we can also select elements based on their place in the document structure. We can select any element descended from another element, for example, any element of `class` `chapter` descended from a `div` element. Or we can get more specific, and specify that the element must be a child element (that is, contained directly within a particular element).

Descendant Selectors

The first of these two new kinds of selector is the *descendant selector*. It selects an element based on the elements that contain it (either directly, as their parent element, or as a container of their parent, and so on up the tree). We can select elements based on one containment relationship, or chain together selectors to make them more and more specific. Let's start with the simplest case, where we have just two elements.

In the last chapter, we cautioned against the indiscriminate addition of `class` and `id` values to elements, suggesting rather it makes sense to give an `id` value to significant, unique parts of a document (for example, the header part of a page, which will usually be a `div` element, which contains a heading and probably page or site navigation). Other common "landmarks" in a page include the main content of the page and footers. We'll look at page layout in great detail in Chapter 9, which will also focus on markup conventions for page layouts.

Let's suppose we have the main content block of our page contained within a `div` with `class` `main` (we've chosen this name from the ARIA landmarks, which we cover in detail in Chapter 6). Now, we can select only elements inside this element—for example, only paragraphs inside the main content—not those inside the footer or header using a descendent selector:

```
div#main p{
}
```

Rather than having to give a `class` of `main` to each paragraph in the main content `div`, we can use this descendant selector instead. Descendant selectors are the single most overlooked aspect of CSS in relation to their value. Learning to use `id` judiciously for marking up landmark elements and descendant selectors for selecting their contents is one of the most useful techniques you'll learn as a web developer.

Child Selectors

Child selectors are closely related to descendant selectors, but they differ both in their syntax, as well as what they select. They select descendant elements of other elements, but *only* when the element is a child of the first selected element—that is, only when it is directly contained within the first selected element. These can be useful in situations like those just discussed, but they give us even more specific ways to select elements based on the structure of the document.

Child selectors, instead of simply having a space between the component selectors, have a greater-than sign (>) between them. So, for example, to select only headings of level 2 that are directly inside the main div, we'd use this:

```
#main>h2{}
```

As mentioned, we can also chain together selectors to make them even more specific.

Chaining

Nested lists are a particularly good example of the ways in which chaining is useful. Lists can be nested several deep. Suppose we have a list such as this one:

```
<ul>
  <li>HTML and XHTML</li>

  <li><ul>
    <li>principles of markup</li>
    <li>syntax</li>
    <li>semantics</li>
    <li>validity</li>
    <li>accessibility</li>
  </ul></li>

  <li><ul>
    <li>HTML versions</li>
    <li><ul>
       <li>HTML 4.01</li>
       <li>XHTML 1.0, 1.1</li>
    </ul></li>
  </ul></li>
</ul>
```

Let's suppose we wanted to style only the list items nested three levels deep. We could do this by adding a class value to each such list item—though that's something we've suggested time and again that we should try to avoid. We should always see whether there's an approach using CSS before adding markup specifically for styling a document. The selector `li` will select every list item in the document, which won't do. Similarly, `ul li` will select all of the list items that are inside an unordered list. Now if we think about the structure, we know the elements we want to select are list items inside unordered lists, inside unordered lists, inside unordered lists. So, working backwards, our selector for these list items would be:

```
ul ul ul li {}
```

Similarly, we can select the second-level indented elements using this:

```
ul ul li {}
```

But, if you think it through a bit, we have a problem. A list that is nested three levels deep is also listed two levels deep. So this statement selects any lists that are nested either two *or* three levels deep. But let's suppose these lists are contained within the same div of `id` `main`. This selector will select the same lists (all of them being descendants of the main `div`):

```
#main ul ul li {}
```

On the other hand, if we want to select only those list items contained inside an ordered list that is itself contained inside an ordered list that is *directly* inside that the main `div`, we'd use:

```
div#main>ul ul li {}
```

This example shows how even seemingly intractable problems of selecting elements without resorting to adding `class` and `id` values solely for presentation can often, with some ingenuity, be solved with CSS selectors. In Chapter 12, we'll see how CSS3 provides microsurgical tools for selecting elements with CSS, but the most important thing is to start "thinking in CSS," which means really understanding and exploring selectors.

But, as you must be expecting by this point, there's just one little hitch. We've mentioned browser support for CSS in passing, and how it's long caused headaches for developers. In Chapter 7 we'll go into this whole issue in significant detail, but here's where we run into the issue in practical terms for the first time.

Although all modern browsers support child selectors, until Internet Explorer 7, Internet Explorer did not. This means that the reasonably large percentage of users who use IE 6 won't see any style applied using child selectors without the use of workarounds such as JavaScript libraries, which add support to IE for features it doesn't support. We'll go into this in detail in Chapter 7, so don't worry too much about the issue now.

Specificity of Child and Descendant Selectors

How does specificity work with selectors like these? Earlier we said that id selectors trump class selectors, which themselves trump type selectors. Often, that's all you need to know, but in the case of child and descendant selectors, which may be made up of type, class, and id selectors, how do we determine which is the more specific selector? Well, each different kind of selector is given a value. Type selectors are worth 1, class selectors are worth 10, and id selectors are worth 100. We then add up the total value of all the component selectors for a child or descendant selector. (Really.)

So this selector:

```
#main ul ul li
```

would be worth 103 (100 for the id selector, and 3 for the three type selectors), whereas this one:

```
chapter ul li
```

would be worth 12 (10 for the class selector, and 2 for the two type selectors). The selector with the highest value is the most specific, and it trumps any selectors with a lower specificity.

Note that this *doesn't* apply to group selectors. Instead of adding up the individual selectors in the group, we treat each of the comma-separated selectors in the group as belonging to different statements. So, for instance, this selector:

```
#main ul li, .chapter p
```

is really two selectors—one with a specificity of 102, and one of 12.

The State of the Browsers

As we've noted, in practical terms, we need to take into account browser support (and more importantly, lack of support) for CSS while developing sites. Throughout this book, I'll refer to various browsers and their support for CSS, and other standards. Here's a quick overview of the current state of web browsers, focusing on the most widely used.

Internet Explorer   At the time of this writing, there were three widely used versions of Internet Explorer. IE 6, released in 2001; IE 7, released in late 2006; and IE 8, released in March 2009. Web developers generally still test for all three versions to ensure that sites work adequately in each.

Firefox   Firefox is a browser from Mozilla, which uses the open source rendering engine (which parses and displays HTML and provides other core functionality) called "Gecko." Gecko is used in a number of browsers other than Firefox. Users of Firefox tend to rapidly upgrade their browsers, and so at the time of writing, developers generally considered that they needed to focus on Firefox 3 and 3.5 in terms of compatibility. Firefox is available on Windows, Mac OS X, and Linux operating systems.

Safari   Safari is a browser from Apple that is available for both Mac OS X and Windows. There is also a Mobile Safari, which runs on the iPhone and iPod Touch. At the heart of Safari is a core engine, WebKit, which parses and renders the HTML and CSS and provides the low-level functionality for the browser, like Gecko does for Firefox. WebKit is in fact used by a number of other projects, such as Google's Chrome browser, the browser in the Android

mobile platform, the browser in the Nokia S60 platform, and the browser in Palm's Pre. It must be noted that these different platforms often use different versions of WebKit (even the iPhone and desktop versions of Safari have significant differences in terms of CSS support). Throughout the book, we'll typically refer to "Safari" to mean WebKit browsers in general. Only where there is a very significant difference between Safari and another prominent WebKit browser such as Chrome will it be mentioned explicitly.

Opera   In addition to a widely used desktop browser (while in Europe and the U.S., Opera market share is in the order of 1% to 2%, it is much higher in countries such as Russia), which we refer to quite frequently in the book, Opera also has a browser for low-powered mobile devices (Opera Mini), and Mobile devices (Opera Mobile). All are quite different, and in this book, we almost exclusively refer to the desktop browsers (versions of which are also used in the Nintendo Wii, some Panasonic televisions, and other devices).

Modern browsers   I frequently refer to "modern browsers," which usually means the latest version of Opera, Firefox, Safari, and Internet Explorer, which at the time of writing were Opera 10, Firefox 3.5, Safari 4, and Internet Explorer 8 (all of which were released during the writing of the book). With the exception of Internet Explorer, users of other browsers tend to upgrade frequently, and so, typically, web developers don't need to be concerned with versions of these browsers older than the previous one.

Common Background Properties

Since CSS1, CSS has provided a number of properties that let us style the background of an element.

It may seem an obvious thing, but before we go on, just what is an element's background? We'll see in a moment that every element has its own box that contains its content; the box includes margin, border, padding, and content, as shown in figure 4.3.

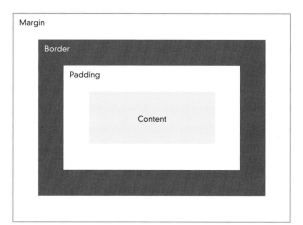

4.3
The box of an element is a rectangle, with margin, padding, border, and content. Note that margin, padding, and border widths and heights may all be zero.

The background of an element starts inside the border box—so applying a background color or image to an element does not apply the background to its margin, as demonstrated in figure 4.4.

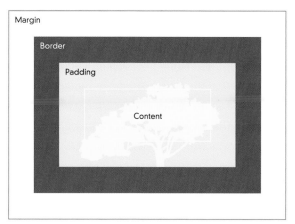

4.4
The background of an element starts at its border box and does not fill the margin.

CSS3 lets developers specify where the background starts, both horizontally and vertically: the border box, padding box, or content box are all options, but the margin box is not. Alas, this and other advanced background properties like multiple background images are not yet widely supported in browsers and can be difficult to use with progressive enhancement.

background-color

The `background-color` property specifies the color of the background of an element. It can take all of the values that we saw for the `color` property, and one more—the keyword value `transparent` (note that this value is not valid for the `color` property). A transparent `background-color` means that the content "behind" the element is visible through the element. We'll look at how to create semi-transparent backgrounds using CSS3 in Chapter 13. To create a light gray background on an element, we use a statement like this:

```
p {
    background-color: #b3b3b3
}
```

It's important, when specifying a background color, to ensure sufficient contrast with the text color so that the text will be legible. We look at this issue in some more detail in Chapter 6, but one good practice is to make sure you always specify a color when you specify a background color (the CSS validator will give you a warning to this effect).

background-image

The `background-image` property, which specifies a background image for an element, is one of the most commonly used features of CSS. It can be used to create patterned backgrounds behind whole pages or large sections of a page; to add icons (such as a PDF icon for a link to a PDF file); even to add "bullets" to lists—although there's another a property designed expressly for this purpose.

A background image might be a single large image, or an image that's tiled horizontally, vertically, or both. Background images can be positioned anywhere on the background of an image, though only in CSS3 can they be resized, and this feature has little support in browsers, so is as yet of little real-world value.

A background image is added to an element using the `background-image` property. This takes a URL value, which is a relative or absolute URL for the image file. The PNG, GIF, and JPEG formats are supported in all browsers, though some browsers also support other formats (such as PDF in Safari and SVG in Opera). Because of the limited support for formats other than these three main formats, only these formats should be used in most situations. As mentioned with the HTML `img` element in the last chapter, PNG is to be preferred for non-photographic images, and JPEG for photographic images.

URL Values

URL values in CSS have the form of a relative or absolute URL inside parentheses, and are preceded by the string `url` wrapped in single or double quotation marks, like this:

```
url("path/to/image.png")
```

Here we'll add the background image in figure **4.5** to the **body** element:

```
body {
  background-image: url("./images/shadow.png");
}
```

4.5
The background image
for our **body** element

And here's the effect [4.6], which is almost certainly not what we want.

Our background image,
tiled horizontally and
vertically

It is a truth universally acknowledged, that a single man in possession of a good fortune, must be in want of a wife.

However little known the feelings or views of such a man may be on his first entering a neighbourhood, this truth is so well fixed in the minds of the surrounding families, that he is considered the rightful property of some one or other of their daughters.

"My dear Mr. Bennet," said his lady to him one day, "have you heard that Netherfield Park is let at last?"

Mr. Bennet replied that he had not.

"But it is," returned she; "for Mrs. Long has just been here, and she told me all about it."

Mr. Bennet made no answer.

"Do you not want to know who has taken it?" cried his wife impatiently.

"_You_ want to tell me, and I have no objection to hearing it."

This was invitation enough.

"Why, my dear, you must know, Mrs. Long says that Netherfield is taken by a young man of large fortune from the north of England; that he came down on Monday in a chaise and four to see the place, and was so much delighted with it, that he agreed with Mr. Morris immediately; that he is to take possession before Michaelmas, and some of his servants are to be in the house by the end of next week."

"What is his name?"

"Bingley."

"Is he married or single?"

background-repeat

So what's going on here? By default, a background image repeats both horizontally and vertically, creating a tiling effect. In this case, that's not what we
want. The effect we are trying to achieve is a shadow on the right-hand side of
the page. So, we'll need to repeat the image vertically but not horizontally. We
can specify how an image repeats with the `background-repeat` property. This
property takes one of these keyword values:

- `repeat`—The default value that repeats the image in both directions.
- `no-repeat`—Means the image is only shown once.
- `repeat-x`—The image is repeated horizontally but not vertically.
- `repeat-y`—The image is repeated vertically but not horizontally.

In this instance, we want to repeat vertically, so we'll use `background-repeat`:
`repeat-y` [4.7].

> It is a truth universally acknowledged, that a single man in possession of a good fortune, must be in want of a wife.
>
> However little known the feelings or views of such a man may be on his first entering a neighbourhood, this truth is so well fixed in the minds of the surrounding families, that he is considered the rightful property of some one or other of their daughters.
>
> "My dear Mr. Bennet," said his lady to him one day, "have you heard that Netherfield Park is let at last?"
>
> Mr. Bennet replied that he had not.
>
> "But it is," returned she; "for Mrs. Long has just been here, and she told me all about it."
>
> Mr. Bennet made no answer.
>
> "Do you not want to know who has taken it?" cried his wife impatiently.
>
> "_You_ want to tell me, and I have no objection to hearing it."

4.7
Our shadow image, repeated vertically

If you can't make out where the shadow has gone, it's now down the left-hand side of the page. What we want to do is position it down the right-hand side of the element, which we can do with `background-position`.

background-position

The `background-position` property lets us specify where the image will be placed, or if it is repeated, where the repeat starts from. We can specify the position of a background image for an element in a number of ways.

Keywords

The `background-position` property can take one or two keywords. If a single keyword is used, it applies to both horizontal and vertical position. If two keywords are used, the first applies to horizontal position, and the second applies to vertical position. Regardless of the keyword chosen, it's important to note that the image tiles to fill the background horizontally, vertically, or in both directions. The keywords are:

- `top`—The image is placed, or repeats, vertically from the top down.
- `center`—The image is placed, or repeats, horizontally from the center of the element left and right, and vertically from the center of the element up and down. Note that the background image when repeated always repeats in both directions (up and down, or left and right).
- `bottom`—The image is placed, or repeats, vertically from the bottom up.
- `left`—The image is placed, or repeats, horizontally from the left-hand side of the element to the right.
- `right`—The image is placed, or repeats, horizontally from the right-hand side of the element to the left.

In this instance, we want the element to be repeated from the top down, and to be placed at the right-hand side of the element. We'd do this by using `background-position: right top`.

Length Values

It's possible to explicitly specify where the image will be placed or repeated from with one or two length values. For example, we might specify that a background image is placed 5 em from the left edge of an element using `background-position: 5em`.

With length values, unless the width of our element is fixed, it's not possible to achieve the objective of putting the image at the right side of the element.

Percentage Values

A particularly technical way we can specify background image position is using percentage values. Unlike length values, where the value specifies a vertical or horizontal offset for the top or left of the element, percentages are more subtle again.

With a percentage value of, for example, 60%:

```
background-position: 60%
```

we aren't specifying that the left edge of the background image is 60% from the left edge of the element, but that a point 60% from the left edge of the image horizontally is aligned with a point 60% from the left edge of the element horizontally, as shown in figure **4.8**.

Figure **4.9** shows these different positioning approaches together.

Although it sounds quite complex, it gives great flexibility when aligning background images with their elements. In the current situation, where we are looking to put the shadow image at the right of the element, we can use `background-position: 100%`.

This doesn't put the left-hand edge of the image 100% across the background of the element—which would essentially hide the image to the right of the element—but rather aligns the point 100% across the image with the point 100% across the element, so that their right edges are aligned.

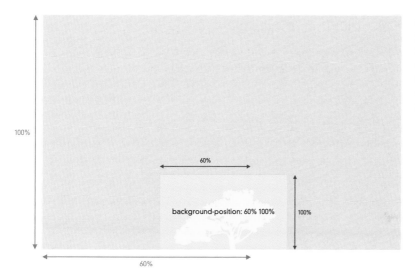

4.8
Percentage **background-position** values align a point on the background image with a point on the element.

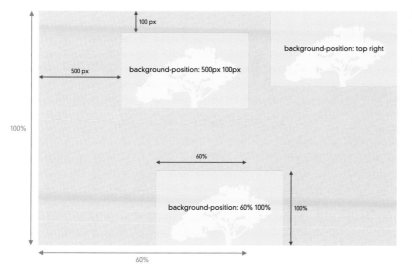

4.9
background-position with keywords, length values, and percentages

Figure **4.10** shows our page with the shadow now aligned with the right edge of the **body** element.

4.10

The shadow image aligns
with the right edge of the
body element.

It is a truth universally acknowledged, that a single man in possession of a good fortune, must be in want of a wife.

However little known the feelings or views of such a man may be on his first entering a neighbourhood, this truth is so well fixed in the minds of the surrounding families, that he is considered the rightful property of some one or other of their daughters.

"My dear Mr. Bennet," said his lady to him one day, "have you heard that Netherfield Park is let at last?"

Mr. Bennet replied that he had not.

"But it is," returned she; "for Mrs. Long has just been here, and she told me all about it."

Mr. Bennet made no answer.

"Do you not want to know who has taken it?" cried his wife impatiently.

"_You_ want to tell me, and I have no objection to hearing it."

background-attach

With the current example it might not make much sense, but it's possible to "fix" an image on the background, so that when the content of the element is scrolled, the image remains fixed in its location on the background. We do this with the `background-attach` property, which takes two possible keyword values: `scroll` and `fix`. For example, if we had a single large watermark-style image as the background of a page:

```
body {
    background-image: url('../watermark.png');
    background-repeat: no-repeat;
    background-position: center;
    background-attach: fix
}
```

then, when the page is scrolled, the watermark remains horizontally and vertically centered on the page, and the text and other content of the page scrolls over the top of it. `scroll` is the default value for the property.

CSS3 Background Properties

CSS3 introduces several new background properties, including the ability to specify multiple background images (we cover this in Chapter 13), to resize the background image, and to specify where the image fills from—the border, padding, or content box, not just the padding box, as is the case now. As noted briefly, none of these properties is very widely supported in contemporary browsers and should be used very carefully if at all at present, as their use can easily render content unreadable.

Shorthand Properties

CSS provides a way for some sets of properties to be specified with a single shorthand. For example, we can specify all of the background properties for a single statement with the one shorthand property `background`. We simply put each of the individual values separated with spaces as the value for the shorthand. For example, our shadow shorthand would look like this:

```
background: url('../shadow.png') repeat-y top right;
```

It's important not to mix shorthand and regular properties in a single statement. When you use a shorthand, *all* of the properties associated with that shorthand are applied—including defaults for any property you've not explicitly set a value for in the shorthand. In our example, the default value of `background-attach` (`scroll`) would be specified even though we've not set it explicitly. Why is this important? Well, if you'd previously specified a `background-attach` value of `fix` in the same statement, the shorthand overrides this, because the shorthand is further down the style sheet. This is a subtle problem that can catch developers and cause considerable confusion. The best way to avoid it is to use either shorthand or "longhand" properties, but to not mix them together.

Dynamic Selectors

HTML elements can be in different states depending on the user's current action (the mouse may be hovering over an element), or past actions (a link may have been visited by the user at some point). CSS provides ways of selecting elements based on these various states. The format for these selectors is to append a colon (:) and the name of the state to an existing selector. For example, to select an element with a `class` value of navigation when the mouse is over it, we'd use the selector `.navigation:hover`. The various states and associated selectors in CSS are:

- **hover**—When the user has the mouse over the element. The associated selector is `:hover`. Any element can be in the hover state, although in IE 6 and earlier only anchor elements in the hover state could be styled with this selector.

- **active**—This is the state an element is in when it is being activated—for example by being clicked, tapped, or when the return key is pressed while the element has the focus. The associated selector is **:active**.

- **visited**—Browsers typically remember for some period of time that a link has been visited, which can help users differentiate between different links on a page. You can style visited links with this selector. Think carefully before removing visual cues that differently styled visited and non-visited links provide the user. The associated selector is **:visited**.

- **focus**—When an element has the keyboard focus—that is, when keystrokes will go to this element—it is in the focus state. A common style for text fields with the focus is some kind of outline. The selector for an element with the focus is **:focus**.

One common "gotcha" with these states is the difficulty getting them in the right order in your style sheet. Elements can be in more than one state—for example, a link in the **hover** state might also be **visited**, or an element with the **focus** might also have the mouse over it. We know that the further down a style sheet a statement is, the more weight it has compared with other selectors of the same specificity. Now if we were to specify four statements like this:

```
a:visited {color: red}

a:hover {color: green}

a:active {color: blue}

a:link {color: black}

a:focus {color: orange}
```

What color would a link be in the **hover** state? The **visited** state? The **active** state? When it has **focus**? The answer is that in all but the last case, it would be black—because the **a:link** selector "trumps" all the others by virtue of it being lower in the style sheet than them—and a link is always a link, regardless of what other state it is in.

The best order for dynamic statements is **link**, **visited**, **hover**, **focus**, **active**. This means that the most significant state to the user at any given time gets precedence when it comes to styling.

Adding **:link**, **:hover**, and so on to a selector increases its specificity over that same selector without the added "pseudo class" (the technical term for these selectors). So, in the following instance:

```
a:link {
  color: red
}

a{
  color: green
}
```

the link in its unvisited state will be red, even though this statement precedes the statement with the selector **a**.

Basic Page Layout

CSS1 introduced the fundamental model of page layout for CSS, along with a number of whitespace properties, and borders. CSS2 extended these properties, with a new model of positioning. We'll look at the basic CSS page layout properties here, and more advanced properties shortly. We also look at the issue of creating page layouts in significant detail in Chapter 9, so here we'll focus on the properties and their values.

Block vs. Inline Elements

In the last chapter, we saw that HTML has two kinds of elements: block elements, which may contain other block elements as well as inline elements; and inline elements, which may only contain other inline elements.

CSS has two main ways of displaying elements, block and inline, which are related to the HTML concepts of block and inline elements, but not exactly.

The CSS **display** property lets us specify different ways in which an element should be laid out on the page by the browser. The two main ways are referred to as **display**: block, and **display**: inline. But be careful, because although setting a **display** of block for an element like **strong** (which is an inline element according to the HTML specification) is quite valid, it does *not* change the rules of HTML—the **strong** element may still only contain other inline elements. So what does display do? It changes how the element is displayed in the page layout.

Elements with a display value of `block` create a new layout block on the page and cannot have content alongside them (unless they are given a float value, which we'll see shortly). Common examples of block elements are headings, and paragraphs. Figure 4.11 shows this in action.

4.11
Elements with a display of block, like the heading and paragraph, create new blocks on the page. Elements with a display of inline don't create a new block.

We are also the founders of the **Web Directions conference series**, with conferences in **Sydney, Australia**, **Denver, Colorado**, and **Tokyo, Japan**

The very best way to contact us is to **use our contact form**. It's rare we won't get back to you within a few hours, often even minutes. If you need to talk to us, get in touch, and we'll get right back to you.

Elements with a display value of inline don't create a new block. Rather, the browser places them alongside the inline elements that come before and after it in the HTML document. Common examples include `strong` elements and anchors.

Changing the display property value of an element will change how the browser lays out the page, but it doesn't, as we said, change the rules of HTML. We'll look at some other aspects of the display property shortly.

The Box Model

When a browser lays out the elements in a document, each element gets its own box. The rules of how these boxes are laid out can get quite complicated, but for now we'll focus on the box of an element. It has four main components, as shown in figure 4.12: a margin, border, padding, and content.

4.12
The box model for an element

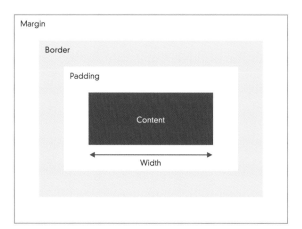

Working from the inside out, almost every element has content whose width and height can be determined in a couple of ways. It can be automatically calculated by the browser based on the actual contents (text, images, and so on), the width and height of the window, and other elements on the page. Or, it can be specified by the developer, using the `width` and `height` properties of CSS, which can take length or percentage values.

Next comes the padding of an element. This can be specified as either a length or percentage value, on all sides or individual sides of an element. As we saw earlier, the background of an element (image or color) fills the padding box of an element, as well as the content box, but that's as far as it goes. Outside the padding box lies the border, which is also part of the element's box. The border can be on all four sides of the element or one or more sides individually.

Lastly, outside the border, but still part of an element's box, is the margin, which too can be on all four sides of the element or on individual sides.

width

The `width` property specifies an explicit width for an element. We can use either percentage values (the element will be this percentage of the current width of its parent element) or length values. For example, we could specify that paragraphs are 40em wide like so:

```
p{
   width: 40em
}
```

Specifying widths of elements in ems means that they remain the same number of characters wide regardless of the size users choose for their text. As we'll see in Chapter 9, this can help make content much easier to read.

However, there's a complication. Inline elements don't take an explicit width (or height). Specifying a `width` for them has no effect on the flow of the document. In fact it's slightly more complicated still. Some inline elements—specifically, "replaced" inline elements (most commonly images, but also embedded content like video)—can take a `width` and `height` that affect the line in which the element appears.

height

The `height` property specifies an explicit height for an element. `height` can be specified as length values such as pixels or ems, or as percentages, though percentage heights are tricky: a percentage height *only* has effect when the containing element for the element has an explicitly specified height. If the containing element's height is calculated automatically by the browser based on the element's content, or if it is specified as a percentage, percentage height won't work on the contained element. This means that centering elements vertically is very difficult. (We'll come back to this in Chapter 9.)

Overflowing Content

If we can specify the `width` and `height` of an element, what happens if the area of the element is not large enough to contain the contents of the element? The `overflow` property allows us to specify what happens in these situations. `overflow` can take the following keyword values:

- `visible`—Although the size of the element and its impact on the page layout doesn't change, the content overflows its element.

- `hidden`—Any content which overflows its element is "clipped" and can't be seen.

- `scroll`—Horizontal and vertical scroll bars are added to the element that enable scrolling to display all the content of the element. Note both scroll bars are shown even if scrolling is only required in one dimension and not the other, and even if the content doesn't overflow its element.

- `auto`—The browser will display scrollbars only for the dimensions that need them—which may mean no scrollbars are shown, or only a horizontal or vertical scrollbar, or both, depending on how the content overflows the element.

The advent of browsers like those found in the iPhone and Palm Pre, which don't feature scrollbars, means that you can't rely on scrollbars being displayed to allow access to overflowing content in all browsers.

margin

The margin of an element is the space between its border and the edge of adjacent elements' margins. We've seen that background colors and images aren't seen behind the margin—so in essence the margin is transparent.

We can specify the `margin` for an element, either on all sides or on individual sides, using length values like pixels and ems, as well as percentages. When we use ems, the margin width and height is proportional to the size of the font for that element as it is currently being displayed. This allows margins that grow and shrink as the user increases and decreases the `font-size`, thus maintaining the proportions of `font-size` to whitespace. Percentages specify horizontal **and** vertical margins as a percentage of the overall width of the element—including margin, padding, and border.

There are four margin-related properties: `margin-top`, `margin-left`, `margin-bottom`, and `margin-right`. We can also use just the shorthand `margin`.

The shorthand can take one, two, or four values separated by spaces. Where it takes a single value, this is the value for each margin—top, left, bottom, and right. Where it is two values, the first value is for the top and bottom margin, and the second value is for the left and right margin. Where it takes four values, we have to be a little more careful. The four values apply to the different edges in the following order—clockwise around the element—top, right, bottom, and left.

Other shorthands, padding in particular, work in similar ways.

Gotcha: Collapsing Margins!

One very confusing aspect of vertical margins is that the top and bottom margins of elements that adjoin so that the two margin edges touch will "collapse" to be not the combined height of the two margins, but the height of the larger of the two. Suppose we have an **h2** element and immediately below it a paragraph element [4.13] with the following CSS:

```css
p {
    margin-top:3em
}

h2 {
    margin-bottom:2em
}
```

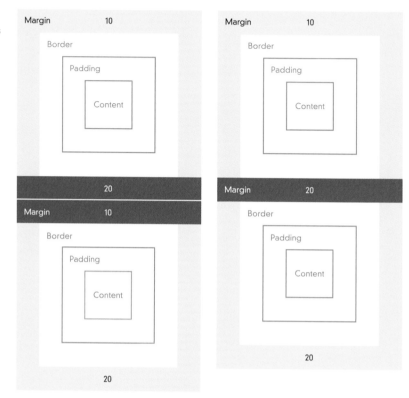

Logically, we'd expect the total space between the two to be 5em. But, because the margins collapse according to the CSS specification, the total space between them is just 3em, the larger of the two widths (if the two widths had been 2em, the width would collapse to 2em).

We revisit this issue in Chapter 7, where we look at various browser bugs, because in some situations, in some versions of Internet Explorer, margins that should collapse, don't.

border

Inside the margin of an element is its border. By default, elements have a border with no style, so in effect no border. Borders are specified using three properties: `border-style`, `border-width`, and `border-color`.

border-style

Browsers can draw borders in a number of different styles, specified with keywords. There are three one-dimensional (`solid`, `dashed`, and `dotted`), and four two-dimensional styles, which seem out of date and are very rarely used (`groove`, `ridge`, `inset`, and `outset`). The CSS3 properties **box-shadow** and **border-image**, both discussed in Chapter 13, essentially make the two-dimensional styles obsolete.

border-color

We can specify a **border-color** in the same ways in which we specify text and background colors—and like background colors, borders can be transparent. If no color is specified for a border, the border is the color of the text in the element (not black, as people often assume).

border-width

The third border property is **border-width**, and it can take three keywords—`thin`, `medium`, and `thick`—the exact widths of which aren't specified and can vary from browser to browser. **border-width** can also be specified using length values, but **not** percentages.

So, we could specify a .1em-wide solid red border for a paragraph with this CSS:

```
p{
    border-style: solid;
    border-width: .1em;
    border-color: red
}
```

.1em is typically the smallest em value or increment that browsers recognize.

We can also use the **border** shorthand, with these three values in any order separated by spaces, for instance:

```
p{
    border: .1em red solid
}
```

Individual Borders

Just as we can specify individual margins for each edge of an element, we can specify individual borders for each edge, with different styles, colors, and widths. It's also possible to specify borders on some but not all edges.

The only complicating factor is that there are a number of different shorthands for doing so. The longhand properties look like this:

- `border-top-style`
- `border-top-color`
- `border-top-width`

But, we can also use a single shorthand for each edge, which takes the three space-separated width properties, for example:

```
border-bottom: .2em groove blue
```

We'll see in Chapter 13 that we can also specify that the corners of our borders be rounded, using the CSS3 `border-radius` property.

padding

The last of our box properties is `padding`, which is inside the border, and behind which background color and images are seen.

Padding is otherwise very much like the margins of an element. We can specify different padding on different edges, using percentages (as with margin, the width of both horizontal and vertical padding will then be a percentage of the overall **width** of the element), or length values. Padding can be specified using the padding properties `padding-top`, `padding-bottom`, `padding-left`, and `padding-right`, or using the padding shorthand, which works just as margin does, taking one, two, or four values. (Refer to the preceding section on margins for how these shorthands work.)

How Wide and Tall Is an Element?

It may seem obvious, but just how wide is an element with a width of 50 em? The logical but not necessarily correct answer is "50em." The `width` and `height` properties specify not the entire width and height of an element's box, but only the width and height of the **content** area of the element. So, the total width of an element is the width of any left and right margins, plus left and right padding, plus any left and right borders, plus the content width. Similarly, the total height is the content height, plus any top and bottom padding, plus any top and bottom border, plus any top and bottom margin.

So, we have to be very careful when we specify an explicit width or height, along with padding, margin, or borders. The height or width we set won't match the actual height or width of the element's box. We'll see in Chapter 7 how this is particularly problematic due to a bug in older versions of IE, where width **does** specify the total width of the element's box. CSS3 in fact has a property, `box-sizing`, supported in all contemporary browsers, including IE 8, which lets us specify which of these two models—`width` and `height` apply to the whole block, or only the content area—the browser should use to lay out a page.

Advanced Page Layout

These CSS1 layout properties provide basic page formatting abilities, but they don't give developers the tools to create complex page layouts. We'll turn to the issue of page layouts in great detail in Chapter 9 (in fact, that's all we cover in that chapter), but here we'll look at the core properties we'll be using to create those layouts, as well as other related properties.

float

As we've seen, CSS can display elements in two ways: as blocks and inline. But in print design, it's very common for text to flow around, for example, images. The `float` property in CSS1 is designed to enable this. Both inline and block elements can be given a float property, of either left or right, which specifies which side the element floats to. When an element is floated, say to the left, it is taken out of the flow of the page (that is how the page would otherwise be laid out), and then moved horizontally to the left, until it touches the left edge of its containing element, or the right edge of another floating element. Content "below" it in the document—that is content that comes after it in the HTML—then flows around the element. Let's see this in action in figure 4.14. In this example, we've floated the portrait image to the left, and it also has a margin, which is why there's a space between the text and the image.

4.14

The image before being
floated (top) and after
being floated (bottom)

Dmitry Baranovskiy

Dmitry has over 8 years experience in creating web applications. Having started as a
back end developer, more recently he has changed his orientation to front end
development and even pure design. These days he spends his working hours trying to
embrace a wide range of front end technologies while working as a JavaScript
Developer for Atlassian. He is also the creator of Optimus, the Microformats
transformer, as well as Raphaël, a JavaScript Vector Library. At any given moment he is
always working on three secret projects, though no one knows where he gets the time
for any of this.

Dmitry Baranovskiy

Dmitry has over 8 years experience in creating web applications.
Having started as a back end developer, more recently he has changed
his orientation to front end development and even pure design. These
days he spends his working hours trying to embrace a wide range of
front end technologies while working as a JavaScript Developer for
Atlassian. He is also the creator of Optimus, the Microformats
transformer, as well as Raphaël, a JavaScript Vector Library. At any given moment he is
always working on three secret projects, though no one knows where he gets the time
for any of this.

Just as elements can be floated to the left, they can also be floated to the right by
using the value **float**: right. We'll revisit **float** in detail in Chapter 9, where
we'll see how it's used to create multi-column page layouts, among other things.

clear

Sometimes, we **don't** want an element's content to flow around a floated element. We can stop this by giving the element a **clear** property of both [**4.15**].
We can also stop floating on one side of an element while allowing it on another
by using **clear**: left (which still allows floating to the right), and **clear**: right
(which still allows floating to the left).

Pete Ottery

Pete has been designing web sites for about 10 years. Having previously worked as the Head of Design at Fairfax Digital and Creative Director at Daemon, he is now working at News Digital Media as the Group Interface Designer. Recently he has been designing carsguide, truelocal, & iphone.news.com.au. He works directly with site owners and execs (the suits!) to help inform requirements and push product design boundaries. He is daily knee deep in photoshop concepts and html/css code.

Follow Pete on Twitter: @c41

Presenting: Designing for suits

4.15

`clear` stops floating to one or both sides of an element—here our heading stops the float beside it.

Positioning

As we'll see in Chapter 9, `float` has become the principal way of creating many page layouts with CSS, but the CSS positioning properties, introduced in an interim "CSS Positioning" specification and included in CSS2, were designed to enable sophisticated page layout with CSS. They are still used for this purpose, often in conjunction with `float` and `clear`. For now, I'll provide a brief overview of the properties and concepts, and we cover them in much greater detail later in the book.

The *position* Property and Positioning Schemes

The position property takes one of four keywords, each of which specifies a different way of placing the element on a page:

- `static`—The default position value, `position: static`, specifies that the element be laid out in the normal flow of the document. The rules for how a browser lays out elements in the flow are complicated, but they should be very familiar, at least intuitively, to anyone who has used the web extensively.

- `relative`—When an element is positioned with a `relative` value, it is first laid out as it would be in the flow, then moved from that position according to its `top` and `left` values (and less commonly `bottom` and `right` values). When the element is moved relative to its place in the flow, very importantly the normal flow of the document doesn't change.

- `absolute`—Elements with a `position: absolute` are taken completely out of the flow of the document and then positioned with respect to the top and left of the first element that contains it that *also* has a `position` of `absolute`, `relative`, or `fixed`. Because the element is taken out of the flow, the rest of the page is flowed as if the element was not present in the document.

- `fixed`—Elements with a **position**: `fixed` are positioned very similarly to those with a **position**: `absolute`. They are taken out of the flow of the document and then positioned according to their `top` and `left` property values always with respect to the window they are in. This means that when the page is scrolled, the element remains exactly where it is with respect to the window.

While these concepts may sound a bit daunting, they are very logical. As mentioned, we revisit them in considerable practical detail in Chapter 9, so we won't belabor them here.

top and *bottom*, *left* and *right*

With the exception of **position**: `static`, the other values of position are typically used in conjunction with the properties `top` and `left`, and—to a lesser extent—`bottom` and `right` to place the element on the page. These properties work in slightly different ways, depending on the value of the position property:

- For `static`, they have no effect.
- For `relative`, a positive `top` value moves the element down the page from where it would otherwise be placed; a negative `top` value moves it up the page from where it would otherwise be placed. Similarly, positive `left` values move the element to the right, and negative to the left of where they would otherwise be. `bottom` and `right` work in the reverse.
- For `absolute`, the effect is similar to `relative`, but in this case, the element is moved with respect to not where it would otherwise be in the flow, but with respect to the top and left of the first element that contains it that also has a `relative`, `absolute`, or `fixed` position value (such elements are said to have a *positioning context*). This will often be the **body** element.
- For `fixed`, again the effect of the `top` and other properties are similar, but in this case move the element with respect to the top and left of the window itself (inside all the browser controls, or chrome).

Mastering positioning takes time, so don't feel you should be able to digest and use all of the information in this section immediately. More important than the actual properties and their values are the techniques we can implement with them, which is what Chapter 9 is about.

Advanced Selectors

CSS2 and CSS3 provide a number of more advanced selectors that give even finer control over the elements we select on a page with them. In Chapter 12, we'll look in detail at some of the CSS3 selectors, but here, we'll quickly touch on three very useful kinds of selectors.

Adjacent Sibling Selectors

Sibling elements are those elements that share the same parent element in the document structure. CSS2 introduced the ability to select two elements that are adjacent to one another. The form of the selector is selector 1 + selector 2 (for example `li+li`), and they select an element that matches the second selector that is directly after an element that matches the first selector in the HTML document. They aren't commonly used but can come in very handy. This type of selector is supported in all contemporary browsers, including IE 7 and onwards, so it needs to be used with care where users of IE 6 are concerned.

Attribute Selectors

The attribute selector was introduced in CSS2 and considerably extended in CSS3. It enables us to select elements based on the value of their attributes.

With CSS2 we can select elements in three different ways:

- **`selector[attribute name]`** (for example, **`img[alt]`**) selects an element matching the selector that also has the named attribute set to *any* value.
- **`selector[attribute name=value]`** (for example, **`img[alt=photo]`**) selects an element matching the selector that also has the named attribute set to exactly the specified value. So **`img[alt=photo]`** selects `<img alt="photo">` but *not* `<img alt="photo of a flower">`.
- **`selector[attribute name~=value]`** (for example, **`p[class~=introduction]`**) selects an element matching the selector that also has one of the space-separated values of the named attribute set to the specified value. This is useful for attributes like `class` that can take multiple values separated by spaces.

Note that we don't put quotation marks around either the attribute name or value.

CSS3 adds several new attribute selectors, including the ability to match substrings in attribute values. For example, we could select a link with the final four characters ".pdf", or the first seven characters "http://". It's also possible to select based on a substring value anywhere in an attribute value; for example, if we wanted to style the links to a particular subdirectory, say "contact" distinctly, we could do that as well.

- `selector[attribute name^=value]` (for example, `a[href^=http://]`) styles any element that matches the selector that also has the named attribute value starting with the specified value. `a[href^=http://]` selects any link with an absolute link, which could be used to style links away from the current site differently from those internal to the site (provided you use relative links internally, of course).

- `selector[attribute name$=value]` (for example, `a[href$=.pdf]`) styles any element that matches the selector that also has the named attribute value finishing with the given value. So `a[href$=.pdf]` selects any anchor that links to a file with the extension .pdf, which could enable us to let users know when they are going to download a PDF.

- `selector[attribute name*=value]` (for example `a[href^=/contact/]`) styles any element that matches the selector where the named attribute value also includes the given value.

These selectors are supported in all contemporary browsers other than Internet Explorer (including IE 8). As such, they need to be used with the consequences in mind of what happens when they aren't supported. We address this issue in detail in Chapter 12.

The Universal Selector

The universal selector (*) selects every element in a document. For example, this statement:

```
* {
  margin: 0
}
```

removes the default margin from every element in the document (we look at default CSS properties in detail in Chapter 8). However, by itself the selector is not recommended, as it can have a significant impact on performance and is usually more heavy handed than required. It's more likely to be used in combination with other selectors, and we'll see it used a number of times in the book. It also played an important role in a hack that hides CSS from some versions of Internet Explorer; see Chapter 7 for more on this and other common hacks.

Display Types

We took a look at the `block` and `inline` values of the `display` property a short while ago. In this section, will look at some other values of this property and the related `visibility` property.

visibility

With `visibility`, we can show and hide an element. It takes the keyword values `visible` and `hidden`, which do pretty much what you'd expect them to. The one thing to note is that even when hidden, elements still take up space in the document flow. If we want the element to completely vanish, and both be invisible and the space it occupies in the document to collapse, we need to use a different property and value: `display`: `hidden`.

hidden

When an element has a `display` value of `hidden`, it is as if the element doesn't exist. The page is rendered as if the element is not there, and its contents are completely invisible as well.

List Items

Just as it is possible to make inline elements like **em** display as block elements—and vice versa—with the `display` property, it's possible to make any element display as a list item. For example, to make paragraphs display as list items, use:

```
p {
  display: list-item
}
```

HTML 4 and CSS2 both support a range of media types, including projection, screen, handheld, and print. The reality is that support for this concept has never been widespread, and even though most browsers support the screen and print style sheets, allowing us to create different style sheets for printing and onscreen display, the other possible values are far less widely supported. Opera supports the projection media type, and uses style sheets with a media type of projection when the browser is in full screen mode. Some mobile devices support the handheld media type, but the iPhone does not use handheld style sheets.

As we'll see in Chapter 14, the concept of targeting different media via CSS has been refreshed with CSS3 and is already well supported. With CSS3 media types, it's the features of the medium, such as color depth or window width, rather than the medium itself that is particularly important. Here we'll touch on the key technical aspects of CSS media types—see Chapter 14 for details.

Media-Specific CSS

There are three ways in which we can specify specific CSS for a particular media type. We can use a `link` to a style sheet that includes a `media` attribute that specifies which media the style sheet is intended for; we can add a `media` attribute to the `style` element in the `head` of an HTML document; or we can use an `@media` statement inside the CSS itself.

Linking with Media Types

When we link to an external style sheet, it's possible to specify the media type using the `media` attribute. This takes one of several values, the most common of which are `all`, `screen`, `handheld`, `print`, `projection`, and `screen`. For example, if we wanted to link to a style sheet for print use only, we could use this statement:

```
<link rel="stylesheet" href="style/style.css"
type="text/css" media="print">
```

We can also specify more than one media type by separating media types with a comma as the value of the `media` attribute.

Embedding Based on Media Types

Similarly, we can add a `media` attribute to an embedded style sheet's **style** element, specifying one or media for which the embedded style sheet applies. As mentioned earlier, embedding style sheets is not the best way to include CSS in an HTML document.

@media

You can also specify CSS inside a style sheet to apply only to particular media, using the **@media** statement. **@media** statements are like subsets of a style sheet. They have the following form:

```
@media projection, screen {
  p {
    color: black
  }
}
```

where one or more statements that only apply to a particular medium or set of media are contained within curly brackets, and the media to which these statements should apply are specified after the keyword **@media** as a comma-separated list of media keywords, taken from the predefined list in CSS2 and HTML 4.

All commonly used browsers support all of these approaches, and there's no enormous advantage of one over the other. We've mentioned that embedding is to be avoided where possible. The **@media** approach has the advantage over linking because it requires fewer individual requests to a server. When there are a significant number of server requests (for example a number of external style sheets, script files, images, and so on), site performance can suffer, so minimizing linked files is a good practice.

To date, using media types to create style sheets for particular media has not been common, but we'll see in Chapter 14 that with CSS3, it's possible to create far more tailored style sheets for devices and media based on their specific characteristics, like window width, color depth, and even orientation. Targeting different media and devices with CSS is likely to become much more common now that these features are widely supported in browsers.

Importing Style Sheets

If you've been wondering throughout the first 15,000 words or so of this chapter just where the word "cascading" in "cascading style sheets" comes in, well, wonder no longer. One of the strengths of CSS is that style sheets can import from other style sheets, enabling us to create, for example, a base style sheet, used across an entire site, and more specialized style sheets, which import from this base style sheet, associated with specific subsections of a site. This way, when the style sheets that are imported into a style sheet change, there's no need to update the style sheets that do the importing—the changes flow, or "cascade" directly into these style sheets, then into the HTML documents they style. The "cascade" is the flow of style from one style sheet into another style sheet via importing.

@import

Any style sheet, whether it's embedded or a stand-alone CSS file, can import another style sheet. We accomplish this with an `@import` statement, which has the form of the keyword `@import`, followed by the URL for the imported style sheet (a relative or absolute URL), and optionally a comma-separated list of media types, as we saw a moment ago.

The URL may take either the form of a URL value, like we saw earlier with the `background-image` and `list-style-image` properties, or simply the URL alone, but in either case should be quoted with single or double quotation marks. Very importantly, if the URL is relative, it must be relative to the style sheet the `@import` statement is in, not to the HTML document. (This may sound obvious, but Netscape 4 got this wrong and treated the URL as relative to the HTML document.) Here's how we might import a style sheet for our typography into a main style sheet for a site:

```
@import url("./style/typography.css")
```

We could import a page layout style sheet for the screen or projection media, and another for printing, like this:

```
@import url("./style/screenlayout.css") screen, projection
@import url("./style/printlayout.css") print
```

Just as the order of statements in a style sheet is important for the specificity of a statement—statements lower down in the style sheet trump those of the same specificity higher up in the style sheet—the same rule applies in the cascade. Statements lower down in the cascade override those higher up in the cascade.

`@import` statements must appear in a style sheet above all other statements, and other @ rules like `@media`. This is so browsers can fetch the imported style sheets before calculating the specificity of all the rules in the style sheet.

Quality Assurance

In the previous chapter, we looked at the various QA tools that are available for ensuring the quality of your HTML. There are two principle concerns when it comes to the quality of CSS. First, we want to ensure our CSS is valid—that is, it conforms to the rules of the CSS language. We also want to ensure that the CSS we use is supported in as many widely used browsers as possible, and if it isn't, that it doesn't impact the ability of users to use the features and access the information of our site.

Validating Your CSS

Just as we can validate HTML, we can also validate CSS to ensure that it is free from errors. The W3C provides a CSS validator at **jigsaw.w3.org/css-validator**, and there are others online as well. Note that in order to validate CSS3, you need to change the default settings of the validator, which is set to validate CSS2.1.

Checking Browser Support

Now that CSS support in browsers is far better than it was even a few years ago, checking browser support is far less of a problem than it used to be. Some development tools, like Style Master, which I developed, include a database of browser support information, which can help you identify which selectors and properties are supported, aren't supported, or are buggy in various browsers. There are also a number of online resources that detail browser support problems, which we link to at the end of the book.

Previewing in Browsers

Testing that sites are acceptable across a broad range of browsers, in particular, current and very recent versions of Firefox, Safari, and Opera, as well as versions of Internet Explorer back to at least version 6—which is still as widely used as any of these other browsers at the time of this writing—is an important quality assurance step. There are a number of services online that can make this a much more productive experience than simply running all these browsers locally. It's particularly tricky to run multiple versions of Internet Explorer on the same version of Windows, and for the many Mac-based developers, it involves using a virtualization solution like Parallels or VMWare, and running Windows inside a virtual machine.

Some of the services available include:

- Browsercam (**www.browsercam.com**) has been around for many years, and it allows you to test your site in dozens of browser versions on various operating systems.
- Browsershots (**www.browsershots.org**) is a free but less sophisticated service that provides screenshots of your site in dozens of browser versions.
- Adobe's new BrowserLab (**browserlab.adobe.com/index.html**) doesn't yet provide the same level of browser coverage but looks like it may become an important tool for web developers. It integrates with Dreamweaver.

Specific Challenges and Techniques

Throughout the rest of the book, we'll cover various development techniques that make heavy use of CSS. But here we'll touch on a number of very common CSS challenges that don't get much coverage elsewhere.

Styling Forms

Using CSS to style form elements has long caused developers headaches. In the past, support for styling form elements in many browsers was patchy, to say the least, and although contemporary browsers support CSS on form elements much better, there are problems stemming from the CSS specification and a lack of clarity about how form elements should be styled in some respects. Eric Meyer, whose knowledge of CSS is virtually without peer, has written on the issue extensively at **meyerweb.com/eric/thoughts/2007/05/15/formal-weirdness**.

This is not to say that developers shouldn't use CSS with form elements, but we should be aware of some of the potential problems and pay particular attention to cross-browser problems, since different browsers interpret the relevant CSS specification in different ways.

Image Replacement

Because of the limited range of fonts available via CSS prior to the widespread availability of downloadable fonts (an issue discussed in Chapter 15), web designers have long used images of text, particularly for headings and other display elements. Initially, this involved simply using an `img` element with the "text" of the heading or other element rendered as an image. This severely impacts both accessibility and search engine visibility, and so it is strongly advised against. After CSS became widely supported in browsers, designers developed a number of "image replacement" techniques that aimed to address these shortcomings, while still enabling the use of text as an image. The first generation of these techniques exemplified by FIR (the Fahrner Image Replacement Technique named after Todd Fahrner, its inventor) were based on the idea of placing the text of an image to be replaced inside a `span` element, and then hiding this text from the reader, while using an image with the text rendered on it via CSS as the background image for the element. So, for example, we'd have this HTML:

`<h1 id="mainheading"><span>`This is the text of the heading`</span></h1>`

We would then hide the text in the span, typically by positioning it absolutely and then giving it a large negative `left` value (some versions of the technique used `display: none`, which may hide the element from a screen reader). We then add a background image to the heading, which contains an image of the text we have hidden:

```
h1.mainheading {
    background-image: url("./images/mainheading.png");
    background-repeat: none;
}

h1.mainheading span {
    position: absolute;
    left: -1000px
}
```

Although this "solves" the problem by letting developers use fonts other than those available on the end user's system for a web page, and still provides text that a screen reader or search engine can recognize, it has several drawbacks:

- The text won't increase or decrease in size when users zoom their text.
- With screen magnifiers, the text will pixilate, rather than magnify smoothly as "real" text will.
- Users often look for key words like "contact" on a page using the browser's find command, and image replacement can interfere with that.
- The font is very likely rendered with a different font rendering engine than that found in the browser, and so there's a mismatch in terms of anti-aliasing and other font hints between the text in the image and other text on the page.
- Site maintenance and development is more complicated, as any change to the text in replaced elements requires creating and uploading new images.

A second generation of techniques, typified by Scalable Inman Flash Replacement (sIFR), used Flash rather than images to replace the text. This addressed issues like magnification and zooming, but the other problems remain.

An even newer solution is Cufón (**wiki.github.com/sorccu/cufon/about**), which uses native browser technologies like SVG and VML—which we cover in Chapter 16—and JavaScript instead of Flash or images.

Despite their challenges, these techniques have been widely used, in part because clients and other decision makers often insist on a particular font being used. With luck, the arrival of widespread font embedding technology, which is covered in Chapter 15, will bring about an end to the need for these techniques.

Page Layout

As mentioned, we devote the whole of Chapter 9 to current practices in using CSS for page layout, so while we haven't touched on how to create multi-column layouts here, we'll cover that in detail there.

Browser Challenges

It's no secret that browser support for CSS for many years left quite a bit to be desired. Even though CSS support in all contemporary browsers is excellent, we'll still be dealing with legacy browsers like IE 6 for some time to come. In Chapter 7, we focus on the challenges of older browsers and techniques for addressing them.

Formatting CSS

In CSS code, whitespace isn't significant, which means we can use spaces, tabs, and returns to improve the legibility of our CSS. Some common techniques for making CSS more readable include:

- Separating the selector from the declaration block with a return
- Putting each declaration on a new line and indenting them with a tab
- Ordering declarations alphabetically by property name

An example statement using these techniques might look like this:

```
p {
    border: solid thin #555;
    color: #333;
    font-family:
"Lucida Sans Unicode", "Lucida Grande", sans-serif;
    line-height: 1.3;
    padding: 1em
}
```

CSS and Site Performance

When using CSS, as with any external resource (images, scripts, and so on), two things can impact the performance of a site: the size of the file, and the number of linked files. While CSS files are typically small in comparison with external resources like images, we can optimize them by removing all whitespace and comments and by using shorthands. Of course, these all make your code far less legible and less maintainable, so rather than using these techniques in your development code, it's best to process your CSS into a production version just before serving it. There are numerous CSS compression tools available, with a good list here: **www.askapache.com/css/online-css-compression-tools.html**.

The other main impact on site performance is the number of external linked files. For production code, it can help to move numerous individual style sheets into a single large style sheet before serving.

Both of these are things that can help improve the performance of heavily trafficked sites, if you find page load times are less than desired.

Style Master

Style Master, the CSS development tool for which I'm the lead developer, is now more than a decade old, and is available for both Mac OS X and Windows operating systems. I originally developed it when teaching CSS and "advanced HTML" in the mid 1990s, not long after CSS1 was released, because then there weren't any good tools for developing CSS. Style Master includes built-in real-time validation, browser compatibility checking, previewing, and other tools that will, I hope, make learning and working with CSS more efficient and enjoyable. You can learn more at **www.westciv.com/style_master**.

chapter five

The DOM

The web began as text. Style—at first via presentational HTML like the `font` element—followed, but with the exception of links and simple forms, there was little real interactivity in the browser, because there was no way of making content interactive on the client side. Any processing—form validation, for example—had to be done on the server, which meant that whole pages had to be refreshed if a single element such as a required form element wasn't filled in.

In 1996, Netscape 2 debuted and brought with it a new programming language, JavaScript (which, despite its name, has little in common with Java). And JavaScript brought with it real interactivity in the browser.

DOM Level 0

Of course, JavaScript in a browser is useless unless it has some way of interacting with the page and its elements—form fields, links, images, and so on. So, along with JavaScript, Netscape 2 implemented an application programming interface (API), which let developers access some of the parts of a web page and change their properties using JavaScript. It also enabled developers to write JavaScript that was sent notifications when certain events occurred (for example the mouse was being hovered over a link) and then respond to these events. This API is the *document object model*, or DOM. Compared with modern DOMs, the Netscape 2 DOM was very limited. Only a small subset of the elements in a document (links, images, and form elements) could be accessed, and only some of *their* properties accessed and changed. These DOMs were typically used for client-side form validation, and most commonly, image rollover effects.

Internet Explorer 3 introduced its own version of JavaScript (JScript) and the DOM later in 1996. These early DOMs are technically referred to as the Legacy, or Level 0 DOM.

Intermediate DOM

The release of Internet Explorer 4 and Netscape 4 in 1997 saw widespread and usable if somewhat flawed support for CSS, and entirely new—though maddeningly incompatible—DOMs in each browser. Like DOM Level 0, these DOMs, now commonly referred to as Intermediate DOMs, were never standardized by the W3C. Nevertheless, they did introduce the capabilities that enable today's Ajax-based websites and web applications: the ability to change an element's CSS programmatically and the ability to access any element and almost any property of any element via JavaScript. It's fair to say that, along with CSS, these DOMs introduced modern web development as we still know it.

Level 1 DOM

After the success of CSS 1 and HTML 4, the W3C turned its attention to standardizing the unruly DOMs. Although Netscape chose Ecma International as the standards body that would standardize JavaScript (hence JavaScript's official name, "EcmaScript"—JavaScript is a trademark of Sun), the W3C brought together Netscape, Microsoft, and other member organizations to develop a standard DOM. DOM Level 1 was published in 1998.

Level 2

The Level 2 DOM introduced the modern event model of the DOM, which developers use to handle user interaction and other events. DOM Level 2 was published in 2000, and has widespread though not perfect support in all modern browsers.

Level 3

DOM Level 3 extends DOM Level 2, but as of this writing, it is not widely supported in browsers. *Some* aspects of DOM Level 3 *are* widely supported and used, however, and are a core aspect of DOM scripting.

The level of the DOM to which a specific feature belongs to is not particularly important, as JavaScript libraries are increasingly becoming the most common way in which developers interact with the DOM.

In this chapter, we'll focus on the DOM itself, and won't discuss JavaScript in detail. The DOM and JavaScript are intimately associated, so this separation may seem odd, but there are two reasons I've taken this approach. The first is that the DOM is defined in a language-neutral way. Languages other than JavaScript may be used—in theory, and to some extent in practice—to access and change the DOM. The second is that JavaScript as a language is far too large a topic to address in a general book such as this one, and it's also been addressed very well elsewhere. From this chapter, you'll gain a solid understanding of what the DOM is, what it does, what you can do with it, and core best practices and techniques for working with it. You'll find resources for learning a lot more about JavaScript itself at the end of the book.

The DOM Tree

An HTML document is made of text that the browser parses into an internal model it uses for rendering pages, responding to user interactions such as clicks, taps, and keystrokes. The DOM standardizes this internal model, making it much easier for developers to interact with a page—for example, we might want to find the label for a form element, and to change its text and background color if the associated element isn't correctly filled out. Let's take a look at a simple HTML document, and how the browser might model it internally using the DOM.

```
<html>
<head>
    <title>Simple</title>
    <link rel="stylesheet" href="style.css"
type="text/css" media="all" />
</head>
<body>
<p class="abstract">It is a truth <em>universally</em>
<a href="index.html">acknowledged...</a></p>
</body>
</html>
```

The browser takes each of the elements, and creates a family tree of *objects* in which an element contained within another element (for example the **a** element) is a child of that element. In this example, **p** is the parent of the **a** element, while the **em** and **a** elements are siblings. These objects may have *properties*; some of these properties are the attributes of the element, such as an **href**, or media type, while others, such as the style, are a consequence of the browser's application of a style sheet, or of other factors outside the element and outside the attributes defined in the HTML. The DOM specifications define the properties of any particular type of DOM object. Figure **5.1** shows how this document might be represented as a tree of objects, with various properties.

5.1

The HTML document as a tree of DOM objects

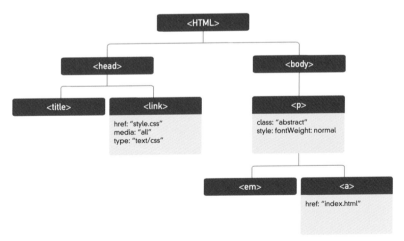

In addition to properties, which developers can get (or read), and usually but not always set (or write)—some properties are read only—DOM objects have *methods*. A method defines something an object can be asked via JavaScript to do—for example to take the keyboard focus or return a value that is not directly one of its properties, but which it can easily calculate. Understanding and using the methods of DOM objects is the heart of working with the DOM.

Let's take a quick look at some example DOM code, using JavaScript, before looking at the most commonly used DOM objects, their properties, and their methods. Now, if you've never really seen any JavaScript before, don't panic! It's not as baffling as it may first appear.

Suppose we've got hold of the **a** element in the example paragraph (we'll learn how to do so in a moment), and we want to access its URL property. We do this with *dot notation*, like so:

```
theLink.href
```

See, not scary at all. We simply add a dot, then the name of the property as defined by the DOM specification. We can change the **href** of this link by setting it with an = sign, like so:

```
theLink.href="http://westciv.com"
```

Or to get the value—here we'll show the value in an alert window using a built-in **alert** method of the **window** object—we'll use this:

```
window.alert(theLink.href)
```

from which we can note that we also use the methods of an object in the same way that we access its properties.

Core DOM Objects and Methods

Now we've got an overview of the core concepts of the DOM, let's take a look at some of the most commonly used DOM objects, and their methods and properties.

Window

The **window** object gives access to the properties and methods of the window containing the document. Getting the **window** object with JavaScript is straightforward: just use the word *window*. The **window** object has quite a few built-in properties that can be read, and sometimes changed, using JavaScript. These include how far the page is currently scrolled horizontally or vertically (**window.scrollX** and **window.scrollY**), the width and height of the content area of the **window**, (**window.innerWidth** and **window.innerHeight**), and a good deal else besides.

JavaScript and the DOM are case sensitive, which means that accessing **window.innerwidth** instead of **window.innerWidth** will cause an error. Note the format of DOM property and method names—where the initial letter of the first "word" is in lowercase, and subsequent "words" are in uppercase. This is referred to as *camel case*, and is the naming convention for all DOM methods and properties, making it easy to remember exactly how these names are written (provided you remember the name of course).

In addition to properties, like all DOM objects, **window** also provides a number of methods that a script can invoke to get the **window** to do things like move, resize, or ask for user input via various built-in dialogs like Alert, Prompt, and Confirmation. For example, we can stop the **window** from loading, perhaps to let the user stop loading a particularly long page, using **window.stop**.

Some methods take *arguments*, and may return *results* that can be used later in the script. For example, here, we can use the built-in **window** method **prompt** to ask a user for some input, and place the response in a variable called **answer**.

```
answer=window.prompt("What is 3+2");
```

We might also use another **window** method, **alert**, to display the user's response:

```
window.alert(answer)
```

OK, so that's a perfectly pointless thing to do, and likely to be *really* annoying, but it's a good basic illustration of how the DOM works.

You'll often see the use of **window** methods like **alert** by themselves, like this:

```
alert(theLink.href)
```

(Window methods are special in the DOM—you can refer to them without explicitly adding **window** to your code.)

Document

The **document** object gives developers access to the contents of the HTML document, and has a number of its own methods and properties that can be particularly useful when DOM scripting. For example, we can get (or set) the **title**, get the **URL**, and get a list of all the **form** elements in the document. The **document** object is also an **element**, which is the next main type of DOM object we'll look at—this means that in addition to its own methods and properties, **document** objects also have all the methods and properties of other elements. To put it technically, the **document** object implements the **element** interface *in addition to* the **document** interface.

Element

Every element in an HTML document is represented in the DOM by an **element** object. Elements have numerous properties, such as **className**, **id**, its location with respect to its containing element (**offsetLeft** and **offsetTop**), its current width and height (**offsetWidth** and **offsetHeight**), and much else. There are numerous methods we can use as well, such as retrieving the value of a given attribute (**getAttribute**) or even all child elements of a particular type (**getElementsByTagName**).

One thing we may well want to do is get or change the style of an **element**, and there are several ways of doing this, which we'll turn to now.

Style

If we simply want to directly change the style of an **element**, for example its background color, we can get the **style** property of the element, which returns a **style** object. We can then directly set the **backgroundColor** property of this object to the color we want.

Suppose we have a paragraph in a variable called **thePar**. We can change its background color like this:

```
thePar.style.backgroundColor="red"
```

There are a few things going on here. Note how we've chained our properties—we get the **style** *property* of the paragraph, which is a **style** *object*. Then we set the **backgoundColor** property of this object to red (we can use any color value we'd use in CSS as the value of the background color). The **style** object has a property for every possible CSS property, though it uses slightly different names for these. Dashes, like those in CSS's `background-color` and `text-align` are removed, and the resultant name is converted to camel case, so in the preceding example, we have **backgroundColor** and **textAlign**.

The **style** object only contains the *inline* style of an element, not those from any linked or embedded style sheet. So, if we get the value of this property, we'll only get the CSS properties set via inline CSS or set directly on the **style** using the DOM. If we set a CSS property via the DOM using the **style** object, this is the same as using inline CSS.

If we want *all* the style properties currently set on an element (including those set via style sheets), we need a function of the **window** object called **getComputedStyle**. After getting an element from the **document** using a method like **getElementById**, we pass the element whose styles we want to the **getComputedStyle** method. The **getComputedStyle** method then returns a **style** object that contains all the CSS properties of the element:

```
theStyle=window.getComputedStyle(thePara, null)
```

The object returned as the value of the variable **theStyle** is the same *type* of object as the **style** property of an element, but the new object contains *all* the currently set values of all the CSS properties for that element, whether from the default style sheet, the user style sheet, any linked or embedded style sheets, or inline styles. (Note that we can't *set* an element's styles with this object— we just get the currently computed values, then use the **style** property of the element to make any changes. We use the **style** property to set CSS properties on an element via the DOM.)

GetElementsByTagName

It might be necessary to get all the elements of a given kind—for example, all the links or all the **input** elements in a document or inside a particular element. We can use the **getElementsByTagName** method on any element object, or on the **document**—remember, the **document** is an element itself—to return a list of these elements. To find all **input** elements, in the document we would use this:

```
allInputs=document.getElementsByTagName("input")
```

We can iterate through this list using a JavaScript standby, the *for loop*, to perform various actions—more on this when we get to event handlers. (Want to know more about the **for** loop? Check out the JavaScript resources at the end of the book.)

GetElementById

One of the simplest and most common DOM methods is locating an element by its **id** value. Because **id**s are meant to be unique, we can very quickly find the element with an **id** of a given value. If more than one element on a page has a given **id** value (which shouldn't be the case), this method will *probably* return the first such element, but that's not guaranteed.

The **GetElementById** method is only a method of the **document** object, unlike **getElementsByTagName**. So, to locate an element with the **id** value site-navigation, we'd use: **theElement=document.getElementById ("site-navigation")**.

One very common gotcha with this method is the capitalization of *Id* in **GetElementById**—the *d* must be lowercase and the *I* uppercase.

Now that we've taken a look at some of the most common objects you'll work with when DOM scripting, we'll turn to how we bring together user interaction (like typing, tapping, and clicking) with our document and scripts using an important part of the DOM called *events*.

Events

So far, we haven't seen how to tell if a user is interacting with our page—or how a script can know anything has happened at all, let alone respond to it. DOM events let us do all these things.

The browser sends an **event** object to the object that is associated with the user interaction or other event when a user:

- Clicks an element
- Moves the mouse over or off an element
- Types a character

Or when:

- A document finishes loading
- A window is resized or scrolled
- And in many other instances

For example, when you click a link, a **click** event is sent to the **a** element, and when you scroll a window, a **scroll** event is sent to the **window** object. All this happens automatically, without intervention from developers—but to take advantage of these events, we need to add *event listeners* that listen for events of a particular type on a particular element, and *event handlers* to respond to events.

Event Listeners

Most web developers have had at least a little exposure to JavaScript and the DOM, even if only through copying and pasting example script into a page. If you're one of those developers, you'll have seen markup like this:

```
<a id="home" href="./" onclick="linkClicked(this)">
onclick="wasClicked(this)"
```

This is an *inline event handler*. It tells this particular **a** element what to do when it receives a *click event*—it calls a function called **linkClicked**, with a reference to itself (`this`) as the argument. If that's getting too far out of your JavaScript comfort zone, don't worry about this part. What's important is that this is an *inline* event handler. We'll see in a moment that these inline event handlers, like inline CSS, are no longer recommended as the best way to respond to events. Rather, we can attach event listeners to any element using the DOM method **addEventListener**. So instead of using the above inline event listener, we'd add a listener to this element to accomplish the same thing like so:

```
document.getElementById("home").addEventListener("click",
"linkClicked", true)
```

What we've done is found the element with an **id** of home in the document, then added an event listener for click events. The event listener will then pass the event to a function we've written called **linkClicked** (we can ignore the "true" argument for now, but we'll get to it in a moment).

You might be thinking that this has gone a bit too easily so far. We haven't mentioned a single browser bug or inconsistency yet, after all. And the bad news is that just as with CSS, we do have browser bugs and inconsistencies to deal with. The good news is that there are many libraries and other resources that largely make these browser inconsistencies go away as though by magic, and we'll look at them soon. In the meantime, just note that Internet Explorer doesn't support the **addEventListener** method, and so we need to separately add an event listener for that browser using an IE-specific method. (Don't worry—we'll cover all of this soon, and you don't need to think about it now.)

Event Propagation

We can add event handlers for the same type of event to many elements in a document, and we can add event handlers for *different* types of events to the same element. But what happens when you click on an element which has a click handler, and whose parent element *also* has a click handler? Which element "gets" the click event? Do they both get the click event? And if so, in which order?

Welcome to the labyrinth.

Capturing and Bubbling Events

There are two *event flow models* in the DOM. The first model, in which an event is handled initially by the parent and then by the child element (and so on further into the tree if there are further descendants with event listeners for the same type of event) is called *event capturing*. All browsers other than Internet Explorer support this event flow model.

The second model, in which the descendants receive the event first before the event "bubbles up" to the parent and further ancestor elements, is called *event bubbling*. Internet Explorer supports *only* this event flow model. All other modern browsers support *both* models, and choose between them based on that third argument in the **addEventListener** method we just saw. If this argument is "true," the capture model is used; otherwise, the bubbling model is used. The implications and differences can be subtle, but far-reaching. Though the fine points are outside the scope of this chapter and aren't always important, they're something to be aware of as a developer.

Best Practices in Modern Standards-Based DOM Scripting

Now that we've discussed the key concepts of the DOM—objects, properties, methods, and events—we'll turn to best practices in DOM scripting. We've already touched on one, the idea of separating scripting such as event listeners from our markup, but there are several others to keep in mind. If you are new to the DOM, you won't need to "unlearn" out-of-date habits and techniques that other developers may have acquired when these were more generally considered to be acceptable. If you are a more experienced DOM developer, it's my hope that this chapter will either confirm that you're doing things in the best way, or reveal that some of your practices may need tuning—in which case, the DOM scripting resources at the end of the book will help you polish up your techniques.

Unobtrusive Scripting

Unobtrusive scripting refers to a set of techniques that are intended to ensure that sites and applications built with JavaScript and the DOM work well for users even in the absence of good JavaScript and DOM support. Support might be missing because a user has chosen (or been forced by their IT department) to disable JavaScript. It might also be missing because a particular device or browser just has limited DOM or JavaScript support, as is the case with many mobile devices (even the iPhone has JavaScript limitations).

The underlying philosophy of unobtrusive scripting is that even when users have no JavaScript support at all, a site's main information and functionality should still be available. If you're thinking this looks a lot like progressive enhancement with CSS, you're spot on. Unobtrusive scripting should enhance the experience for users with more sophisticated browsers without becoming a barrier to those with less sophisticated browsers.

Is JavaScript Really Needed?

The first step in unobtrusive scripting is to consider whether JavaScript is really needed at all. Many techniques that might once have required JavaScript to implement are now possible using CSS and HTML alone. Rollover techniques, for example, once required JavaScript, but have been possible with CSS for many years now. The same thing is true of table-row zebra striping, which until recently could only be achieved by using additional markup on `tr` elements, or by using JavaScript to dynamically add this markup. As we'll see in Chapter 12, CSS3 structural selectors now allow us to "stripe" table rows without using JavaScript or touching our HTML markup.

Separation of Behavior from Presentation and Markup

Just as we always want to separate structured, semantic content (in our markup) from presentation (via CSS), we also want to separate our behavioral code (DOM scripting) from our CSS and markup. One important way in which we can achieve this is to use event listeners, which we can add to elements using JavaScript after a page has loaded, thus allowing us to avoid inline event handlers that entangle behavior and content.

Usually, we'll want to wait until the document model for the page is ready (which happens when a page finishes loading) before attaching the event listeners. When a page finishes loading, an **onload** event is fired for the **window** object. We can add an event handler for **onload** events to the **window** in our JavaScript, which then calls an "initializing" function, which adds all the event listeners.

```
1. function initializeControls() {
2. //add an event listener to all links
3.   var allLinks = document.getElementsByTagName('a');
4.   for( var i=0; i < allLinks.length; i++ ){
5.     allLinks[i].addEventListener("click", "linkClicked",
       true)
6.   } //end for
7.} //end initializeControls
8.
9. window.onload=initializeControls;
```

Again, don't let the JavaScript put you off if you are new to it. This snippet of code tells the browser that when the page is finished loading, the browser should perform the function **initializeControls** on line 9. That function (which is defined on line 1 and onward) collects all the links in the document in a variable called **allLinks** (line 3). It then *iterates* though the entries in this collection (lines 4 through 6, the "for" loop), and adds the event listener to each entry (line 5).

With this technique, we've now separated our event handlers out from our HTML.

Forms and Links

There are two places where we need to take special care when it comes to using the DOM, if we want to ensure our pages are usable without JavaScript. Links *must* allow the user to follow them to their destination when JavaScript is disabled. This is a particular challenge when the link reveals hidden content via JavaScript, as in figure **5.2**.

One solution is to make all the hidden content visible initially, and then hide it in an initialization function once the page is loaded. Whatever the solution, which will vary from situation to situation, it's important to consider what happens when JavaScript is not enabled.

A similar caution applies to form elements. Client-side form-field validation can be very helpful, but the form must still be able to be sent to the server even if fields could not be validated because of the absence of JavaScript. And for security purposes, regardless of any client-side validation, user-entered data must always be validated on the server as well.

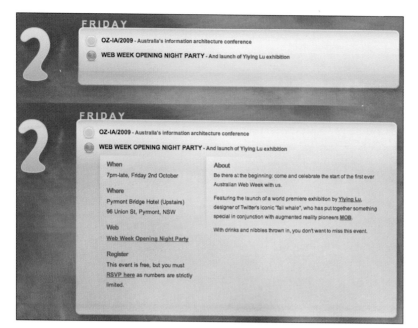

5.2
JavaScript associated with a link reveals additional content when the link is followed. Above the link has not been clicked, while below, the content is revealed by clicking the link.

Browser Incompatibilities

We've mostly avoided the elephant in the living room so far, but yes, Virginia, there are browser inconsistencies when it comes to the DOM. Not every browser supports even all of the Level 2 DOM, while Internet Explorer has a good many DOM-like features that aren't entirely compatible with the standard DOM. This is bad news, because it makes it much harder to write cross-browser DOM scripts, but the good news is that it is almost always possible to find equivalents across all browsers of various DOM features. Until the last couple of years, this essentially meant any DOM scripter needed to be familiar with the intricacies and idiosyncrasies of all the major browsers. (Joy!) But recently, several wonderful libraries that provide a common layer of functionality for developers to access, and which hide the inconsistencies between browsers, have emerged. Before looking at these libraries, let's briefly consider how best to address the situation when one or more browsers don't support a standard DOM feature.

There are two strategic responses to dealing with a browser that doesn't support a feature widely supported in other browsers we want to also target:

- We can use the progressive enhancement approach of simply not providing that feature for browsers that lack the relevant capabilities, but in many cases, this is not feasible—particularly because the most commonly troublesome browser is Internet Explorer, which is still the market-share leader.
- We can write JavaScript that addresses different browsers in different ways.

To do the latter, we need to distinguish between browsers. For example, if we know that Internet Explorer 8 and older versions don't support **addEventListener**, but do support **attachEvent**, then we can use the latter with IE, and the former with other browsers. But this could get complicated very quickly: What do we do about IE 9? What do we do about obscure, or new browsers that support **attachEvent** but not **addEventListener** (for example)? We can try to "sniff" for the user agent of the browser using the **userAgent** property of the **navigation** property of the **window** object, but as we'll see several times in other chapters, browser sniffing, or "user agent sniffing" is a fragile and undesirable practice. Browsers frequently identify themselves as other browsers, and they also improve between versions—IE 9 might support a feature that IE 8 does not. Plus, the matrix of even just current browsers and their DOM support is enormous. Do you really want to test and track all of the DOM support in all of the commonly used browsers and their different versions? (Clearly, you don't.)

Luckily, with the DOM, you don't need to.

With the DOM, we can test for the presence of *features*, rather than for a particular browser. That way, we only need to handle a small number of cases—for example the presence of support for **addEventListener** or **attachEvent**—rather than the many different possible browsers. Here's how we do it: using JavaScript, we ask if a method like **addEventListener** is supported by invoking the method *without any arguments* in a Boolean expression, like so:

```
(window.addEventListener)
```

Note that in JavaScript, Boolean expressions are contained within parentheses. If the method is supported, this expression will be true; otherwise it will be false. We can then use this information to separately target browsers that support **addEventListener**, browsers that support **attachEvent**, and browsers that support neither. Our code will look something like this:

```
if(window.addEventListener)          { //DOM Level 2 Events
element.addEventListener(type, expression, bubbling);
}
else if(window.attachEvent) { // Internet Explorer
  element.attachEvent('on' + type, expression);
}
```

Detecting feature support, rather than browser versions, is a far more robust and "future proof" method. It only causes problems when a browser incorrectly claims to support a feature—that is, when a browser returns "true" in the Boolean test expressions. Such instances are very uncommon, though Firefox has been known to report support for some CSS properties in the style object even when it doesn't really provide that support.

innerHTML vs. DOM methods

One of the more polarizing debates among DOM scripters is the issue of whether or not to use **innerHTML**. The **innerHTML** property is an as-yet unstandardized element property (though it is part of the draft HTML5 standard) that can set or get the HTML of all descendent elements of a given element as a string. You can easily create all the descendants of an element as follows:

```
thePara.innerHTML="this is the text of the paragraph
with some <a href='http://google.com'>links<a> and
some <strong>other elements</strong>"
```

The browser takes the string value (**"this is the text of the paragraph"** and so on), parses it as it would an HTML document, then adds the resultant elements (a link and a **strong** element, along with the rest of the content) as the descendants of the **thePara** element, replacing any current descendants of that element.

The `innerHTML` property is polarizing in large part because it is non-standard, and thus poses philosophical problems for many developers. But in practical terms, the lack of standardization means that there are differences in `innerHTML` implementations across browsers. It's a very powerful property, because it lets you take any text, which may or may not be valid HTML, and pass it to `innerHTML`, and rely on the browser turning this into part of the DOM. Note that this includes removing all of the existing descendent elements of the element. As a consequence, in particular when using it to create HTML, `innerHTML` needs to be used very carefully.

The alternative is to use DOM methods like **`createElement`** and **`setAttribute`**. With this approach, each element and attribute is explicitly created by the JavaScript, rather than inside the blackbox of `innerHTML`, making the results more predictable. Methods like **`createElement`** will return exceptions if they fail—for example, if they try to add an `href` attribute to a `p` element, which isn't allowed. This makes it easier to handle invalid markup without having to write a parser of your own in JavaScript to ensure sensible markup is passed to the browser via `innerHTML`.

The downside of DOM methods is they are currently far slower than `innerHTML`. So where performance is an issue, `innerHTML` is superior in that respect. Additionally, creating DOM-based solutions requires considerably more effort than simply passing a string to a method. It's possible to make `innerHTML` more robust by preprocessing the input, but that will affect performance and ease of implementation as well.

You should decide which of these approaches is appropriate for your projects by considering whether robustness is more or less important than performance and ease of implementation. In reality, you might find yourself using either of these approaches, depending on the situation at hand.

Security

Browsers are designed to be as secure as possible, and typically implement policies and approaches that attempt to ensure that malicious code can't execute outside a web page, interact with the local system, or grab information from other open browser windows. Nevertheless, the incentives for malicious coders are so great that we can't simply rely on the browser to ensure security. And as websites become more like applications and increasingly rely on server-side databases and processing, we have another vector for malicious code. While the issue of DOM and JavaScript security merits entire chapters and indeed books, it's worth focusing on one fundamental principle that all DOM scripters should be aware of.

Don't Trust User Data

Every time a user is able to input data, there are potential security risks—particularly when that data is to be stored on the server in a database. These risks can be mitigated by:

- Validating the data on the client using JavaScript (but keep in mind JavaScript may be disabled). A simple example is to not allow `<script>` elements within user input, which may then be executed by the browser.
- Validating the data on the server (far more secure). Even if data is validated on the browser, it should *always* be validated on the server.
- Encoding user input (for example, encoding < and > as `&gt;` and `&lt;`).

If you are interested in knowing more about JavaScript and DOM security issues—and you should be—you'll find plenty of resources at the end of this book.

The Rise of the Libraries

The last two or three years have seen the meteoric rise of JavaScript libraries as a core part of web development. Initially many developers were skeptical about libraries, seeing them as valuable prototyping tools that were not to be relied on in production environments—or as a dangerous trend that puts, as one developer (in)famously said at the 2006 @media Conference, "guns in the hands of children" by giving developers with little JavaScript and DOM knowledge too much power (something many other developers think may actually be a good thing). Other concerns are that libraries are typically quite large and involve downloading additional files, both of which have performance implications for a site. There's also the concern that, given the complexity of much of the code used in libraries, it is much more difficult for developers to diagnose and address problems caused by the libraries themselves.

These debates have largely subsided as it has become apparent that the underlying code of these libraries is usually very good, and that they provide very helpful functionality. Rather than having to write all the cross-browser code it takes to have DOM scripts work in all common browsers, developers can use libraries to do the heavy lifting. The major libraries are also quite well documented, and are being adopted as part of development environments such as Visual Studio, which incorporates support for the JQuery library (**www.jquery. com**), and Palm's new webOS, which features the Prototype library (**www. prototypejs.org**). Additionally, many libraries are supported by thriving communities, which means that support and bug fixes are readily available. Meanwhile, performance issues can be addressed by "minifying" and compressing the library files, and by amalgamating them into a single file.

Just as no one would consider developing desktop applications without using an application development framework, it's likely that, within a very short time, little serious web development work will be done using the DOM without using at least one major JavaScript library.

There are different types of JavaScript libraries. Some, like JQuery, are general purpose—essentially an entire platform that enable plug-ins to extend the functionality of the library. Others, like qooxdoo (**www.qooxdoo.org**), are "widget libraries," providing a number of JavaScript-based controls (like data grids, tree lists and so on). Still others, like Moo.fx (**moofx.mad4milk.net**), are effects libraries, providing easy to use cross-browser effects like element zooming, fading, and so on. There are also numerous small libraries that help manage cookies, browser history, graphics, and much else besides. We'll list some of the most commonly used libraries here, and there are references to many other libraries at the end of this book.

As mentioned earlier, all these libraries are widely used, and almost all of them are developed by a core team of full-time, paid developers. Most are open source, and most have thriving communities of developers and users. Each is well worth considering, depending on your needs. But keep in mind that once you've chosen a library for a project, replacing it with another will typically require a lot of work, so choose wisely.

Choosing a Library

High-profile developer Brian Reindel has compiled a widely referenced series of questions to help developers decide which library to choose. Some of the criteria Reindel raises include:

- Does the framework support A-Grade browsers?
- Is there a core team of developers?
- How mature is the framework?
- How often are updates publicly released?
- How friendly is the documentation?
- Is there an active community?
- Are benchmark tests performed regularly?
- How extensible is the framework?
- Do you like the API style?

It's well worth checking out the whole list at **blog.reindel.com/2007/10/30/how-to-choose-a-javascript-framework**.

JQuery

www.jquery.com

The increasingly popular JQuery has recently gained the backing of Microsoft, which has built support for the library into the ASP.NET Ajax Framework, and from Nokia, which has incorporated JQuery into its Widget Development Platform for the S60.

JQuery is highly modular, with a plug-in architecture that enables third-party developers to easily extend the library's functionality. JQuery has a thriving community, and is open source. It is considered to be one of the best-performing and most compact of popular general purpose libraries.

Prototype

www.prototypejs.org

Prototype, which has close ties with Ruby on Rails, was one of the earliest general purpose libraries to gain prominence. It provides core DOM functionality, with libraries such as MooFx and Script.aculo.us built on top of it to provide effects and widgets. Prototype is an open source library with a strong community of developers and users.

Script.aculo.us

script.aculo.us

Script.aculo.us provides effects and widgets on top of Prototype. It too is widely used, is open source, and has a strong community. It adds animation, controls, and drag and drop functionality among other things to Prototype.

Yahoo User Interface Library (YUI)

developer.yahoo.com/yui

From Yahoo Developer Network, YUI is a core set of DOM functionality, along with effects and widgets such as datatables, menus, color pickers, and calendars. It also features utilities for cookie management, history management, and much more. YUI is widely used by Yahoo sites.

Inspecting the DOM

These days, most browsers ship with or have as extensions very powerful debugging tools that can help inspect the DOM, and otherwise debug your web development. Here's a very brief overview of some of the most widely used tools for popular browsers.

IE Developer Toolbar for IE 6 and 7

tinyurl.com/2vaa52

The IE developer toolbar, which can be downloaded and installed for IE 6 and 7, has the ability to inspect the DOM, validate HTML and CSS, check accessibility and much more. For developing and debugging in Internet Explorer, it's a must-have.

Internet Explorer 8 Developer Toolbar

IE 8 has built-in developer tools, accessible from the tools button menu (F12 opens these tools). The IE developer tools have similar features to the IE 6 and 7 toolbar, and once again is indispensible for developing and debugging with IE 8.

Firefox Firebug and Web Developer Toolbar

www.getfirebug.com
www.chrispederick.com/work/web-developer

These two Firefox extensions are essential tools for web developers using Firefox. The Web Developer toolbar is similar to the IE developer toolbar, while Firebug provides a huge array of functionality for debugging and developing HTML, CSS, and JavaScript, including a sophisticated DOM inspector.

DragonFly for Opera

www.opera.com/dragonfly

DragonFly is a developer extension from Opera Software for the Opera browser, and features a rich DOM inspector in addition to other script, HTML, and CSS development tools.

Safari Web Inspector

www.apple.com/safari

Apple's Safari browser for Windows and Mac OS features the Web Inspector, which is similar to DragonFly, Firebug, and the IE 8 developer tools, and it includes a DOM inspector.

With each of these browsers and the developer tools mentioned above you can select an element in the DOM, inspect its properties, such as current CSS, and traverse the DOM (going up to inspect parent elements, sideways to inspect sibling elements, or down to inspect child elements). For example, figure 5.3 shows the DOM as a collapsible tree on the left, with the properties for the selected element on the right. These DOM inspectors can help you quickly determine the structure of a document, which can greatly aid in the development of DOM scripts (and their debugging when they don't work).

Until recently, DOM and JavaScript debugging were very poorly supported in browsers. Though these web development tools still lack the sophistication of those available to desktop application developers, we're making huge strides.

5.3
Safari's Web Inspector in DOM inspection mode

Ajax?

In many ways, Ajax is really a brand name for rich browser-based interfaces. Although the A stands for *asynchronous* and refers to the ability (via the clumsily named **XMLHTTPRequest** DOM object) to update only part of a web page rather than requiring a full page refresh as would have been the case a few years ago, many Ajax interfaces don't in fact use this capability. Interestingly, **XMLHTTPRequest**, introduced by Microsoft in IE 5, is still unstandardized, although it is supported across all modern browsers and is currently in the process of standardization by the W3C.

While the term *Ajax* has served a great purpose as a brand name for dynamic rich browser-based experiences, I suspect in time the term will become less common, as we'll come to expect rich browser-based user experiences from web sites and applications.

The Wrap

This chapter has been a whirlwind tour through the DOM. If you are already familiar with the DOM and JavaScript, I hope the chapter has helped solidify your understanding and introduce you to practices you may not be aware of. If you are brand new to the DOM and scripting, it's my hope you'll see that it's not nearly as daunting as you may have imagined, and you are now keen to learn more. If so, you'll find (as always) resources outlined at the end of the book to help.

Much of modern web development is heading away from static, page-based designs toward more dynamic, interactive, application-like experiences, and the key to developing these experiences is the DOM. So, like it or not, the DOM is something we're going to have to learn to live with... and, hopefully, to love.

But a commitment to accessibility should be a core part of the ethics of our emerging profession: something we willingly strive to achieve, not something we do grudgingly and only when legislation requires it. If you've had much contact with someone with a disability, you may understand how difficult it can be to gain access to vital information, social networks, and services. If you haven't, consider limiting your own access so you can experience for yourself some of the challenges faced by people with disabilities. Spend a week making all your purchases and commercial interactions online. Use a screen reader to check your email and catch up on your daily reading. Navigate with only your keyboard, or only your mouse. You'll quickly gain an appreciation for the immense challenges most websites and internet interactions pose for people with disabilities—challenges you are in a position to do something about.

The leading role that the web has played in improving the lives of so many people with disabilities is one of the reasons I'm a web developer. That won't be true for everyone, but whether you're motivated by altruism or by the threat of lawsuits like those involving Target and RiteAid in the U.S. (and going back to the Australian Human Rights and Equal Opportunities Commission legal action involving the Sydney Organising Committee for the Olympic Games in 1999), you'll find that accessibility is a core goal of professional web development.

Fortunately, it's much less confusing and difficult to achieve than you may have been led to believe.

In this chapter, we won't be able to cover accessibility-related areas in great detail, but we'll cover the central issues, recommendations, and technological challenges, and look at some straightforward steps we can take to help make our sites as accessible as possible with little additional effort.

The Business Case for Accessibility

There's a solid business case to be made for accessibility in web development. Accessible development can improve the lives of those who visit our sites, but it also translates into direct cost savings (fewer people calling customer service phone lines, for example), and lets businesses reach many more people, thus increasing sales and revenue. The number of people with disabilities in our communities is far greater than most people imagine. For example, the U.S. Department of Health & Human Services recently reported that one in five U.S. citizens has some form of disability, and one in eight has a severe disability.

When we speak about people with disabilities, we're talking about tens of millions of people—and about a market segment that is often more likely to use e-commerce than many other groups. Addressing the needs of this community can directly impact the bottom line of a company.

Beyond these direct commercial benefits, accessible development techniques can also have many other positive results. Google and other search engines are, in a sense, blind. When they index a site, the only text they perceive is actual *text*—not images or Flash files that only people without visual disabilities can interpret as text. Sites that use good clean semantic structure, avoid table-based markup, and embrace other accessibility practices are, therefore, likely to benefit from improved findability and search engine ranking.

The Global Legal Framework

Throughout the world, anti-discrimination legislation addresses discrimination against people with disabilities. Such legislation generally covers many aspects of life, but increasingly also expressly addresses the web and website accessibility. The issue is complex, and any attempt to provide a simple overview will likely be more confusing than not. You'll find sources of more complete information on the situation worldwide at the end of this book.

Accessibility and the W3C

Since its early days, the W3C has attempted to develop accessibility recommendations, guidelines, and policies, and to build accessibility directly into standards like CSS and HTML. In 1999, the W3C published the Web Content Accessibility Guidelines version 1 (WCAG 1), and in 2008, they published an updated version, WCAG 2. Additionally, to address the growing need for accessibility guidelines for web applications, the W3C's Web Accessibility Initiative (WAI) developed the Accessible Rich Internet Applications Suite (WAI-ARIA), a standard we'll turn to shortly.

WCAG 1

Published in 1999, in the days of version 4 browsers, WCAG 1 was the first major attempt to codify a set of practices to ensure more accessible websites. The goal of WCAG 1 was to show "how to make Web content accessible to people with disabilities" (**www.w3.org/TR/WCAG10**).

WCAG 1 is divided into fourteen guidelines, each of which is subdivided into checkpoints, and each of these checkpoints has a priority, from A to AAA (usually called "triple A"). Conformance to WCAG 1 guidelines can be measured by conformance to these checkpoints. A document has a conformance level A if it meets all of the level A checkpoints. Likewise, a document is considered AA ("double A") if it meets all the AA checkpoints, and triple A if all of the AAA checkpoints are met.

Before we delve a little more deeply into these guidelines and checkpoints, it's worth noting that AAA compliance is widely considered to be difficult to attain, and not always worth the effort: many AAA checkpoints are highly subjective, and AAA compliance produces little practical value. As a result, AA compliance is the level most experts (and some official government guidelines) recommend aiming for.

Guidelines and Checkpoints

As noted above, each of the fourteen guidelines of WCAG 1 has several checkpoints. In this chapter, we'll examine *only those checkpoints* that most commonly cause difficulties. The WCAG 1 guidelines (and an accompanying "Techniques" document) are quite straightforward, so don't be afraid to read them yourself.

Guideline 1: Provide Equivalent Alternatives to Auditory and Visual Content

This guideline addresses the needs of people with hearing or visual disabilities. One of the most common errors developers make is to omit appropriate `alt` content for images. In HTML 4, all `img` elements must have an `alt` attribute, though the attribute value may be empty (that is `alt=""`) when an image is purely decorative—though we should really be using CSS, rather than markup, to add such images.

Rich audio and video content accessibility requires far more than simple textual equivalents, and the requisite captioning techniques go quite some way beyond the scope of this book. You'll find links to resources on audio and video captioning and related accessibility techniques at the end of this book.

Guideline 2: Don't Rely On Color Alone

This applies to CSS more than HTML, as style should always be applied using CSS, not presentational markup. Up to eight percent of the male population has some form of difficulty discerning the difference between colors, while people using monochrome devices (such as Amazon's Kindle) will not be able to discern between many different colors. Instead of, for example, using green to indicate safe and red to indicate danger, use shapes, text labels, and other indicators to convey the information.

Guideline 3: Use Markup and Style Sheets and Do So Properly

This guideline suggests that we should use the technologies of the web according not just to the letter of the law (table-based layouts will, after all, validate), but according to its spirit as well. Checkpoints here include ensuring documents are valid, relative units like `em` and `%` are used instead of `px` in CSS, and the appropriate semantic and structural elements of HTML are used (for example headings, lists, quotations, and so on).

Guideline 5: Create Tables That Transform Gracefully

Tabular data can cause significant problems for people using assistive devices like screen readers. Guideline 5 has several checkpoints to help improve the accessibility of such data.

These checkpoints include using `row` and `column` headers in data tables, and for complex data tables, use features like **thead**, **tfoot**, and **tbody** to group rows, **col** and **colgroup** to group columns, and the `axis`, `scope`, and `headers` attributes to show the relationships between cells and headers. We look at techniques for improving the accessibility of data tables later in this chapter.

Guideline 9: Design for Device-Independence

Guideline 9 focuses on the importance of being able to use a site or page no matter what input device you're using—a keyboard, a voice input device, and so on—instead of only with a mouse.

These are just a few of the guidelines, but many major sites fail to comply even with this limited set. Conformance to WCAG 1 level AA is mostly straightforward, and is usually machine testable using tools we'll cover in a moment. It is, therefore, relatively easy to assess a site's level of conformance with these guidelines—and developers have little excuse for failing to meet them.

Quality assurance tools for WCAG 1

Not all of the WCAG 1 guidelines can be machine tested—several require human judgment to measure conformance—but for those guidelines that are machine testable, a number of tools exist to make the process easier. They include:

- CynthiaSays from HiSoftware—**www.cynthiasays.com**
- HERA—**www.sidar.org/hera/index.php.en**
- WAVE from Webaim—**wave.webaim.org**
- Total Validator—**www.totalvalidator.com**
- ATRC Web Accessibility Checker—**www.achecker.ca/checker/index.php**

WCAG 2

WCAG 1 is focused on the web technologies that existed when it was published. In the years that followed, some of these technologies matured, while others—like DOM scripting—became more prominent. The second release of WCAG, WCAG 2, is structured rather differently.

Principles, Guidelines, Success Criteria, and Techniques

WCAG 2 was developed with the aim of creating guidelines that are less bound to particular technologies, more objective, and thus more readily testable (by software or people), and more adaptable to changes in web technologies. According to the Web Accessibility Initiative, WCAG 2 is intended to apply to "different types of Web technologies and to more advanced technologies" as well as technologies that "develop in the future." It is also designed so that compliance with its success criteria will be "more precisely testable with automated testing and human evaluation" (**www.w3.org/WAI/WCAG20/wcag2faq.html**).

Where WCAG 1 was a series of guidelines with associated checkpoints, WCAG 2 is divided into four major principles. Each principle has a number of guidelines, and each guideline has several checkpoints, called *success criteria*. Each success criterion is associated with *sufficient* techniques (recommended ways of meeting the success criteria) and *advisory* techniques (methods that are not by themselves sufficient to meet the criteria, but which are still encouraged). None of these techniques are *required* to meet the criteria. The "Techniques for WCAG 2" document also identifies *common failures*, which the working group defines as "authoring practices known to cause Web content not to conform to WCAG 2.0."

WCAG 2 is not without its critics in the accessibility arena, and its uptake as the primary reference criteria for web accessibility has been slower than the W3C might have expected. It does appear, however, that it will eventually supplant WCAG 1 as the primary guideline for web accessibility. For an overview of some of the industry's concerns with WCAG 2, see Wikipedia's entry on web accessibility, which at the time of this writing was surprisingly good (**en.wikipedia.org/wiki/Web_accessibility#Criticism_of_WAI_guidelines**).

WCAG 2 is a much larger document than WCAG 1, and has been criticized for being vague and jargon-filled—for a taste of these criticisms, check out **www.alistapart.com/articles/tohellwithwcag2** and **www.webcredible.co.uk/user-friendly-resources/web-accessibility/wcag-guidelines-20.shtml**. It is, however, accompanied by very detailed documentation to help developers understand and meet each success criterion. It's also designed so that pages that currently meet WCAG 1 A and AA criteria should mostly continue to meet WCAG 2 criteria with little or no additional effort.

The depth and complexity of WCAG 2 put its details far beyond the scope of this book, but you'll find links and other resources related to the guidelines in the Resources section at the back of this book.

Quality Assurance Tools for WCAG 2

Because WCAG 2 is still in its relative infancy, there are far fewer automated tools available for it than for WCAG 1. Of the list of tools for WCAG 1 testing discussed earlier, only ATRC Web Accessibility Checker also does WCAG 2 testing.

ARIA

As web content and sites have become more sophisticated and application-like, it has become increasingly challenging to maintain, and even to define, accessibility. The WAI's Accessible Rich Internet Applications Suite, or WAI-ARIA, more commonly called ARIA, is designed to meet exactly this challenge. ARIA is a set of HTML extensions that can be used to annotate elements, thus identifying each annotated element's role, states, and properties in ways that increase a page's accessibility.

In this section, we'll take a quick look at what ARIA enables to get you started. Although ARIA is still in its early days, there's at least some non-trivial support in all contemporary browsers, including IE 8 as well as a number of screen readers, and it seems clear that browser developers are solidly behind the technology. ARIA is here to stay.

Keyboard Access

To be accessible, a page or web application needs to be fully usable with devices other than a mouse. ARIA enables applications and pages to be used via a keyboard—no mouse required.

In HTML 4, *focus* is a term that describes which element on a page is first in line to receive input from the user's keyboard or other input device. A limited number of elements such as `a`, `area`, `button`, `input`, and `select` can receive focus, and users can press the tab key to cycle through these elements. The *tab order* of these elements (the order in which they receive focus as the user presses the tab key) is determined by their order in the HTML source, or by the `tabindex` attribute, which specifies via an integer the tab order: the lower the number, the earlier the element comes in the tab order.

In HTML 4, it is possible for developers to create their own application controls, or *widgets*, as they are called in ARIA, with elements that don't receive focus, and thus cannot be used via the keyboard alone. With ARIA, any visible element can have a `tabindex`, and thus can receive focus and be used with the keyboard.

This aspect of ARIA is now supported in IE 8, Opera 9.5, Safari 4, and Firefox 3.5.

Roles

HTML largely relies on element names to provide semantic information about documents; although clever developers use the `class` and `id` attributes to add additional information about elements, this use is merely conventional, and isn't an official part of HTML. As such, HTML is impoverished in terms of its semantic capabilities. ARIA extends a feature of XHTML 1.1, the `role` attribute, to allow developers to describe the function an element plays, in addition to what it is. For example, lists are `li` elements, but can play the role of—among other things—navigation. ARIA provides a set of possible values for the `role` attribute: a set of names for the types of roles that elements can play. To get technical, it provides an *ontology* for `role`.

By using the `role` attribute to describe the role played by a particular element, developers can allow browsers that understand ARIA roles to better communicate the structure of a document to the user. The `role` attribute can also provide standard, user-expected behavior and appearance for specific types of controls—checkboxes, for example—that are implemented by the developer using elements other than the expected HTML element (which would be `<input type="checkbox">`, in this case).

The roles of ARIA fall into a number of categories including:

- **Landmark roles**, which describe regions of a page for navigational purposes. These roles include `application`, `banner`, `main`, `navigation`, and `search`.

- **Document structure roles**, which describe the part played by the element in the structure of the document. These roles include `navigation`, `section`, `note`, and `heading` (as we'll see in Chapter 11, these are often closely associated with new structural elements of HTML5).

- **Application structure roles**, which describe the part an element plays in the structure of an application, including `alert`, `alertdialog`, `progressbar`, and `status`.

- **User interface elements** such as `treegrid`, `toolbar`, and `menuitem`.

- **User input roles** like `checkbox`, `slider`, and `option`.

Using `role` is simple: we add one of the defined `role` values as a value of the `role` attribute of an element, just as we might add a `class` value. For example, suppose we want to use an **input** element of **type** `image` as a button. We'll just add a role of `button` to describe the role this input element is playing:

```
<input type="image" alt="font-weight: bold" src=
"./images/bold-unpressed.png" role="button">
```

Just what a browser will do with the information that this is a button is left up to that browser's developers. But the information is now there, and we can imagine how browsers and assistive devices might make use of this knowledge for the benefit of not only users with disabilities, but all users.

States and Properties

In addition to allowing developers to annotate the roles an element plays, we can also explicitly declare the state of an element—for example, whether it is currently pressed—as well as other information about that element. States provide dynamic information such as whether or not a checkbox is checked, whereas properties provide information that is essential to an object's nature. That said, the distinction between properties and states isn't that important, since they work in very similar ways. It is, however, important to note the difference between states and properties on one hand and the `role` attribute on the other. When we use `role`, we apply values to the `role` attribute itself, but there are many state and property attributes, and each has its own name—in other words, there's no ARIA attribute named `state` or `property`. ARIA property and state attribute names include the `aria-` prefix: the `aria-disabled` state, for example, which can take the values `true` and `false`, and the `aria-flowto` property, which identifies the next element in the recommended reading order.

Returning to the input example, if the element in question were a button that toggled between two states (pressed and unpressed), we could communicate this using the ARIA state `aria-pressed`.

```
<input type="image"
alt="font-weight: bold" src="./images/bold-unpressed.png"
role="button" aria-pressed="false">
```

We could then change the `aria-pressed` using JavaScript when the element was clicked or received an *enter* keydown event.

CSS and ARIA

All modern browsers, including IE 8, allow us to style elements based on their ARIA properties and states (and their `role` attribute values) using attribute selectors. For example, to change the background color of an element when that element is pressed, we'd use the following CSS:

```
[aria-pressed=true] {
  background-color: #cfb725;
}
```

Adding ARIA roles, properties, and states to a website or application requires extra work, but not much more than we'd already do if we used `class` or `id` values to accomplish the same tasks. And instead of having to come up with our own approach to capturing the state and properties of a widget or other part of a page or application, we can simply reuse this well-thought-out, standardized approach. Not only will we be helping improve the accessibility and overall usability of our part of the web, we'll be writing more maintainable and consistent code as well.

Because developers are increasingly using libraries and frameworks like Dojo, JQuery, YUI, and others we touched on in Chapter 5, and because these libraries increasingly support ARIA, much of the effort to increase support for ARIA is already being done for us by the developers of those libraries. Some of the efforts in this area include:

- JQuery—The core team has begun the work of supporting ARIA, and there is a plug-in, jARIA, which adds full support for setting and getting roles, properties, and states via JavaScript using JQuery syntax.
- Dojo—The Dojo 1.0 toolkit has full ARIA support for the core DojoX widget set.
- YUI—A number of the YUI widgets include support for ARIA.

Browser and Assistive Device Support

So what level of support is there in current browsers for features in ARIA? We've already seen that `tabindex` and the ability for any visible element to receive the focus is widely supported, including in Internet Explorer from version 5 on. Here's the story for other features:

- IE 8 includes support for ARIA roles, properties, and states.
- Firefox 3.5 has the most comprehensive support for ARIA of all contemporary browsers, including roles, properties, and states.
- According to Opera Software, "Opera 9.5 supports parsing ARIA in HTML… This support is experimental, while the ARIA standard stabilizes."

- Safari 4 has limited support for ARIA, supporting a number of common roles, but not states or properties. Because Safari supports CSS attribute selectors on any attribute, whether it is part of a current HTML standard or not, it is possible to style HTML in Safari using the value of ARIA property and state attributes—and this is actually the case for Opera, Firefox 3.5, and even Internet Explorer 8 as well.

- Perhaps most importantly, the two most widely used screen readers, Window-Eyes and JAWS, have solid support for ARIA in their most recent versions.

The demonstrated commitment of these developers to implementing ARIA indicates widespread support on the web. In addition, a number of very high-profile websites and applications including Google's Google Reader feed reader and Gmail use ARIA extensively. Consequently, developers can feel confident that ARIA is a technology worth investing time and effort in.

Validation and ARIA

So how can we use ARIA in our markup today? We know that simply adding attributes that aren't part of the HTML specification to our markup will make our documents invalid. There are several ways to use these features that will let our documents validate, though they can be a little more complicated than simply choosing a **DOCTYPE**.

It's possible to use custom **DTD**s (document type definitions) that include the attributes of ARIA. At present there are no such reference **DOCTYPE**s for HTML or XHTML, though there have been calls for the W3C to provide them. The Paciello Group, a well known and respected accessibility consultancy, have an experimental HTML 4.01+ ARIA DTD (**www.paciellogroup.com/blog/?p=107**) that can be used with the W3C's HTML validator.

The experimental HTML5 validator at **www.validator.nu** also validates ARIA and HTML5. It will give errors with non–HTML5 **DOCTYPE**s, but is a useful tool for ensuring ARIA is used correctly. It has limitations as to what aspects of ARIA it will test, one of which is a lack of recognition of "landmark" roles.

The emergence of ARIA raises a bigger question, however: is validation always an important goal? After all, despite ARIA's tremendous potential value and solid browser support, without a good method of creating valid documents that incorporate ARIA, the technology falls at the validation hurdle. When it comes to the use of new web technologies, validation is a bit like driving while looking in the rearview mirror. Henri Sivonen, one of the more influential figures in the development of HTML5 (and the developer of the HTML5 validator) makes this observation:

> [G]etting new features is much more important than validating against a legacy validation target. ARIA adds markup, so ARIA can't validate against a legacy validation target such as XHTML 1.0 (without retroactively changing what XHTML 1.0 is). (**wiki.codetalks.org/wiki/index.php/ Web_2.0_Accessibility_with_ARIA_FAQ**)

If validation is absolutely required because of internal or regulatory requirements, there are solutions. But if validation is essentially a quality assurance mechanism, it's possible to intelligently use the output of HTML 4 or the HTML5 validators to check the quality of your ARIA-enabled markup, even if the document doesn't strictly validate.

Common Accessibility Problems (and Solutions)

We'll finish this chapter by addressing some of the most common accessibility problems, and ways of addressing them simply with HTML and CSS.

Links and Titles

Links are extensively used by screen readers and assistive devices to give users quick access to the contents of a page. While they only constitute a small percentage of the text on a page, they are a key way for many users to access a page's content. The text of a link is an important guide to where a link will take a user. For optimum accessibility, link text should "clearly identify the target of each link" (WCAG 1), and avoid assumptions about users' input devices revealed by use of terminology like "click here" as the link text. When several links on a page use the same text, they should all point to the same location.

The `title` attribute on link elements, although considered by many to add valuable accessibility information, can in fact be harmful: it can obscure other content in browsers that display `title` information as a tooltip, it isn't accessible unless a mouse is used, or users of screen readers have their settings so that title values are read out. There is no consensus in the industry as to whether the `title` attribute should be used, but it should definitely not be the only way for users to identify a link's destination.

Headings

Screen readers often use the headings on a page to create a "table of contents" to help users scan the page and jump to relevant areas. If you use heading elements *as headings* and use the heading order sensibly, you can make these screen-reader behaviors more usable. Don't skip heading levels (from `h2` to `h4` for instance). The visual style of headings can always be changed by CSS, so there's no need to skip a heading level.

alt text

Any non-textual content should have a textual alternative. With images, you can do this using the `alt` attribute. (A pedantic note from an old-timer: it's not the alt "tag.") Any `alt` content should be succinct, and although all `img` elements require an `alt` attribute in order for a page to validate, purely decorative images should have an empty string as the value of their `alt` attribute. Better still, purely decorative images (list-item bullets, for example, or decorative background images) should be included via CSS, not markup, which should be reserved for semantically useful content.

Color Contrast

The rather vague term *color blindness* leads to the common misconception that people who are color blind see the world in grayscale. This kind of vision impairment ("monochromasy") is in fact extremely rare; the majority of people with color blindness see in color, but have difficulty *distinguishing* between certain colors that are easily distinguishable by people without color blindness.

Although it's important that we avoid using only color to convey meaning (for example, using red as a warning, in the absence of additional shapes, text, or other information), there are other color-related accessibility concerns to consider. A lack of sufficient visual contrast between the text and its background is a commonly neglected problem. A text-background pair that appears "obviously" high contrast to someone without color blindness may be illegible to someone with color blindness or another visual deficiency.

Many tools will report whether a pair of colors has a sufficient contrast for legibility, but using these can be time consuming, since you must manually test each foreground and background color combination for a site. Tools like AccessColor from AccessKeys (**www.accesskeys.org/tools/color-contrast.html**) analyze an entire document by looking at the DOM and highlighting possible contrast problems. Most contrast-testing tools only work when text is set against a background color (not an image), however, and they don't test dynamic effects like hovering, so they can't provide a foolproof test of color contrast.

Tables

Tables present particular challenges for visually impaired users. The structure of a table, which may appear obvious to sighted users, can be confusing when read by a screen reader. HTML provides several elements and attributes to help screen readers read out the contents of tables more sensibly.

In addition to the standard `td` (table data) elements, tables may also have table header (`th`) elements, as we saw in Chapter 4. To make tables as accessible as possible, `th` elements should be used for the cells that are the headers of rows or columns.

caption and summary

The table `caption` element exists to provide a short description of the table, which is used both visually by a browser, and by screen readers. It's recommended tables have a caption, which is marked up immediately after the opening tag of the table. Tables may only have a single caption.

```
<table>
<caption>Timetable for Day 1 of the conference</caption>
```

In addition, the table element may have a `summary` attribute, which provides an overview of the contents of the table for users of screen readers. Sighted readers can also get a sense of the table and its contents at a glance; the `summary` attribute exists to help readers with visual disabilities do so as well. Unlike captions, summaries are not rendered by visual browsers—they are exclusively used by screen readers.

```
<table summary="Full timetable for all three tracks of
the first day of Web Directions South 2009">
<caption>Timetable for Day 1 of the conference</caption>
```

abbr and scope

Already we've given the browser a good deal of information that will make our tables more accessible. But particularly for complex tables, HTML has a number of under-utilized but helpful features that screen readers can use to help their users make more sense of data tables.

Because screen readers usually read each cell (including header cells) linearly, each header will be read many times, which may become time consuming and annoying. We can use the `abbr` attribute of the `th` element to define abbreviated text to be read in place of the full contents of the `th` element.

```
<th abbr="design">Design Track</th>
<th abbr="business">Business Track</th>
<th abbr="development">Development Track</th>
```

It's not always clear from the structure of a table whether a `th` element is the header for a row or a column of cells. The `scope` attribute allows us to specify which cells the `th` element is the header of. In our case above, the headers are for columns, and so our markup would be:

```
<th abbr="design" scope="col">Design Track</th>
<th abbr="business" scope="col">Business Track</th>
<th abbr="development" scope="col">Development Track</th>
```

For relatively simple tables, a screen reader can use the `scope` attribute to read out the header (or abbreviated header if we've added an `abbr` attribute) in front of the contents of a cell.

For example, in **figure 6.1**, the screen reader might read the highlighted cell as "design Font Embedding and Typography Mark Boulton." But, as this example shows, this is far from the whole picture. What the reader really needs to hear is something along the lines of "10.45am–11.40am design Font Embedding and Typography Mark Boulton." In essence, we need to associate more than one header with the cell. We can do this by adding an `id` to each header, and then using the `headers` attribute for `td` elements to associate `th` elements with a `td` element.

THURSDAY, OCTOBER 8, 2009			
TIME	DESIGN TRACK	BUSINESS TRACK	DEVELOPMENT TRACK
7:00AM – 9:00AM	Registration		
9:00AM – 9:10AM	Opening comments		
9:10AM – 10:15AM	Opening keynote		
10:15AM – 10:45AM	Morning tea		
10:45AM – 11:40AM	Font embedding and typography Mark Boulton	Beyond SEO Cheryl Gledhill & Scott Gledhill	Best practices for speeding up your site Mark Stanton

6.1

A sighted person can easily deduce that the font embedding session is in the design track at 10.45. For those using screen readers, it can be far from easy, unless we use the right markup.

```
<table summary="Full timetable for all three tracks of
the first day of Web Directions South 2009">
<caption>Timetable for Day 1 of the conference</caption>

  <tr>
    <th>Time</th>
    <th abbr="design" scope="col">Design Track</th>
    <th abbr="business" scope="col">Business Track</th>
    <th abbr="development" scope="col">Development
    Track</th>
  </tr>

  <tr>
    <th id="time1">7:00am - 9:00am</th>
    <td colspan="3">Registration</td>
  </tr>
```

continues on next page

```
<tr>
   <th id="time2">9:00am - 9:10am</th>
   <td colspan="3">Opening comments</td>
</tr>

<tr>
   <th id="time3">9:10am - 10:15am</th>
   <td colspan="3">Opening keynote</td>
</tr>
<tr>
   <th id="time4">10:15am - 10:45am</th>
   <td colspan="3">Morning tea</td>
</tr>
<tr>
   <th id="time5">10:45am - 11:40am</th>
   <td headers="design time5"><a href="http://south09..."
   >Font embedding...</a>
   <a href="http://south09...">Mark Boulton</a></td>
   <td headers="business time5"><a href=
   "http://south09...">Beyond...></a></td>
   <td headers="development time5"><a href=
   "http://south09...">...</a></td>
</tr>
```

While this additional information requires extra effort to mark up, the impact on accessibility for people using screen readers can be substantial. Like most development practices, when first encountered and used, these techniques may seem like a burden, but using appropriate attributes and elements soon becomes second nature.

Forms

You can directly and significantly improve the accessibility of your pages by marking up forms correctly. A few simple practices will greatly increase the usability of forms for people with various disabilities.

Form field labels provide absolutely vital information for users of screen readers. Although visual cues make it easy for those of us with good vision to determine what a field is for, unless form fields are explicitly and correctly associated with labels, users of screen readers may be unable to determine how a form works.

Some form elements—**button** elements, for example—have their own labels. For these elements, the value of the **value** attribute is the label for the element. When there is no implicit label, which is the case for most form elements, the **label** element should be used, and associated directly with the element it is the label for using the **for** attribute of the **label**. Here's how we can ensure maximum accessibility for our labeled text input field:

```
<label for="last-name" id="last-name-label">Last Name
</label> <input type="text" id="last-name" aria-labelledby=
"last-name-label">
```

Note that we're also using the ARIA attribute **aria-labelledby** in the form element itself—the **input** element, in the preceding example—to give the browser the **id** of the element that labels the present element. So in our example, we have indicated that an element (the **label** element, appropriately enough) with the **id** of last-name-label provides the label for the **input** element whose **id** is last-name.

Sharp-eyed readers may note that **aria-labelledby** works just like the HTML 4 **for** attribute, but backward: with **for**, the labeling element identifies the labeled element by its **id**; with **aria-labelledby**, the labeled element identifies the labeling element by *its* **id**. Note too that **labelledby**, though not standard U.S. spelling, is correct in this instance.

When a **label** element cannot be used, WCAG 2 suggests that it is sufficient to use the **title** of the element as the label. For example, we'd need to use **title** for a search box in the toolbar of a page, where a label would take up more horizontal space than is available.

Grouping Field Elements

More complex forms may make more sense when related fields are grouped together with a heading for each group. HTML provides the **fieldset** and **legend** elements for precisely this purpose. A *fieldset* is simply a **fieldset** element that contains all of the related form elements. The first element of the **fieldset** should be its **legend**, which is similar to a caption for a table.

```html
<fieldset>
  <legend>Billing Contact</legend>
  <p>But first we need to know, <strong>who'll be paying
for the tickets?</strong></p>
  <ol>
    <li>
      <label for="billing_name"><em class="required">*
Name</em></label>...
</fieldset>
```

The techniques we've covered here address many of the most common accessibility difficulties that users face on the web. Implementing them is typically not onerous, and goes a long way to improving the experience of your sites by people who are most reliant on the web. It will also go a long way to addressing the legal and institutional obligations you or your organization may be required to meet.

The Wrap

In this chapter, we've taken a high-level overview of accessibility, including the underlying legal and ethical framework, existing W3C standards, and specific accessibility problems and solutions. Besides these points, what should you take away from this chapter? The most central concept is the idea that, rather than being a checklist of corrections to be made at the end of the development process, true accessibility arises from a holistic approach to web design and development—one that not only benefits users with disabilities, but all users. (The same techniques that improve accessibility often improve usability as a whole.)

The prominence of accessibility in web development has increased significantly in the last decade, due in large part to individual evangelists within the industry. There's little doubt that legal frameworks and social expectations are all headed in the direction of greater accessibility to more people. Rather than worrying about the "stick" of legislation and legal action, think of the "carrots": the opportunity to reach the many people with disabilities who visit your site, the built-in search-engine friendliness of accessible code, and the satisfaction you'll derive from doing something to improve the online lives of so many others.

Part II

REAL-WORLD DEVELOPMENT

Working With, Around, and Against Browsers

Anyone who develops for the web quickly learns that it is a challenge to develop sites that work consistently across browsers. As browsers have matured, and particularly now that Internet Explorer 7 and 8 are starting to replace IE 6, this challenge is receding, but browsers have bugs, and always will. So why do browser bugs cause us so many headaches?

Like operating systems, web browsers provide the underlying technologies that applications (in this case, web pages and web apps) use to present themselves. Of course, unlike desktop applications designed to run on a single operating system, web pages and applications must run on all common browsers. When there's a bug in an OS, application developers can use workarounds to avoid the consequences of that bug, because the operating system they're developing for is effectively unique. On the web, however, a workaround for a problem with one browser might cause problems in another browser, or in future versions of the same browser. In essence, we must target multiple operating systems (browsers) with the same code base (our markup, styles, and so on), which is very difficult to do.

Over the last decade, a body of *browser hacks* has been developed to work around browser bugs and shortcomings—but while some of these methods may "work," we should nevertheless avoid them, because they are likely to fail in future browsers.

In this chapter, we will focus on some of the most common browser bugs, the reasons why they exist, and sensible, standards-compliant, long-term solutions that work across all browsers.

I hope that future editions of this book will include less and less of this kind of information, as old browsers fade away and new browsers improve their support for standards. The day that Internet Explorer 8 (or even 7) is the baseline version of IE will be a watershed moment in the life of professional developers; when that happens, we'll be able to turn our backs on many of the challenges addressed in this chapter. Until then, though, we'll need to find the best way forward that we can.

What's a Browser Hack?

The term *hack* has two quite different connotations in the wider development world. In one sense, a hack is a positive thing—an elegant, unorthodox solution to a problem. But the older connotation of the word is of a quick and dirty, inelegant solution to a problem.

For web development, because we aren't developing for a single, controlled environment like an operating system, but for numerous different browsers, many solutions to specific browser limitations can easily become hacks in the second sense. When choosing a solution to specific browser problems, we need to be mindful not only of other browsers and how they respond to the technique, but of the ways in which future browser versions might undo a hack and break our sites.

Three Kinds of Browser Shortcomings

Developers usually need to contend with three different kinds of browser shortcomings:

- Complete lack of support for a feature
- Partial support for a feature

- Buggy support for a feature—that is, support inconsistent with a specification and implementations of the same feature in other browsers

Of these, buggy support is often the most problematic. In the absence of support for a feature in one browser, the progressive enhancement approach suggests that we simply don't concern ourselves with browsers that lack support (see Chapter 2 if you need to brush up on progressive enhancement). This isn't always feasible, because some features are fundamental to the way a page works—for example, using CSS3 table display properties to create page layouts will work fine in IE 8 and all other contemporary browsers, but will leave IE 7 and older user agents with broken pages. But on the whole, it's buggy support, rather than missing support, that causes the most difficulty.

In the pages that follow, we'll largely focus on Internet Explorer, and particularly on its older versions that are still in use. We'll do so not because we are anti-Microsoft, but because those browsers—especially IE 6—are the ones that cause the most problems, in large part because some of them are nearly ten years old. The upgrade cycles of other browsers (both on the side of browser makers and browser users) tend to be much shorter than those of IE, so bugs in browsers like Firefox and Safari tend to have a smaller impact on web development.

Browser Modes

Many of the problems developers encounter, particularly with IE, are due to its "backward compatibility mode"—and most of the problems we'll discuss in this chapter simply go away if we used standards mode to render our pages. So what exactly are these modes?

Quirks Mode and *DOCTYPE* Switching

Until Internet Explorer 5 for the Mac was released in late 1999, browser support for CSS was, to be blunt, pretty dire. We could style pages with CSS to an extent, but browser inconsistencies made it difficult to do all but simple styling, like colors and fonts. IE 5 for the Mac faced a major challenge when it was launched. If it used a strictly standards-driven approach to rendering web pages, the vast majority of websites online at the time (most of which had been authored to suit buggy browsers) would appear "broken" in IE 5. Alternatively, if IE 5 simply rendered all pages as the older, buggy browsers did, there really wasn't any point to its support for CSS standards. So IE 5's makers developed a technique that would allow the best of both worlds.

They introduced the concept of two rendering modes: a standards mode, which provided full standards support, and a non-standards, or Quirks mode, in which the browser tried to emulate the broken rendering of older browsers. The browser developer's biggest challenge was figuring out how the browser could determine which mode to use for a particular site.

The ingenious hack (in the good sense of the word) that they hit on was the observation that the developers who used a *document type* in their pages tended to be the same developers who designed with standards in mind (DOCTYPEs, which we saw in Chapter 3, were then considered an optional extra and were only widely used by standards-focused developers). The combination of IE 5's excellent support for CSS rendering and its ability to switch modes is probably one of the most significant steps in the evolution of the standards-based web, though ironically the whole concept of using DOCTYPEs in this way is still viewed critically in some quarters as being nonstandard. Over time, other browsers, including Internet Explorer versions 6 and higher for Windows, adopted the concept of Quirks mode and DOCTYPE switching.

Rendering modes, useful as they once were, have served their purpose, and are no longer really needed. Quirks mode was always intended to be used for older content, with the presumption that newer content should be written in conformance with standards. Still, these modes do exist, and we need to actively let browsers know we want to use standards mode.

Choosing Standards Mode

Any HTML document with a full DOCTYPE will be rendered by all modern browsers (back to IE 6 for Windows) in standards mode. With rare exceptions, this is the mode you should use. In IE 6 and up, Quirks mode effectively triggers the same rendering as IE 5.5 for Windows, which is a huge leap backward. In other browsers, such as Opera, Safari, and Firefox, Quirks mode causes yet another set of rendering behaviors that certainly won't be identical to one another or to that of IE 5.5. Quirks mode is triggered by using no DOCTYPE or a DOCTYPE with no URL. For example, this DOCTYPE:

```
<!DOCTYPE html PUBLIC "-//W3C//DTD HTML 4.01//EN"
"http://www.w3.org/TR/html4/DTD/strict.dtd">

<head> ...
```

will cause any browser to render the document in standards mode.

On the other hand, this one:

```
<!DOCTYPE html PUBLIC "-//W3C//DTD HTML 4.01//EN">
<head> ...
```

will cause browsers to use Quirks mode, as will leaving off the DOCTYPE entirely (which we'd never do, since it would prevent us from validating our pages). With Internet Explorer, there are additional constraints: if anything (such as a comment) precedes the DOCTYPE declaration, IE will use Quirks mode:

```
<-- this will put IE into Quirks mode but all other
browsers into standards mode-->
<!DOCTYPE html PUBLIC "-//W3C//DTD HTML 4.01//EN"
"http://www.w3.org/TR/html4/DTD/strict.dtd">
<head> ...
```

Lastly, if you want to trigger Quirks mode *only* in IE 6, you can add an XML prolog to an XHTML document, like this:

```
<?xml version="1.0" encoding="utf-8"?>
<!DOCTYPE html PUBLIC "-//W3C//DTD XHTML 1.0 Strict//EN"
"http://www.w3.org/TR/xhtml1/DTD/xhtml1-strict.dtd">
```

IE 8's New *DOCTYPE* Switching Model

Internet Explorer 8 has introduced a new DOCTYPE switching model, which caused considerable controversy before the browser's launch. The fuss has since died down, but "compatibility mode switching" in IE 8 (and in future versions of IE) is more complicated than **DOCTYPE** switching. Firstly, IE 8 supports several compatibility modes:

- IE 5 mode—Essentially the same as IE 7 in Quirks mode
- IE 7 mode—A mode that renders content "as if it were displayed by the Internet Explorer 7 standards mode." This is often referred to as "almost standards mode."
- IE 8 mode—Internet Explorer's current top-of-the-line page rendering

To tell the browser which mode we want it to use, we'll need to use a new **meta** element—X-UA-Compatible—with various content values to tell IE 8 (and newer browsers) which rendering engine to use. The **meta** element appears in the **head** of a document before any elements other than **title** and other **meta** elements; it comes before any **link** or **script** elements. Its **http-equiv** attribute value is X-UA-Compatible, and its **content** attribute tells IE which rendering mode to use:

```
<meta http-equiv="X-UA-Compatible" content=
"IE=EmulateIE7" />
```

It's also possible to specify the same information via an http header by setting this up in your web server (such as Apache or IIS).

The possible values of the content attribute are:

- IE=5 (aka Quirks mode)—IE will use the IE 5 rendering model, regardless of the **DOCTYPE**.
- IE=7 (also known as IE 7 standards mode)—IE will use the IE 7 in standards mode rendering model regardless of the **DOCTYPE**.
- IE=EmulateIE7 (IE 7 emulation mode)—IE will use IE 7's standards or Quirks mode, depending on the **DOCTYPE** (essentially the browser pretends to be IE 7).
- IE=8 (IE 8 standards mode)—IE will use IE 8 standards mode, regardless of the **DOCTYPE**.
- IE=EmulateIE8 (IE 8 emulation mode)—IE will use IE 8's standards mode or Quirks mode, depending on the **DOCTYPE**.

- `IE=edge` ("latest mode")—IE, from version 8 and up, will always use the latest standards mode regardless of the `DOCTYPE`.

There are further potential complications, but they're rarely a problem, and you can follow up on them if you need to using the Resources section at the end of this book.

So what does this all mean? Essentially, you can choose to target different rendering modes using a combination of X-UA-Compatible instructions and `DOCTYPE`s. Which should you use? In an ideal world, you should use standards mode for newly developed sites, so `IE=8` is the recommended mode—Microsoft advises against using `IE=edge` except in experimental projects. If you need to use a particular rendering engine for legacy content, you can use the various values of the content attribute as outlined.

What happens if no X-UA-Compatible `meta` element is present? Then matters get really complicated, and depend on such factors as whether users have chosen Compatibility View in their browsers, whether Microsoft has added your site to a list of sites for which they maintain compatibility information (typically only heavily trafficked sites), the air-speed velocity of an unladen swallow, and other factors. (OK, not the swallow thing, probably.) The best thing to do is include an X-UA-Compatible `meta` element or serve your pages with an X-UA-Compatible http header.

Common Browser Bugs

Here we'll delve into a number of the most common browser rendering bugs, possible workarounds, and other solutions. Some of these, like the Box-Model Bug, will only show up in Quirks mode, and we only look at these bugs if they are historically significant. Why cover them at all? Because these bugs and their workarounds have had such an effect on web development that developers, even if they never need to deal with the bugs themselves, will likely be seeing leftover workaround code in legacy markup for years to come.

The Box-Model Bug

Probably the most vexing of all browser bugs is the Box-Model Bug in Internet Explorer 5 and 5.5, and in Internet Explorer versions 6 and higher in Quirks mode. The good news is that it's easily avoided using standards mode rendering. But for historical purposes, let's take a quick look at the bug that launched a thousand hacks.

If I specify the following CSS rule:

```
p {
    width: 200px;
    margin: 20px;
    padding: 5px;
    border: 2px solid;
}
```

…then how wide should the p element be when rendered? (For now, we'll leave aside the issue of whether we should be specifying all those values in pixels.) The obvious—and wrong—answer is 200px. It's wrong because, according to the CSS specification, the element should be 254px wide, counting from the left edge of the left margin to the right edge of the right margin [7.1]. This might seem counter-intuitive, but the CSS specification says that width applies to the *content* of an element—and padding, margins, and borders are all added to make the total width of the element. The same approach applies to the height property.

7.1
The standard CSS box model

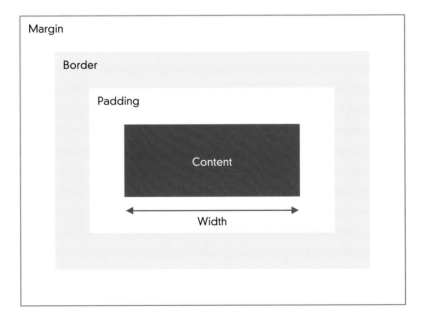

Internet Explorer 5, 5.5 (and later versions in Quirks mode) calculate the width of an element differently. Given the CSS just provided, these versions of IE would calculate the width of the element as, logically enough, 200px, making the content box 146px wide (200px minus 40px for the `margin`, 10px for the `padding`, and 4px for the `border`) [7.2]. This method may seem more logical, but `width` in CSS applies to the width of the *content*, not the whole width of the element (though with the CSS3 `box-sizing` property, it's now possible to specify the box-model calculation to use either the standard model, or the IE model).

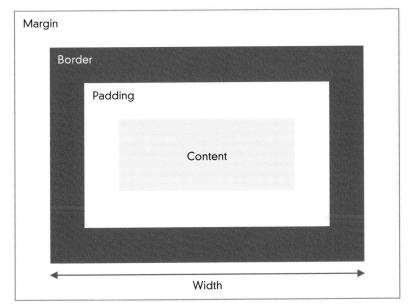

7.2
The IE CSS box model

In many situations—and particularly with the `float`-based multi-column layouts discussed in Chapter 9—this discrepancy is highly detrimental to the sanity of web developers. So what are we to do about it? Fortunately, the bug vanishes if we use a full **DOCTYPE** and thus trigger standards mode, in which all versions of IE since version 6 use the standard box model. Before later versions of IE provided this solution, many hacks were developed to address this problem, and we'll look at a few that are relevant to developers who must maintain legacy code.

The Doubled Float-Margin Bug

Fixed in IE 7, the IE Doubled Float-Margin Bug once wreaked havoc on `float`-based multi-column layouts as they came into prominence. In a nutshell, in certain situations, the horizontal margin between a floated element and the element in which it is floated is doubled, and thus takes up twice the amount of room specified in the CSS [7.3].

7.3
In IE 6, the horizontal margin between an element and the edge of the element within which it floats is sometimes doubled by this bug.

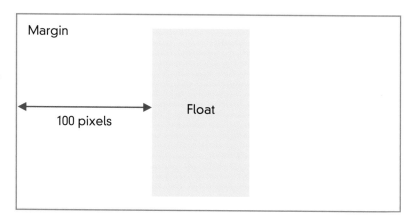

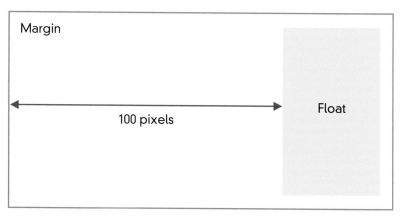

The fix, should you require one, is straightforward—just set the floated element's `display` property value to `inline`. This will have no effect in other browsers, because inline elements, when floated, automatically become block-level elements. But in IE 6, simply adding this value to all floated elements fixes the problem.

The Non-Collapsing Margins Bug

Just as the standard box-model calculation of `width` and `height` may seem counter-intuitive, so too is what happens to adjacent vertical margins on elements. As we saw in Chapter 3, when two vertical margins of block-level elements touch, and the elements don't have padding or borders adjacent to the

vertical margins, these margins should collapse so that the combined margin
is only the size of the larger of the two margins [7.4].

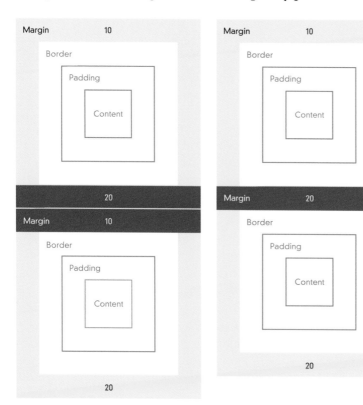

7.4
In the absence of pad-
ding or borders, adjacent
vertical margins should
collapse.

As you may have guessed, Internet Explorer 6 and 7 don't *always* collapse
adjacent vertical margins, even if you trigger standards mode: when certain
properties are applied via CSS, the margins just don't collapse. This has to
do with a magical IE-only property of HTML elements, `hasLayout`, which is
part of no standard, but which Internet Explorer uses as a built-in or internal property when it renders pages. Some CSS properties, including `width`,
`height`, `position: absolute`, `float`, and `display: inline-block`, give their
associated element a `hasLayout` property with a value of `true`. Some HTML
elements, including `html`, `body`, `img`, and many table- and form-related elements, have this property by default. When an element has a `hasLayout` property with a value of `true`, its vertical margins won't collapse when they should.

It's nearly time to jump in and look at workarounds for this and other bugs—
but first, we need to take a detour and learn more about the wonderful world
of `hasLayout`.

IE and *hasLayout*

Over the years, Internet Explorer 6 and (to a lesser extent) 7 have caused a lot of layout problems. Over time, intrepid developers including Holly Bergevin and John Gallant discovered that IE's internal `hasLayout` property is behind many of these problems. Although this is mostly a legacy problem, we'll take a brief look at `hasLayout` in case you have to deal with it in the coming years.

Deep Within Your Browser

Internally, the rendering engine of Internet Explorer for Windows (known as Trident) manages the layout of the page in part using the `hasLayout` property. Because—as mentioned earlier—`hasLayout` is not part of any standard, developers shouldn't really need to worry about it. But this property can have significant consequences for page layout. In a nutshell, when an element has a `hasLayout` value of true, then it is responsible for its own layout, and the layout of its descendent elements (except for those which have `hasLayout`). If an element has this property set to false, then its layout is determined by the nearest ancestor element with `hasLayout` set to true.

In practical terms, when an element has a `hasLayout` value set to true, *many* of the common Internet Explorer (6 and to a lesser degree 7) layout bugs go away. Occasionally, particularly in IE 6, an element having layout *causes* browser bugs. As mentioned, with the release of IE 8, this issue has largely been relegated to one of historical interest, and even with IE 7 was much less of an issue than in IE 6. But it's something developers should know about, as much as anything to understand strange features of some legacy CSS which exist to circumvent these problems.

How Does an Element Get Layout?

There are two ways in which an element can *get layout* (the term developers use for giving an element's `hasLayout` property a value of `true`). It can either be one of a number of elements that have this property value by default, or it can have certain CSS properties set for the element. The following elements have a default `hasLayout` value of `true`:

- `applet`
- `body`
- `button`

- `embed`
- `fieldset`
- `html`
- `hr`
- `img`
- `input`
- `legend`
- `object`
- `table` (and `td`, `th`, and `tr`)
- `textarea`
- `select`

Several CSS properties can also cause an element to get layout. These properties include:

- `float` (of `left` or `right`)
- `min-width`, `max-width`, `min-height`, and `max-height` (IE 7 only)
- `overflow` (IE 7 only)
- `position`: `absolute`
- `position`: `fixed` (IE 7 only)
- `width` or `height` with values other than `auto`
- `zoom` (this is a nonstandard, IE-only CSS property)

Fixing (and Triggering) Bugs with *hasLayout*

Setting `hasLayout` to `true` for elements associated with layout rendering bugs is widely considered to be a cure-all for many such bugs. Nevertheless, because `hasLayout` is an internal feature of Internet Explorer, developers' understanding of the property is based on reverse-engineering, and is necessarily imperfect.

Many bugs are fixed by giving layout to an element—usually the element that contains the page's floated elements. You can often do this safely in IE 6 and 7 by giving the element one of the standard CSS properties and values listed above, or by conditionally linking to an IE-only style sheet and giving an element a `zoom` property value of `0`.

To fix other bugs, such as the Non-Collapsing Margins Bug mentioned earlier in this chapter, we need to set the `hasLayout` property to `false` (thus *taking layout away*). But there's a catch: because `hasLayout` is not a CSS property, we can't use CSS to set `hasLayout` to `false`—nor can we do it via JavaScript. We *can* set the `hasLayout` property value to `false` for elements that do not have layout by default simply by not using any of the previously listed CSS properties that set `hasLayout` to `true`. But we *can't* set `hasLayout` to `false` for elements that do have it by default. Fortunately, elements that do have layout by default are rarely the elements that cause problems like the Non-Collapsing Margins Bug.

Although giving an element layout can make page layouts more stable in IE, it can also introduce a serious `float`-related bug: when a block-level element has layout *and* an explicit width and an element is floated beside it, rather than the content of the element flowing around the floated element, this element stays completely rectangular, and is itself displaced [7.5].

7.5

When a block element with a **hasLayout** value of `true` has an element floated by its side, rather than its content flowing around that element (right), it remains rectangular and is displaced by the floated element.

Lorem ipsum dolor sit amet, consectetur adipisicing elit, sed do eiusmod tempor incididunt ut labore et dolore magna aliqua. Ut enim ad minim veniam, quis nostrud exercitation ullamco laboris nisi ut aliquip ex ea. Duis aute irure dolor in reprehenderit in voluptate velit esse cillum dolore eu fugiat nulla pariatur. Excepteur sint occaecat cupidatat non proident, sunt in culpa qui officia deserunt mollit anim id est laborum tempor incididunt ut labore et dolore magna aliqua.

Lorem ipsum dolor sit amet, consectetur adipisicing elit, sed do eiusmod tempor incididunt ut labore et dolore magna aliqua. Ut enim ad minim veniam, quis nostrud exercitation ullamco laboris nisi ut aliquip ex ea. Duis aute irure dolor in reprehenderit in voluptate velit esse cillum dolore eu fugiat nulla pariatur. Excepteur sint occaecat cupidatat non proident, sunt in culpa qui officia deserunt mollit anim id est laborum tempor incididunt ut labore et dolore magna aliqua.

As you may have guessed, the whole problem is complicated, and a close examination is beyond the scope of this book. Fortunately there's a very detailed discussion at Position Is Everything (**www.positioniseverything.net/explorer/floatmodel.html**), a fantastic resource for understanding and working around browser bugs.

Other (In)famous *hasLayout* Bugs

Internet Explorer has the distinction of having whole websites like **www.positioniseverything.net** devoted almost entirely to its rendering quirks—and of having loads of bugs with idiosyncratic names documented and dissected all over the web. Before we leave `hasLayout` behind, here are three more notes about the bugs it's often used to cure:

- The 3-Pixel Text Jog Bug, which shows itself in some floated contexts, is fortunately cured by giving layout to the containing element of the floated element.

- The Peek-A-Boo Bug is difficult to pin down, and fortunately appears only in IE 6. It causes text with a floated element alongside it to simply vanish, then strangely appear when the page is scrolled, and in other circumstances that cause the window to be redrawn. Giving layout to the containing element of the floated element usually fixes the problem.

- The Double-Margin Float Bug, which we just discussed, can also be fixed by giving layout to the floated element.

Bug Fixing: To Hack or Not To Hack?

In many ways, "hacking" is at odds with the concept of progressive enhancement. Hacking is all about making websites look the same in every browser, usually at the cost of considerable effort, while the goal of progressive enhancement is to deliver information and features to browsers based on their capabilities. But getting pages to look the same across browsers is still an unavoidable necessity in many real-world projects, and some bugs are such showstoppers that we need to deal with them. So how should we go about working around browser bugs?

The traditional approach has been to use hacks with names like the Tantek (Box-Model) Hack, the Holly Hack, the Tan Hack, and so on. These methods, however, are increasingly of historical interest only, and typically rely on the fragile strategy of using one bug in a browser to work around other bugs in the same or different browsers. This method is fragile because if the bug we are trying to avoid gets fixed, but the bug we are relying on as a workaround doesn't get fixed, our CSS must be rewritten. Worse, if the bug we are relying on as a workaround gets fixed, but the original rendering bug remains, our pages will break—and again, our CSS will have to be rewritten.

Instead of using hacks, when we need to specifically target a particular browser—either to provide browser-specific CSS to it or to hide CSS from it—we can break out this CSS into separate style sheets and use more stable work-arounds. For example, consider the famous Box-Model Hack (more on that soon), which delivers different widths to different browsers by relying on parsing bugs in Internet Explorer 6. It looks like this:

```
div.content {
    width:400px;
    voice-family: "\"}\"";
    voice-family:inherit;
    width:300px;
}
```

These days, we'd be better off putting the IE-specific styles into a separate style sheet and linking to it in such a way that other browsers will not see the link.

So, in our IE-specific style sheet we'd have

```
div.content {
    width:400px;
  }
```

while in our "regular" style sheet we'd have

```
div.content {
    width:300px;
}
```

Know Your Enemy

Because there is a great deal of code out there that uses these sorts of hacks, here's a quick summary of the functions and uses of web development's most common hacks. Again, you shouldn't be using these in new sites, but you may find examples of them in your code if you're maintaining large, aging code bases, so some knowledge of the techniques is worth having.

Selector-Parsing Hacks

Selector-parsing hacks rely on the absence of support for some types of CSS selectors in certain browsers (usually IE), and thus allow developers to hide specific statements from those browsers by using a selector that the browser doesn't support. For example, IE 6 doesn't support the universal (*) selector. So adding * to a selector hides the statement from Internet Explorer. If we wanted to specify a width of `400px` for a particular element for IE versions 6 and older, and a width of `300px` for all other browsers, we could use this CSS:

```
.content {
  width: 400px
  }

* .content  {
  width: 300px
  }
```

The rules of CSS specificity say that the second statement takes precedent over the first, so browsers that recognize the selector `* .content` will apply a `width` of `300px` to elements with a `class` value of `content`. IE 6 ignores that statement, because it doesn't recognize the universal selector.

There are other well-known selector patterns for other versions of IE, but again, this method relies on two bugs working in tandem (or being fixed in tandem in future browser versions), so it's too fragile to use in most production code.

Statement-Parsing Hacks

The original hack used for targeting CSS to a particular browser was devised by Tantek Çelik, who led the development of the rendering engine in IE 5 for the Mac. Çelik's extremely clever hack, which we saw earlier, relied on a somewhat baffling CSS-parsing bug in IE for Windows. Subsequently, other, more compact hacks have been developed which rely on the same principle, which is that a parsing bug in a browser makes them ignore perfectly valid (if usually odd-looking) CSS.

Today, the Box-Model Hack is mostly used to work around the Box-Model Bug in older IE versions (and in Quirks mode to this day). Here's the CSS rule again:

```
div.content {
  width:400px;
  voice-family: "\"}\"";
  voice-family:inherit;
  width:300px;
}
```

Its distinctive markings are obvious from a mile away: it uses the
voice-family property of CSS to trick IE's parser into thinking that the statement is broken. When parsers detect an invalid property declaration in a
statement, they must skip to the next statement. Because IE 6 and 7 wrongly
consider the first voice-family declaration to be invalid, they miss the second
width declaration entirely.

Because it relies on a pair of bugs (one that causes a problem and one used to
fix it), this and other statement-parsing hacks are just as fragile as selector-
parsing hacks, and should also be used with extreme caution, if at all.

So, given that it's strongly recommended to avoid all such hacks, how should
we target specific browsers? Read on to find out.

Targeting Browsers

Sometimes it *is* necessary to serve specific style sheets to specific browsers—or
to hide certain style sheets from certain browsers. It may be because we wish to
serve minimal styles to an older browser, or because we want to group together
all the workarounds specific to a browser in a single style sheet for easier
maintenance (and to avoid using statement-level hacks like the ones we've
just looked at).

There are two principal ways of serving or hiding specific style sheets. We'll
classify these as workarounds, rather than hacks, for a couple of reasons: First,
they don't rely on complementary bugs in the way that the hacks we've just considered do. Second, the "bugs" they rely on either won't be fixed (for example, a
bug in Netscape 4) or aren't bugs at all, but features designed to work precisely
as we are about to use them.

The first of these workaround techniques relies on legacy browser bugs, such as Netscape 4's lack of support for the **@import** statement. The second, conditional comments, is specific to Internet Explorer, and allows for linking to style sheets that only Internet Explorer will pay attention to (with conditional comments, you can even target specific versions of IE).

Hiding Style Sheets from Older Browsers

One approach to managing the poor support for modern CSS in older browsers is to hide most or all your CSS from these browsers. Although the idea of serving a very minimal style to older browsers is unnerving to some developers, anecdotal evidence suggests that users of these older browsers—who are also highly likely to be using older computers and operating systems, and to have slower network connections—actually often appreciate these less heavily styled pages, which download more quickly and don't tax their limited system resources.

Hiding Styles from Netscape 4

Netscape 4 doesn't support linking to style sheets with the **@import** rule. So, instead of linking to a style sheet with a **link** element in the **head** of a document, we can link using an embedded style sheet in our document that contains an **@import** rule—or use an **@import** rule in an external style sheet—and then put any style we want to hide from Netscape 4 in the imported style sheet. So instead of a simple linked style sheet like this:

```
<link rel="stylesheet" type="text/css" href="style.css">
```

We might separate out CSS into two style sheets— one containing core style for all browsers, and one for non-Netscape browsers—and use this code:

```
<link rel="stylesheet" type="text/css" href="core.css">
<style type="text/css">
  @import "advanced.css";
</style>
```

Alternately, we might link to a style sheet and place the **@import** statement in the linked style sheet.

A related technique is to link to external style sheets with a media type of `all`, like this:

```
<link rel="stylesheet" type="text/css" href=
"nonnetscape.css" media="all">
```

Netscape 4, and some old versions of Internet Explorer, will ignore these links. There's some suggestion that **@import** statements can impact page loading performance, so the second of these two methods would be recommended.

Conditional Comments for IE

Microsoft implemented a feature in Internet Explorer that lets developers target specific pieces of HTML to specific versions of IE while hiding it from all other browsers using conditional comments. The contents of conditional comments are ignored by other browsers, but are visible to various versions of IE, depending on the form of the comment, and although conditional comments only apply to HTML, we can give specific versions of IE-specific style sheets by using conditional comments in conjunction with the **link** element in the head of an HTML document.

Here's how conditional comments work. Regular HTML comments look like this:

```
<!-- this is a comment -->
```

Conditional comments use this syntax and extend it to add instructions telling Internet Explorer to either use or ignore the contents of the comments; other browsers will continue to ignore them just as they ignore other HTML comments. Conditional comments specify a target in square brackets right after the opening of the HTML comment. For example, to target only IE 6, we'd use a comment like this one:

```
<!--[if IE 6]>
  <link rel="stylesheet" type="text/css" href=
  "ie6style.css">
<![endif]-->
```

We can use the following targets in conditional comments:

- `[if IE]`—will be used by any version of IE from 5 and up (conditional comments were introduced with version 5)

- `[if IE 5]`, `[if IE 7]` and so on (note the space between *IE* and the browser number), targets specific browser versions

- `[if gt IE 6]` (`gt` stands for *greater than*—this example targets versions after version IE 6)

- `[if gte IE 7]` (`gte` stands for *greater than or equal to*—this example targets version IE 7 or more recent)

- `[if lt IE 8]` (`lt` stands for *less than*—this example targets versions of IE older than IE 8)

- `[if lte IE 6]` (`lte` stands for *less than or equal to*—this example targets IE 6 or older)

Conditional comments can only be used inside HTML—we can't conditionally comment our CSS with this approach. So, we *can't* say something like this inside a linked style sheet:

```
<!--[if IE 6]>
  p {
    width: 250px
  }

<![endif]-->
```

Conditional comments are less fragile than hack-based techniques for working around browser limitations and bugs, although they've been less popular than hacks, probably because they require developers to separate out styles for Internet Explorer (or for specific versions of IE) into their own style sheets, which can complicate code maintenance. As with all workarounds, they need to be used as sparingly as possible, and style sheets linked using these techniques should be very well documented so that the interaction between statements and properties in different style sheets is clearly noted. For example, if we are specifying a width for IE browsers in one style sheet, and all other browsers in another, it would make sense to note this in the respective style sheets like this.

In the style sheet only for IE 6 and older:

```css
.content {
  width: 300px
  /* this width is also specified in modern.css for
  browsers other than IE 6 and older*/
  }
```

In the style sheet for all other browsers:

```css
.content {
  width: 200px
  /* this width is also specified in IE6lte.css for IE 6
  and older*/
  }
```

When Feature Support Is Missing

The techniques we've covered so far deal with browser inconsistencies due to buggy support for CSS in one or more browsers and good support in others. The second significant challenge developers face is the absence of support in one browser for a feature that is supported in other browsers. This is more common as Firefox, Safari, and Opera introduce support for CSS3 features and Internet Explorer continues to offer limited CSS3 support. (We look in detail at CSS3 in Chapters 12 through 15.)

In many cases, progressive enhancement is the way to go. If a browser doesn't support `border-radius`, text shadows, box shadows, or other CSS3 features, we can usually just ignore the lack of support for such cosmetic properties. But, there are often features that go beyond the cosmetic—in particular, CSS3 selectors—that are well supported in browsers other than Internet Explorer, and which can radically improve the quality of our markup (as we'll see in Chapter 12). In the absence of support for such features in a widely used browser like IE, can we use them at all?

Happily, the answer is yes. Using JavaScript—and popular JavaScript libraries whose use requires little actual scripting knowledge—we can add support for many features that are not natively supported in web browsers. Let's take a look at some of these libraries.

Dean Edwards's IE 7 (and IE 8)

The best known JavaScript library for enhancing IE 6 and 7's support for features of CSS2 and CSS3 is Dean Edwards's ie7-js (**code.google.com/p/ie7-js**), which was originally known simply as "ie7." This popular library has been updated and is now offered as a superset library, ie8-js, which includes all the functionality of ie7-js and adds support for IE 8 and features of CSS (and HTML) still missing even from IE 8.

The library's goal is "to make Microsoft Internet Explorer behave like a standards-compliant browser," and it adds support for:

- CSS selectors like the child, adjacent sibling, structural, and attribute selectors
- CSS properties including `max-width`, `min-width`, `max-height`, and `min-height`
- Alpha transparency in PNG graphics

…as well as fixing common bugs like the Double Margin and Peek-a-Boo bugs we saw earlier in the chapter, via a related bug-fixing library, ie7-squish.

When introduced, the idea of JavaScript libraries for extending and fixing browsers was quite radical, but in the years since ie7-js was first released, the idea of using JavaScript for this sort of purpose has become widely accepted. Still, two possible drawbacks remain. First, many people still use the web with JavaScript disabled, either because of personal security concerns or because of security policies in large corporate, government, and institutional networks. Because of this limitation, all JavaScript libraries should be used in conjunction with *unobtrusive scripting* techniques like those discussed in Chapter 5. The second potential drawback is that use of the library may harm site performance, particularly for very high-traffic sites. If you use one of these libraries in a production environment, you'll need to consider the potential negative performance effects for your specific project.

Both ie7-js and ie8-js are easy to use. They're hosted on Google Code, so in many cases you won't even have to host them yourself. It's a good idea to use conditional comments to link only to Internet Explorer, so that other browsers don't download the unnecessary file. Here's what that might look like if we wanted to use the ie8 version of the library along with the ie7-squish bug-fixing library:

```
<!--[if lte IE 8]>
  <script src="ie7/IE8.js" type=
  "text/javascript"></script>
  <script src="ie7/ie7-squish.js" type=
  "text/javascript"></script>
<![endif]-->
```

And presto! Internet Explorer now supports all of the features that the library adds as though that support were native in the browser. These libraries are used on large, popular websites, and have been refined over several years, so they're safe to use in just about every situation. The only real surprise is that more developers don't use them.

The Wrap

Even a few years ago, if you had asked developers—even most standards-oriented developers—they'd probably have told you that they developed sites first to work perfectly in Internet Explorer, and then worried about validation and support in other browsers. Today, the tide has turned. Developers overwhelmingly develop to the standards first and then work on support for various browsers.

Only a few years ago, the web developer's lot was that of a constant battle with browser bugs and inconsistencies. Although it may sometimes still seem so today, the reality is that browser support for CSS and other standards has improved dramatically in all browsers. We'll still be dealing with browser inconsistencies for some years to come, but if the improvements of the last few years are any indication, this will become less and less a concern. With luck, this chapter will soon be outdated—used only to help new developers understand what that strange-looking CSS in their ancient legacy was actually for, back when it was still needed.

We live in hope.

Best Practices for Modern Markup

At the heart of any site, at the heart of the web, is markup. It's what browsers see, it's what search engines see, and it's what we as developers look at day in and day out. Writing clean, meaningful markup has many benefits:

- It makes our code much easier to maintain—for us and for other developers months or years after we've gone.
- It can help search engines index and rank our sites.
- It can help users find content on our pages more easily.
- It helps make more web content more accessible to people with disabilities.

In this chapter, we'll look at some of the techniques, practices, and technologies that can help us produce cleaner, more maintainable markup that is easy for browsers, search engines, JavaScript, and other developers to interact with. First, though, let's consider these benefits in greater detail.

Code Readability

All code, whether it's written in a programming language such as C++ or JavaScript or in a markup language like HTML, has two audiences. The most obvious audience is software: compilers, interpreters, browsers, search engines, and so on. But code has another important but often overlooked audience: developers. We're likely to revisit our own code many times during its development and maintenance, and on most web projects, many other developers will also need to view and maintain our code.

Code that is easy to read is usually easier to maintain, to debug, and—by virtue of its intelligibility—easier to get right in the first place. The past four decades of software engineering have produced many practices that we can apply to our markup (and our CSS and JavaScript), including the use of sensible names and naming conventions, the use of formatting to aid legibility, and the use of commenting to explain coding decisions and aid readability.

Naming

Once upon a time, computer memory was rare and precious. As a consequence, brief variable names and compact code were necessary. These days are gone, but many of us code as if they weren't. Yes, more compact code can improve website performance, but these improvements can be attained without compromising readability by compressing code served to browsers while maintaining legible, "verbose" versions of files for development. (You'll find links to performance improvement resources at the end of this book.)

We'll consider semantic naming practices in a moment, but for now, let's just note that names should not be so short that they become cryptic. Make names meaningful, and where conventions exist—whether they're public, like Electronic Commerce Markup Language (ECML) or microformats, or for internal use only—reuse those conventions.

Formatting, Commenting, and Consistency

Sensible code formatting enhances readability, and unlike many programming languages in which whitespace is significant, HTML and CSS allow us to format markup (with tabs, carriage returns, and spaces) as we please, with no impact on the way browsers parse the code.

The simplest and most important HTML formatting technique is to indent child elements so that the document's hierarchy is clear at a glance. Compare the readability of this block of markup:

```html
<div id="header">
<h1>Welcome to ACME Devices Inc</h1>
<div class="navigation">
<ul>
<li>Home</li>
<li>Devices</li>
<li>Widgets</li>
<li>Contact</li>
</ul>
</div>
</div>
```

to the readability of this one, which is identical except that it's formatted using indents to indicate element nesting:

```html
<div id="header">
  <h1>Welcome to ACME Devices Inc</h1>
  <div class="navigation">
    <ul>
      <li>Home</li>
      <li>Devices</li>
      <li>Widgets</li>
      <li>Contact</li>
    </ul>
  </div>
</div>
```

Commenting can further aid the readability of such code. Although it's relatively easy to match the opening and closing tags of the two **div** elements in this example, in more complex real-world situations in which **div**s may be nested several layers deep, matching opening and closing tags can be quite difficult. The resultant mistakes can produce invalid pages with unpredictable and difficult-to-debug rendering problems. A simple way to overcome this problem is to add a comment to each closing tag of deeply nested elements, like this:

```html
<div id="header">
  <h1>Welcome to ACME Devices Inc</h1>
  <div class="navigation">
    <ul>
      <li>Home</li>
      <li>Devices</li>
      <li>Widgets</li>
      <li>Contact</li>
    </ul>
  </div> <!-- navigation -->
</div> <!-- header -->
```

Consistency of formatting, commenting, and other markup practices—always using the same `class` and `id` naming format, always quoting attribute values, and so on—is another quality of readable code. And whether we do it for that reason or not, consistent coding practices also make it easier for us tell when there's something not quite right about our markup.

Readable code is easier to maintain and is less likely to be invalid or otherwise incorrect. The preceding techniques, simple as they are, can save hours of development time and make even small web projects run more smoothly.

Plain Old Semantic HTML

As we've noted before, the semantic toolset of HTML is limited. We have headings, paragraphs, lists, and a few other basic building blocks for any document. Fortunately, HTML does provide a mechanism for adding richer semantics to our documents via the `class` and `id` attributes. But before we dive into some of the current best practices in using these techniques to enrich our markup, note that the semantics we add to our documents in this way are only *conventions*—they aren't part of any official standards. Although web applications, browsers, and even search engines are beginning to take advantage of some of these conventional semantics (particularly microformats), the best reason to use them now is that they produce more readable and maintainable markup. Markup written this way also tends to work better with JavaScript—and to be more easily styled using CSS—than markup written without attention to conventional semantics.

"Plain old semantic HTML" (POSH) is a recently coined term for the practice of using the core aspects of HTML intelligently to create clean, meaningful, readable markup. To write POSH, you should:

- Use valid HTML or XHTML.
- Avoid any presentational markup, including tables used for layout.
- Use the most semantically suitable HTML elements and attributes for your document.
- Use meaningful `class` and `id` values where appropriate.

We've already considered the first two of these three guidelines in Chapter 3, so let's focus on the third and fourth.

Using HTML Elements, *class* and *id* for More Meaningful Semantics

Beyond commonly used elements like paragraph and headings, HTML provides a number of other elements and attributes that help us produce more meaningful markup.

Quotations

HTML has two elements that are intended to be used for quotations: `q` for inline quotations, and `blockquote` for block quotations. Both may contain a `cite` attribute, whose value is a URL for the source of the quotation.

Definition Lists

In addition to ordered and unordered lists, HTML includes the definition list, which is designed for marking up definitions and their descriptions. You might use these elements to mark up, for example, a dictionary entry with a word being defined and one or more definitions. Here for example is how we might mark up a dictionary entry (definition courtesy of Wiktionary, **www.wiktionary.org**):

```
<dl>
  <dt>Pedant</dt>
    <dd>A person who is overly concerned with formal rules
    and trivial points of learning.</dd>
    <dd>A person who emphasizes his/her knowledge through
    the use of vocabulary</dd>
</dl>
```

Note how here we have two definition descriptions for the single definition term. `dt` elements appear first in a definition list but may have any number of associated `dd` elements.

rel and rev

In HTML, the `link` and `a` elements can include `rel` and `rev` attributes, which describe the relationship of the link's destination to the document containing the link. For example, we can link to a document and use a `rel` value of "license" in the link to indicate that the document we are linking to is the license (which might contain, for example, copyright conditions) for the document that contains the link. Here's what that markup would look like:

```
<a href="http://creativecommons.org/licenses/by/2.0/"
rel="license">cc by 2.0</a>
```

Bonus point: the preceding example is both a microformat and a widely used convention.

The much less frequently used `rev` attribute is used to describe relationships that go the other way: it describes the relationship of the document containing the link to the link's destination. (If you find this confusing, you are far from alone. At the time of this writing, the `rev` attribute is slated for removal from HTML5.)

abbr

The `abbr` element can be used to mark up an abbreviation or acronym. The `title` attribute of the element can then be used to mark up the long form of the abbreviation. For example, we might write:

```
<abbr title="Plain Old Semantic HTML">POSH</abbr>
```

class and id

The `class` and `id` attributes are perhaps the most commonly used "hooks" for extending the semantics of an HTML document. Any HTML element can take these attributes, and they are both central to microformats and a useful way of marking up a document so that it can be styled easily with CSS.

As we saw in Chapter 3, we need to follow some syntactical rules when using the `id` attribute. Values for this attribute must begin with a letter, and may contain only upper- and lowercase letters, numbers, underscores (_), hyphens (-), colons (:), and periods (.). They should also be meaningful and should focus on the semantic nature of the element, not its appearance. For example, if the left-hand column of a page is used for site-level navigation, it makes much more sense to mark it up as:

```
<div class="site-navigation">
```

than as:

```
<div class="left-column">
```

Why is this important? As we've said before in this book—and will say again—we should always separate presentation for the underlying content of our markup as much as possible. It's far more likely that a site's appearance, rather than its underlying content, will change. There will almost certainly be site-level navigation on your site for years to come, but it may not always be on the left side of the page. If we use sensible, non-presentational names, markup will continue to be meaningful for far longer than it would be if we encode presentational details into the HTML.

Less is More

Just how much should we annotate our elements with `class` and `id` values? Does it make sense to add a `class` or `id` attribute to most of the elements on a page? Some of them? And which ones? And when should we be using `id` instead of `class`?

We'll start with the last question. `id` attributes identify *unique* elements on a page, so any given `id` value may only be used once on each page. Some components, like **divs** used for page headers and footers, will naturally occur only once per page, so it makes sense to use `id` attributes for these elements. When a page component may appear on a page more than once (even if it only appears once on some pages), then `class` is the appropriate attribute to use.

Which elements should we mark up using `class` and `id`? Developers often use `class` and `id` extensively to provide "hooks" for styling their pages with CSS. The groundbreaking and rightfully famous CSS Zen Garden (**www.csszengarden.com**) provides the following `class`- and `id`-enhanced markup as the basis for its CSS gallery:

```
<div id="quickSummary">
  <p class="p1"><span>A demonstration of what can be
  accomplished visually through <acronym title=
  "Cascading Style Sheets">CSS</acronym>-based design.
  Select any style sheet from the list to load it into
  this page.</span></p>
  <p class="p2"><span>Download the sample <a href=
  "/zengarden-sample.html" title="This page's source HTML
  code, not to be modified.">html file</a> and <a href=
  "/zengarden-sample.css" title="This page's sample CSS,
  the file you may modify.">css file</a></span></p>
</div>
```

class Attributes in the Zen Garden

Although the `id` on the `div` element in the CSS Zen Garden markup is appropriate—it identifies a unique part of the document—the `class` values on the `p` elements have become extraneous due to recent developments in the world of CSS.

Dave Shea, the developer of the Zen Garden, created the site's markup to provide a demonstration of what can be achieved via CSS. When the Zen Garden was launched, CSS3 structural selectors like **nth-child** (which we'll examine in Chapter 12) didn't exist, so if a designer wanted to style an individual paragraph, something like these hooks was required. With the advent of CSS3 selectors, which are now widely supported, this approach is no longer required.

A rule of thumb: When an element is a significant part of the document structure (a section like a blog post, an article, a block of navigation, and so on), `class` or `id` values should be used to "annotate" it and provide semantic information about its role and contents. The roles that the Web Accessibility

Initiative's Accessible Rich Internet Applications Suite (WAI-ARIA) specifies for its `role` attribute—turn to Chapter 6 if this doesn't look familiar—provide good examples of the sort of semantics we might add. Additionally, HTML5 (discussed in Chapter 11) introduces new structural elements that provide great examples of the kinds of elements we should consider annotating with the `class` and `id` attributes. (Some examples from HTML5 include `nav`, `header`, `footer`, `section`, and `search` elements.)

As we'll see later in this chapter, the microformats project also provides a number of models for marking up the sort of content that is commonly found on the web, such as contact details and calendars.

Electronic Commerce Markup Language (ECML)

Most browsers feature "auto filling" of form fields, which is a great timesaver when you're filling in details such as your name and address. Different browsers have different ways of deciding how to auto-fill fields, but many now support the curiously little-known ECML, which provides a standardized set of form field names that can be used as the value of the `name` attribute of form elements.

ECML covers a very broad range of information commonly required for e-commerce transactions, including shipping information, billing information, credit card information, user and order ID numbers, and much more.

It's easy to use ECML names as values in `name` attributes—we simply find the appropriate ECML value for a given field and mark it up:

```
<input name="Ecom_BillTo_Postal_Name_First" type="text" />
```

Markup and SEO

You'll find a great many search engine optimization experts (and web developers for that matter) who extol the virtues of a particular markup practice for improved search engine placement. The truth is far more complex. Search engine developers—especially Google—keep the exact nature of their ranking algorithms secret to minimize the impact of people trying to "game" their algorithms.

So how can we gain better search engine visibility through better markup? The first thing to note is that markup is one piece of the puzzle. The *content* of a site is a key determinant in a search engine's assessment of that site. On the whole, search engines consider visible content just as important as—if not more important than—metadata such as `meta` element keywords.

A semantic, standards-based approach usually produces simpler, less obfuscated markup, making the content-to-code ratio much higher—something often considered to have search engine placement benefits.

Although there's no conclusive proof that using semantic markup will produce specific search engine benefits, it certainly won't hurt—and given the attention Google and Yahoo are paying to structured content like microformats, it would seem that search engines will increasingly value structured semantic content.

Microformats

The microformats project (**www.microformats.org**) is one of the biggest and most exciting areas of semantic innovation on today's web. The project is a loose, collaborative effort to create patterns of markup and then use these patterns to create specific formats for commonly found types of information. By providing these formats and promoting their adoption, the project hopes to standardize—by convention, rather than through a standards organization such as the W3C—the markup of common information on the web. It also seeks to encourage interoperability between web content and applications such as address books, calendars, and mapping services, and to foster the development of services that can consume this structured semantic data.

The Benefits of Microformats

For developers, there are three significant benefits to using microformats. First, microformats provide sensible formats for marking up common types of information (such as addresses and other contact details, event details, and locations) that developers are likely to mark up on many if not most of their projects. Rather than developing your own markup patterns for these kinds of information, you can simply use the appropriate microformat. Microformats are designed to be very flexible—they frequently don't require you to change your current markup at all, other than to add `class` attributes to existing elements.

The second main benefit of using microformats is that once you've implemented microformats, you can use various services and JavaScript libraries
with very little effort. For example, you can use the X2V service (**www.suda.
co.uk/projects/X2V**) to add a special link to any page that has event details or
contact details marked up with the appropriate hCard and hCalendar microformats. This link will enable users to add these details to their own calendars
or address books with one click, and if you're already using microformats, it
takes almost no development effort to add the service to your site. You might
also use a library like Oomph (**www.visitmix.com/lab/oomph**) to add a toolbar
to your pages that lets users perform various actions on microformatted content at your site—and again, you can do so with very little effort on your part.

One of the biggest long-term benefits of using microformats in your markup
is that, as mentioned briefly in an earlier section of this chapter, Google now
indexes some microformats, and Yahoo's SearchMonkey and BOSS search
engines index many different microformats.

Google indexes, among others, the following microformats, and uses them to
display additional "Rich Snippets" of results [**8.1**]:

- **hCard** for contact details
- **hReview** for review details
- **hProduct** for product descriptions

Kellari Taverna - **Midtown** East - **New York**, NY
☆☆☆☆☆ 46 **reviews** - Price range: $$$
I dropped just a little less here for two people than our **hotel** room rate for one night. .... **New
York**, NY. 5 star rating. 4/14/2008. This **review** is only from one ... bowl of olives at the bar and
the occasion **snippets** of background music. .... I tried one of the Greek wines, Stelios Kenkris,
which was **rich** and not ...
www.yelp.com/biz/kellari-taverna-**new-york** - Cached - Similar - ⚲⊞☒

8.1
Google displays some
results, like reviews
marked up with the
hReview microformat,
as a Rich Snippet.

Through two search APIs (SearchMonkey and BOSS) that developers can use
to build their own targeted search applications, Yahoo indexes various micro-
formats and makes these indexes accessible to third-party developers. Yahoo
indexes, among others, the following microformats:

- **hCard** for contact details
- **hReview** for review details
- **hCalendar** for event details

- **geo** for locations
- **adr** for addresses

Microformats in Action

So, how do we actually *use* microformats? Each of the now two dozen or so draft or fully specified microformats is designed to provide a sensible, interoperable way to mark up common information for the web. When possible, existing formats, such as vCard (the standard format for contact details, supported by most address-book software and online services) and iCalendar (the standard format for calendar-based information, supported by most calendar software and online services) are used as the basis for a microformat—a practice that greatly aids interoperability between web-based content and applications and services.

Let's look at an example in which we'll use microformats to mark up contact details.

Adding Contact Details with hCard

Let's start with contact details as they might be marked up without microformats:

```
<p>Web Directions Conference Pty Ltd</p>
<p>5/50 Reservoir St</p>
<p>Surry Hills NSW</p>
<p>2011</p>
<p>Australia</p>
```

In a few short steps, we'll mark this up using the hCard microformat. hCard takes the semantics of the vCard specification and brings it to HTML, using the field names defined for vCard, but placing them inside HTML syntax. Here's an example of the fields found in the vCard specification:

```
BEGIN:VCARD
VERSION:2.1
FN:Web Directions Conference Pty Ltd
ADR:5/50;;Reservoir St;Surry Hills;NSW;2010;AUSTRALIA
EMAIL;INTERNET:info@webdirections.org
ORG:Web Directions
END:VCARD
```

To turn that into HTML, we'll use what's called the "class design pattern" micro-format. Make a note: This is the single most important pattern for microformat markup. Using the class design pattern, we'll borrow the vCard field names and add them to HTML elements using the `class` attribute. For example, we would mark up the formatted name (the FN field in vCard) like this:

```
<p class="fn">Web Directions Conference Pty Ltd</p>
```

As you can see, we've simply taken the name of the field from vCard and added it as the value of the `class` attribute of the element that contains, in this example, the formatted name. We don't have to add additional elements for each field: where there's existing markup for a field, we can simply add to it.

Here's how we'd take the earlier markup and turn it into hCard:

```
<p class="fn">Web Directions Conference Pty Ltd</p>
<div class="adr">
  <p class="street-address">5/50 Reservoir St</p>
  <p><span class="locality">Surry Hills</span> <span
  class="region">NSW</span></p>
<p class="postal-code">2011</p>
<p class="country-name">Australia</p>
</div>
```

You'll notice that in a couple of places, we *had* to add additional markup, because some of the needed elements didn't exist. We've wrapped the region and locality information in **span** elements and then added the relevant `class` values to these. We've also added a **div** of class adr around the address markup, thus mapping the address details into the hCard microformat. Depending on the nature of your existing markup, you may or may not need to do this; your existing markup can usually remain largely as it is. Microformats don't require you to drastically change your markup to support them.

Got Root?

"But," you might be asking, "how does anyone know this is really an hCard microformat, not just a collection of elements with class values?" The answer is that we need to add one more bit of markup to finish the job of making this address microformatted using the hCard format.

Compound microformats, like hCard, that comprise more than one element, require a root element that contains all of the microformatted content. In this case, we don't have an element that wraps up all our address details (though we will have one in many cases). For this example, we'll add a **div** element to contain the address, and we'll give it a class value of vcard to specify that what it contains is hCard-formatted content. (We use vcard rather than hCard because hCard is simply the vCard specification reformatted for HTML.)

```
<div class="vcard">
  <div class="adr">
    <p class="street-address">5/50 Reservoir St</p>
    <p><span class="locality">Surry Hills</span> <span
    class="region">NSW</span></p>
    <p class="postal-code">2011</p>
  <p class="country-name">Australia</p>
  </div> <!--adr -->
</div> <!--vcard -->
```

And there we have it: our contact details marked up as an hCard. hCard also provides fields for URLs, email addresses, phone numbers, and fax numbers—all the kinds of things you'd expect from contact details—and all of these are marked up very similarly to the address here.

Microformats Tools

Over the four years or so since their inception, a vibrant set of tools for working with microformats has emerged (created by everyone from individual developers all the way up to major companies such as Microsoft and Yahoo). There are tools to simplify the creation of various kinds of microformatted content, services that ease the process of adding functionality to your microformatted sites, tools for "validating" microformatted content, and JavaScript-based tools for adding features to your microformatted sites. We list these at the end of the book, along with books and online resources for learning more about microformats.

Much, Much More

There's a great deal more to microformats than this—indeed, I wrote an entire book on them in 2007 that is still highly relevant, and which, if you are keen to dive deeper, you may find very helpful. You can find a reference to it at the end of this book.

The Wrap

Web developers spend a lot of time focusing on users and user experience, but we rarely consider software and other developers as users of our sites. (This despite the fact that every time a site is visited, software in the form of a browser "uses" it.) And of course, search engines are perhaps the single most important user of any but the most private of sites—if a site's content is hidden from search engines by bad coding practices, the consequences can be catastrophic.

In this chapter, we've looked at some of the needs of our software users and some of the techniques and practices we can use to take care of these needs. As an added bonus, these techniques also produce more readable code—and whether you are returning to your own code after weeks away or approaching someone else's code for the first time, you'll find that clean, readable, well commented code is far more maintainable and comprehensible than the other sort, and you'll be thankful that you spent the time to make it that way.

CSS-Based Page Layouts

In the early years of CSS, web developers were restricted to using style sheets for superficial styling—fonts, colors, and sometimes margins and padding—but continued to lay out their pages using the tables-and-spacer-GIFs method championed in David Siegel's famous (or infamous) book, *Creating Killer Web Sites* (Hayden, 1996).

It wasn't until well after the release of Internet Explorer 6 in 2002 that Douglas Bowman's groundbreaking CSS-based redesign of *Wired* magazine's website debuted and demonstrated that high-traffic, high-profile sites could successfully use CSS to control page layout. The use of tables for layout has since fallen out of favor; table-based layouts mix presentation and structure, making it much more difficult to maintain pages, and harm sites' accessibility and search engine visibility—often dramatically. Nevertheless, table-based layouts persisted for years after 2002, and are still occasionally seen today, though usually not on professionally developed sites.

The persistence of table-based layouts wasn't simply a sign of stubbornness, nor of the unwillingness of developers to learn new tricks. Many common web layout patterns were closely tied to the table model, and the CSS layout model was not designed to replicate the layout model of tables. The classic multi-column layout with a header at the top and footer at the bottom of the page is a perfect example. This kind of layout is easy to achieve with HTML tables, but the real cost of this design method shows up later in the form of major accessibility, search-engine optimization, and maintenance problems. The same layout is superficially more difficult to create with CSS, and requires techniques that it took years to discover and perfect, but the payoff of CSS-based design is well worth the extra time.

In this chapter, we'll look at common layout challenges and the best ways to achieve them with CSS. We'll build on the CSS features we covered in Chapter 4, so if any of the features we cover here look unfamiliar, you may wish to flip back to that chapter for a refresher. Page layout usually requires fine control over element width, margins, padding, and borders, so we'll also use browser-wrangling techniques introduced in Chapter 7 to mitigate problems caused by Internet Explorer's unusual box model. Again, if you need a refresher, have a quick look at that chapter before continuing.

Horizontal Centering

Centering a block of content horizontally is a very common design request, and CSS offers two ways of accomplishing it. We can use the `text-align` CSS property to center the inline content of an element (or to set that content flush left, flush right, or justified), but this property isn't designed for centering block-level elements. To center a block-level element (for example, a paragraph) inside its parent element (a `div`, perhaps, or the `body` element itself), we'll use the `width` CSS property.

Suppose we want to make paragraphs that are half the width of the body, and are centered horizontally on the page. We can do this by creating a CSS rule that selects paragraphs and uses the `width` and `margin` properties, setting the width at 50 percent of the parent element and using the margin value `auto` for the element's left and right margins. This works because when it's used to define horizontal margins, `auto` specifies that the margin space inside the containing element be divided evenly between the left and right margins.

Here's a CSS rule that would make paragraphs half as wide as the parent element and center them horizontally:

```
p {
   width: 50%;
   margin: 0 auto;
}
```

Since we're defining the element's width using a percentage value, we could also use this rule instead:

```
p {
   width: 50%;
   margin: 0 25%;
}
```

These two rules are functionally identical because we know the width of the p element as a percentage of its parent's width. If we specified the element's width using something other than a percentage—ems, for example—we would have to use auto for the left and right margins, because we wouldn't know how much horizontal space there would be between the edges of the p element and those of its parent element.

Easy, right? Sadly, there's one more step. Internet Explorer in Quirks mode doesn't support the auto value for the margin property, so we need a workaround for Internet Explorer in Quirks mode. Luckily, we can rely on a text-align bug in IE to center our elements in IE/Quirks mode without affecting browsers that properly support auto values for margin.

If you aren't clear as to what exactly Quirks mode and standards mode are, we go into this in detail in Chapter 7.

I mentioned that `text-align` is not designed to center block-level elements. In IE Quirks mode, however, `text-align` *does* center block-level elements. We can use this bug to counter the effects of IE's lack of support for `auto margin` values in Quirks mode without confusing more CSS-capable browsers. Here's how:

First, we'll use `text-align: center` on the containing element of the elements we wish to center (in this instance, we want to center paragraphs inside the `body`):

```
body {
    text-align: center
}
```

This rule will center the paragraphs in IE, but will also center all text on the page in other modern browsers, because `text-align` is inherited. To overcome this problem, we'll set the `text-align` of paragraphs to `left` (we could also use `right` or `justified`). This ensures that the text itself will not be centered—and because `text-align` aligns an element's contents, not the element itself, the paragraph elements themselves will be centered in IE. Here's what our CSS rules look like:

```
body {
    text-align: center
}

p {
    text-align: left;
    width: 50%;
    margin: 0 auto
}
```

Because there's no single CSS property for centering block-level elements horizontally, this design request is often a frustrating problem for CSS newcomers. Once you know how to do it, though, it's very easy to achieve in all modern browsers with the tricks I've just described. Vertically centered elements, on the other hand, are more difficult to implement—but not impossible.

Vertical Centering

Just as developers are often asked to center a block of content horizontally, we're frequently given the task of centering content vertically—a far more challenging problem to solve with CSS alone.

CSS offers a `vertical-align` property, but this property is designed to align inline elements in relation to the line of text they're associated with. You might use it to indicate, for example, that the contents of a `span` element should be set as superscript, as in figure **9.1**. Here's an example rule:

```
.note {
  vertical-align: super;
  font-size: .8em;
  font-weight: bold;
}
```

It's a truth[1] universally acknowledged

9.1
`Vertical-align`; super used to create footnote links.

The `vertical-align` property can also be used to align images in relation to a line of text, and to align the contents of a table cell (`td`). The property is not, however, designed for aligning block-level elements within their containing elements. The CSS page layout concept was originally based on the idea that layouts would be fluid, with the width of elements changing as the browser window shrank and grew and the height of elements changing to accommodate their content. As a result, it remains difficult to vertically center an element within its parent element in ways that work across all modern browsers.

All the widely used methods have challenges, and none is especially straightforward, so you should select the method that is most appropriate for your situation. A good overview of the situation can be found at **www.student.oulu.fi/~laurirai/ www/css/middle**, where Lauri Raittila details several types of content (inline content, images, block content) and outlines strategies for vertically centering each type. In short, there's no really good solution, but depending on the particular circumstances, there may be an adequate solution.

CSS Positioning

CSS1 lacked features specifically designed for page layout, beyond the ability to modify the whitespace of an element via **margin**, **padding**, and **border**. However even version 4 browsers implemented at least some of the then–non-standardized positioning properties of CSS2. Popularized as layers in Dreamweaver, these properties allowed developers to position a limited set of elements absolutely or relatively in Internet Explorer 4 and Netscape 4.

Ironically, CSS1 did contain the **float** *property, which was originally created to solve a non-layout-related problem, but has become a staple of CSS layouts.*

Initially, positioning was considered *the* way in which all CSS-based layouts would be developed. But although positioning is sophisticated, it was not designed with common page-design patterns in mind, and over time, positioning has given ground to float-based techniques. Positioning continues to have its uses, which we'll focus on now, and there's no reason not to combine position properties and float-based techniques to lay out pages.

Positioning Schemes

All elements on a page are positioned according to one of three positioning schemes. We detailed various positioning properties in Chapter 4, so we'll focus on more advanced CSS layout and positioning concepts. First, let's define the three primary positioning schemes used to lay out pages using CSS:

- Normal flow. This term describes the way browsers typically lay out elements on a page. Block elements begin their own new block, and inline elements are laid out inline within their containing block element. Elements with a static or relative **position** property value are in normal flow. (Remember: static is the default value of the **position** property.)

- Absolute position. When elements have a **position** property value of absolute or fixed, they are said to be absolutely positioned. Such elements are taken entirely out of normal flow—in other words, the browser ignores absolutely positioned elements when laying out other elements on the page.

- Floated. A floated element has a **float** property value of left or right, and is shifted to the left or right within its current line until its edge reaches the edge of its containing block (or the edge of another floated element within the same containing block), as shown in figure **9.2**. Unlike absolutely positioned elements, floated elements are not removed from normal flow. They affect the flow of the page, with content below them flowing around them.

Beyond SEO

Presenters:
Cheryl Gledhill **and** Scott Gledhill

Search engine optimisation (SEO) is a unique mix of marketing, usability and technology which can often cause confusion on how it is implemented across different organisations. An important part of your SEO strategy is getting the most out of your SEO dollars. This session will explain what your developers, designers, producers, content authors and marketers should all know about SEO to ensure you're getting the maximum return on your SEO.

9.2
Here two images are floated to the left. The first, of Cheryl, is shifted to the left until it touches the edge of the containing element. The second, of Scott, shifts to the left until it touches the right edge of the first floated element. The gap between the floated elements is due to margins on them.

Positioning Properties

Confusingly, these positioning schemes don't correspond *exactly* to the values of the CSS `position` property. As we saw in Chapter 4, `position` takes four possible values:

- `static`—Elements are in normal flow. This is the default positioning of an element.

- `relative`—Relatively positioned elements are laid out as if they were statically positioned, then moved from that position, while the document flow remains unchanged. Relative positioning has one other magical difference from static positioning which we'll see in a moment.

- `absolute`—Elements with a **position** value of `absolute` are taken out of the flow entirely, and then positioned with respect to their containing block-level element.

- `fixed`—Elements with a **position** value of `fixed` are taken out of the flow entirely, and then positioned with respect to their viewport (typically the window, but some browsers such as those found on the iPhone and Wii lack windows).

Absolute Positioning in Action

Float-based layouts have largely superseded absolute positioning when it comes to creating multi-column layouts, but absolute positioning can still be used for this purpose, and in some ways it's easier to use than float-based techniques. It does however have one significant drawback compared with those layouts, which we'll turn to when we deal with floated multi-column techniques.

For our example, we'll use a common document structure that includes a header, a content area that contains content and navigation columns, and a footer. Please note: This example is intended to illustrate features of CSS positioning properties, rather than to model a perfect approach to page layout. I wouldn't recommend copying this particular code as the basis for your own layouts.

```html
<div id="header">
  <h1>This is the header</h1>
</div>
<div id="container">
  <div id="navigation">
    <h2>Navigation</h2>
    <ul>
      <li>one</li>
      <li>two</li>
      <li>three</li>
      <li>four</li>
      <li>five</li>
      <li>six</li>
    </ul>
  </div> <!--navigation-->
  <div id="content">
    <h2>Content</h2>
    <p>Lorem ipsum dolor sit amet, consectetur ....</p>
  </div> <!--content-->
</div> <!--container-->
<div id="footer">
  <h2>Footer</h2>
  <p>Lorem ipsum dolor sit ...</p>
</div> <!--footer-->
```

Creating the Columns

The first step will be to create our main columns. We'll give the content `div` a width of 70% and position it absolutely.

```
#content {
  width: 70%;
  position: absolute;
}
```

Figure 9.3 shows the page as it appears if all the elements are statically positioned. In figure 9.4, however, it's been taken out of the flow of the document, so the footer element is now placed where it would be if the content element didn't exist at all. Note too that the content element is not located in the top left corner of the page, as you might expect, because in the absence of a `top` value, an absolutely positioned element's top and left corners remain where they would be in normal flow.

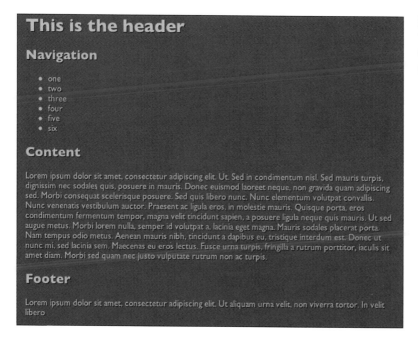

9.3
The page layout with all elements in static position.

9.4
An absolute element is taken out of the flow, but must have `top`, `left`, or other position values to be moved from its position in the flow.

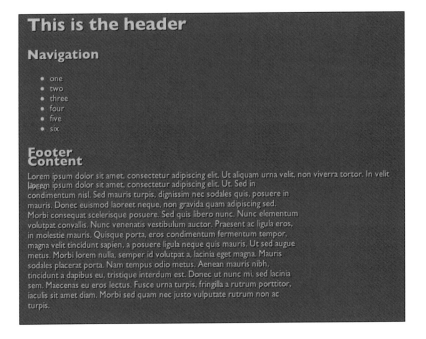

In order to properly position the content element absolutely, we need to give it a `top` value. At the same time, we'll also give it a `left` value of `25%`.

```
#content {
   width: 70%;
   position: absolute;
   top: 0;
   left: 25%
}
```

As we can see in figure **9.5**, we have, in effect, created a column for the main text—though this column is currently positioned on top of the header element, and if we zoom the text size or add long entries to the navigation list, then some of the navigation would also be obscured by the content element.

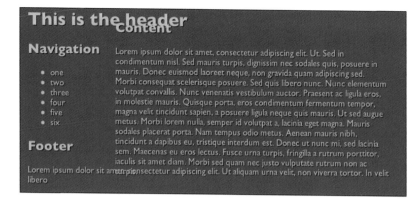

9.5
The absolutely posi-
tioned content element
now covers the header
element, and may cover
parts of the navigation
element.

We can fix the problem with the navigation element by giving that element an explicit width of, for example, `20%`.

```
#navigation {
  width: 20%
}
```

Once we've done this, if any of the contents on the navigation element are wider than 20% of the page, they will wrap instead of going under the content element.

Rescuing the Header

Next, we need to prevent the content element from obscuring the header. We could change the `top` property for the content block from 0 to another value to account for the height of the header, but what value should we use? The height in pixels of the header will change if the text is zoomed by the user, and will also vary between platforms because of differing default resolutions. Using ems would be a little safer, but if we do that, there's no way to precisely align the top of the content element with the top of the navigation block, which is being flowed by the browser. What we need is some way of taking advantage of aspects of the normal flow and absolute positioning schemes.

Enter `position: relative`. We mentioned earlier that when an element is positioned relatively it remains in the flow, and is only moved relative to its position in normal flow. But it's another vital aspect of `position: relative` that will help us now: a relatively positioned element creates a new positioning context for any descendant elements that are absolutely positioned. So if an element is contained inside a parent element with **position**: relative, when we give that contained element a **position**: absolute, it will be absolutely positioned *with respect to its relatively positioned parent element.*

This is powerful stuff, though it can take a bit of work to understand its implications and uses. Let's turn to our example, which will, I hope, clarify matters. Our content **div** is absolutely positioned. At present, none of its ancestor elements—the container **div** and the **body** element—have a **position**: absolute or **position**: relative. As a result, if we give the content element a **position**: absolute, it will be absolutely positioned with respect to the viewport. But if we give the container **div** a **position**: relative, the container **div** will remain where it is (provided we don't give it a left or top value), and the content **div** will now be absolutely positioned *with respect to the container element.* In other words, if we use this rule:

```
#container {
    position: relative
}
```

...then the content element will be positioned at the top of the container element. Because the container element is in the document flow, if the header increases in size, the page will be re-flowed, and the container element's position will be adjusted to accommodate the new header height [**9.6**]. And when the container element's position is adjusted, the content element's position will *also* be adjusted, because the content element is absolutely positioned with respect to the container element.

9.6
As the header element changes size, so too does the location of the container element—and, as a consequence, the location of the absolutely positioned content element.

This is the header

Navigation

Content

- one
- two
- three
- four
- five
- six

Lorem ipsum dolor sit amet, consectetur adipiscing elit. Ut. Sed in condimentum nisl. Sed mauris turpis, dignissim nec sodales quis, posuere in mauris. Donec euismod laoreet neque, non gravida quam adipiscing sed. Morbi consequat scelerisque posuere. Sed quis libero nunc. Nunc elementum volutpat convallis. Nunc venenatis vestibulum auctor. Praesent ac ligula eros, in molestie mauris. Quisque porta, eros condimentum fermentum tempor, magna velit tincidunt sapien, a posuere ligula neque quis mauris. Ut sed augue metus. Morbi lorem nulla, semper id volutpat a, lacinia eget magna. Mauris sodales placerat porta. Nam tempus odio metus.

Footer

Lorem ipsum dolor sit amet, consectetur adipiscing elit. Etiam urna velit, non viverra tortor. In velit Aenean mauris sapien, tincidunt a aliquam eu, tristique interdum est. Donec libero ut nunc mi, sed lacinia sem. Maecenas eu eros lectus. Fusce urna turpis, fringilla a rutrum porttitor, iaculis sit amet diam. Morbi sed quam nec justo vulputate rutrum non ac turpis.

*If you are wondering why the Navigation and Content headings don't align vertically, it's because of the margin on the **h2** element inside the content element. If you set this element's **margin-top** to 0, the headings will be aligned*

Keeping Things on Top

As you lay out a page using CSS, you'll frequently need to answer several questions about the page elements' position in the imaginary stack defined by the **z-index** property. Elements with absolute and fixed positioning have a **z-index** property, and the higher the **z-index** of an element, the closer to the front an element is rendered. (We covered **z-index** in Chapter 4, so take another look at that chapter if you need to revisit the property.) Some of the questions you may need to consider are:

- How, in relation to other elements on the page, is a particular absolutely positioned element drawn?
- Does it obscure the elements rendered below it, or is it obscured by them?
- If there are several absolutely positioned elements, which is on top?

These questions can be difficult to answer. Elements positioned absolutely or as fixed elements are rendered in front of elements in the normal flow, which is one of the disadvantages of using absolute position to create page layouts.

By itself, absolute positioning is very powerful, but because absolutely positioned elements are completely disassociated from the normal page flow, the technique lacks finesse. However, if we use relative positioning to create elements that are in the normal flow and that provide a positioning context for absolutely positioned descendant elements, we have a combo system that looks almost ideal.

So what's the problem? Well, take a look at the example page as shown in figure **9.7**.

Footer

Lorem ipsum dolor sit amet, consectetur adipiscing elit... libero

ac ligula eros, in molestie mauris. Quisque porta, eros condimentum fermentum tempor, magna velit tincidunt sapien, a posuere ligula neque quis mauris. Ut sed augue metus. Morbi lorem nulla, semper id volutpat a, lacinia eget magna. Mauris sodales placerat porta. Nam tempus odio metus. Aenean mauris nibh, tincidunt a dapibus eu, tristique interdum est. Donec ut nunc mi, sed lacinia sem. Maecenas eu eros lectus. Fusce urna turpis, fringilla a rutrum porttitor, iaculis sit amet diam. Morbi sed quam nec justo vulputate rutrum non ac turpis.

9.7
Even when they're contained in relatively positioned elements, absolutely positioned elements don't affect the normal page flow.

The footer element is still being styled as if the content element were not in the page. That's because even if an absolutely positioned element is contained within a relatively positioned element, it still doesn't affect the flow of the page. As a result, the height of the container element includes the height of the navigation element, but *doesn't* include the height of the content block. That's why the footer element is all the way up underneath the navigation element. And here's the real challenge of absolutely positioned layouts like this: if the taller of two (or more) elements that comprise the columns of a layout is absolutely positioned, any element further down in the markup will suffer the same fate as the footer in figure 9.6. It may be possible—as, in fact, it is in this case—to absolutely position another of the "columns" instead of the content element, but this won't always help. So although this approach to multi-column layouts is at times useful, it has serious limitations. We'll look at ways to get around this roadblock using float-based layouts in just a moment.

Fixing Navigation on Screen

Some common page designs keep a subset of the navigation or a small set of tools constantly onscreen. This is often implemented with JavaScript, but can be more simply achieved using the `fixed` value of the `position` property. Like absolutely positioned elements, fixed elements are taken out of the page flow. But unlike absolutely positioned elements, fixed elements are *always* positioned with respect to the *viewport*, even if it is contained within an element that has a positioning context.

Using the preceding absolutely positioned example, if we made the navigation element (instead of the content element) absolutely positioned, we could give it a `position: fixed` to have it remain onscreen no matter how far down the page the user scrolls. The CSS rule would look something like this:

```
#navigation {
  width: 20%;
  position: fixed;
  top: 5em;
}
```

With fixed positioning, we need to be even more careful to prevent elements from overlapping and obscuring other elements on the page, because as the page scrolls, the fixed element remains where it is with respect to the viewport, and the rest of the page scrolls underneath the fixed element. As figure **9.8** shows, when the page is scrolled to the top, the navigation element doesn't overlap the header element, but when the page is scrolled to the bottom it *does* overlap the footer.

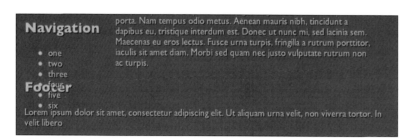

9.8
Ensuring that fixed elements don't overlap other page elements can be difficult.

Float-Based Layouts

To get around the limitations of positioning-based layouts, web developers have discovered and refined several other ways to create multi-column and other layouts using the `float` property of CSS. Float-based layouts don't have the problems associated with `z-index`, and because floated elements still affect the normal flow of the page, the footer problem we saw a moment ago is much less of a problem.

We'll begin by looking at a simple layout: we'll create a horizontal navigation bar from a list of links, then turn to using the techniques learned here to create full-page multi-column layouts.

Horizontal, Floated Navigation Lists

Site-level navigation arranged in a horizontal bar across the top of the page is a very common page design pattern [**9.9**]. Many developers agree that the most sensible approach to marking up such navigation is to use a list of links, since navigation is essentially a list of linked pages. Here's the markup for the navigation shown in figure 9.9.

```
<ul class="sitesections">
    <li><a href="http://westciv.com/style_master/index.
    html">style master</a></li>
    <li><a href="http://westciv.com/tools">tools</a></li>
    <li><a href="http://westciv.com/style_master/house/
    index.html">resources</a></li>
    <li><a href="http://westciv.com/westciv/downloads.
    html">downloads</a></li>
    <li><a href="https://order.kagi.com/?WC4">store
    </a></li>
    <li><a id="feeds" href="http://westciv.com/
    style_master/blog/feed">RSS</a></li>
</ul>
```

9.9

A classic horizontal navigation bar.

We'll take what would otherwise be displayed as a plain list of links [**9.10**] and display it horizontally with just a small amount of CSS—and along the way, we'll go over some powerful aspects of CSS that will be useful in many page layouts.

9.10

The default display of a list of links.

The secret to the technique is to float all the list items. As we saw in Chapter 4, if an element lacks an intrinsic width (as list items do), we need to give it an explicit width if we want to float it. In this instance, we want each list item to have the same width, so we'll divide 100 percent by the number of list items (six), and we come up with a width of 16.6%:

```
li {
    float: left;
    width: 16.6%
}
```

We could also float each of the list items to the right, like this:

```
li {
  float: right;
  width: 16.6%
}
```

Doing so reverses the order of the list items, as we can see in figure **9.11**:

9.11
Our floated list items floated to the right (top) and to the left (bottom).

With floated layouts, it always pays to leave a little bit of breathing room, because browsers need to convert percentages into pixels, and may round up to do so, thus making the total width (in pixels) of all the list items greater than the width of the containing element (in pixels). In this situation, the right-most list item in the layout wraps around under the left-most list item [**9.12**]. This applies to any adjacent floated elements inside the same parent element, and is a challenge for all float-based layouts.

9.12
When the total width of the list items exceeds the width of the containing element, one or more of the list items will move down directly beneath the first line of floated elements.

As you'll recall, older versions of Internet Explorer (and IE 7 and 8 in Quirks mode) calculate the width of an element differently from all other modern browsers. This is almost certain to give rise to the problem shown in figure 9.11, which means one or more of the solutions I mentioned back in Chapter 7 will be required to make your float-based layouts work across common browsers.

Filling the Box

At this point, if we viewed our example page in a browser, you'd notice that the links don't fill their parent list items—as inline elements, they are only as wide and tall as their content requires. But it can be useful to make inline content fill the dimensions of its parent elements, and our example provides just such a scenario. Users will expect the whole navigation bar to be clickable, but as it stands, unless the cursor is directly over the text of a link, clicking won't do anything.

It's easy to make these links fill their containing list items—we simply give them a **display** value of block. Elements with a **display** of block fill the entire height and width of their parent elements, all the way to the padding edge. Here's what such a rule looks like:

```
li a {
   display: block
}
```

A Border Around the Navigation List

Let's now put a border around this navigation list. This should be easy. We just add a border to the list:

```
ul {
   border-style: solid
}
```

But now we have a problem. Figure **9.13** shows how the page now looks in a browser.

9.13
The list border doesn't surround the list items.

This happens because when an element is floated within its parent, it no longer "counts" when the browser calculates the parent element's height. So, when all the children of an element are floated as here, then the element effectively has no height.

It's a giant headache, and for years, developers struggled to find a solution.

Happily, there is now a very simple fix for this problem that works in all modern browsers: give the containing element an **overflow** of `auto` (you can also use `hidden`, or `scroll`, but `auto` is what developers tend to use) and an explicit **width**, and all browsers will magically include the height of the floated elements when calculating the height of the containing element. Here's the code:

```
ul {
    border-style: solid;
    overflow: auto;
    width: 100%
}
```

Now that we've seen how float can be used to create page layout, we'll use it to create common multi-column page layouts. This technique is very widely used, and has been explored in great detail by many developers over several years. While there has been some controversy as to whether using float for these outcomes is in some sense in violation of the CSS specification (float was not expressly designed for the purposes we are putting it to in this chapter), this approach to creating page layout is widely considered to be best practice in CSS layout, and without a doubt the most widely used set of techniques for CSS page layout.

Floated Multi-Column Layouts

Multi-column layouts are ubiquitous on the modern web. We've seen that such layouts can be achieved using absolute positioning, but that this approach comes with substantial limitations. The principal advantage of **float** over absolute positioning is that floated elements aren't removed from the flow of the document, so we can let the browser worry about the impact of floated elements on the rest of the page instead of writing complex CSS and markup to control these interactions ourselves.

Float-based multi-column layout techniques use the same principle we've just seen with horizontal navigation bars. The so-called columns are elements that share the same containing element, and these are floated within their parent element [9.14]. (And as we know, a floated element floats out of the flow of its parent element, and to the edge of that parent, or until it touches the edge of another floated element.)

9.14
Both of the images are floated to the left. The first floated image touches the edge of its containing element, and the second floated element touches the edge of the first image (a margin separates them slightly). The content in the heading and paragraphs that follows these images flows around the floated images.

Beyond SEO

Presenters:
Cheryl Gledhill **and** Scott Gledhill

Search engine optimisation (SEO) is a unique mix of marketing, usability and technology which can often cause confusion on how it is implemented across different organisations. An important part of your SEO strategy is getting the most out of your SEO dollars. This session will explain what your developers, designers, producers, content authors and marketers should all know about SEO to ensure you're getting the maximum return on your SEO.

For our float-based layout example, we'll construct perhaps *the* classic modern page layout: three content columns with a header and footer. As always, our goal is to change the original markup as little as possible to achieve the desired layout, and we'll begin with simple, logical, semantic markup.

```
<div id="header">
  <h1>This is the header</h1>
</div>
<div id="container">
  <div id="navigation">
    <h2>Navigation</h2>
    <ul>
      <li>home</li>
      <li>store</li>
      <li>help</li>
      <li>contact</li>
    </ul>
  </div> <!--navigation-->

  <div id="content">
    <h2>Content</h2>
    <p>Lorem ipsum dolor sit amet, consectetur ....</p>
  </div> <!--content-->
```

continues on next page

```
    <div id="advertisements">
      <h2>Buy Stuff</h2>
      <ul>
        <li>Software</li>
        <li>Hardware</li>
        <li>T-shirts</li>
        <li>Caffeine</li>
      </ul>
    </div> <!-- advertisements -->

  <div id="footer">
    <h2>Footer</h2>
    <p>Lorem ipsum dolor sit ...</p>
  </div> <!--footer-->
```

We'll float each of the three column divs—navigation, content, and advertisements—and give each a different width. Again, we have to make sure the total width of these elements adds up to less than 100 percent—otherwise, the right-most column will wrap around underneath the other columns, breaking the layout and making us weep and rend our garments. So how should we specify the widths? We can use percentages, pixels, ems, or a combination of any of these, but the combination approach can get very complicated—each method results in different behavior when text is zoomed or the window size changes. Before implementing the layout, we'll take a quick look at the strengths and weaknesses of each method.

Fixed-Width Layouts

The most common way to specify the width of columns in a multi-column layout is to use pixels. The resulting layouts are commonly called fixed-width layouts. Because column widths are specified using pixels, when the window is resized or the text zoomed, the column sizes remain unchanged.

One drawback of this method is that the length of lines of text shortens as text size increases, which can result in unreadable pages if the user needs to magnify the text by more than a few sizes. Additionally, fixed-width layouts are typically tuned for specific screen sizes, and as the range of screen sizes increases to include everything from tiny mobile device displays to mammoth 1980-pixel, high-resolution monitors, a single fixed-width layout is increasingly less likely to provide a reasonable solution to page layout. One way around this problem is to use JavaScript to change the pixel widths of columns based on the size of the window. Another is to use CSS3's media queries, which we'll cover in Chapter 14, but this method it not yet supported in any version of Internet Explorer, so it won't be useful for every project.

Another trap for beginning CSS developers is that fixed-width layouts can be very fragile: if the window width is less than the total widths of the columns, the columns will wrap and one or more will be pushed below the other columns. This problem is easy to solve. If the columns are contained inside an element with a pixel-based width that is greater than or equal to the combined widths of the columns, the browser will add a horizontal scroll bar when the window width is narrower than the combined pixel width of the columns instead of breaking the layout. We could add an extra **div** to contain all our column elements, and give that **div** a fixed width, but in many situations, we can just plaster a fixed width on the **body** element. Here's how we'd achieve a bulletproof fixed-width three-column layout.

```css
body {
    width: 1000px;
}


#navigation {
    float: left;
    width: 200px
}


#content {
    float: left;
    width: 600px
}

#advertisements {
    float: left;
    width: 200px
}
```

The bottom line: Fixed-width layouts are still the most common type of floated layout, but as screen sizes continue to diversify, this may change.

Fluid Layouts

Fluid layouts, also known as liquid layouts, specify the width of columns using percentages. With this method, the pixel widths of the columns automatically adapt to the width of the window or viewport. Fluid layouts have several advantages over fixed-width layouts: they'll never break when the window size is changed, and given the growing range of web-capable devices, their ability to adapt to a range of screen sizes makes them very attractive. On the other hand, viewed on very wide or very narrow screens, the line-length of text within fluid columns can become long or too short for easy reading.

Happily, we can combine the best of fixed and fluid layouts using the overlooked `min-width` and `max-width` CSS properties. As you might guess, these properties specify a minimum and a maximum width for an element, and you can use them alongside percentages to ensure that once the maximum or minimum width is reached, the layout stops growing or shrinking. If you're thinking that this simple trick sounds too good to be true, however, you're at least partially right.

With one exception, all the CSS features used in this chapter are supported across all modern browsers from IE 6 on. That exception is the `max-width` and `min-width` properties, which are supported in all modern browsers except for IE 7 and 8, which support them *only in standards mode*.

Because these layouts are somewhat fixed, and so may break as the window becomes narrow, it again makes sense to use the technique we used for fully fixed layouts of fixing the width of the `body` (or other element containing these columns). Here, instead of using the `width` property to do that, we'll use the `min-width` property, with a value that is the sum of the minimum widths of each column. This means that in IE 6, we don't get quite the robustness that the `min-width` on the containing element provides, and for narrow window sizes the layout may break in that browser. But for almost all browsers, our layout will be robust, regardless of the width of the window.

```
body {
   min-width: 640px;
   margin: 0 auto}

#navigation {
   float: left;
   width: 20%;
   max-width: 200px;
   min-width: 120px}

#content {
   float: left;
   width: 60%;
   max-width: 800px;
   min-width: 400px}

#advertisements {
   float: left;
   width: 20%;
   max-width: 200px;
   min-width: 120px}
```

Elastic Layouts

A third, somewhat less common layout method is the *elastic* or em-driven layout. These specify column widths in (naturally) ems. The advantage of this
method is that lines of text will contain approximately the same number of
characters as the user zooms the text size up or down, which means that elastic
layouts are less affected by text resizing than are fluid or fixed layouts.

Fully elastic layouts, in which each column's width is specified in ems, are
uncommon and suffer from the fact that as a user zooms the text, they may have
to use horizontal scrolling. But a combination of em-based width for the main
column of text and fixed or percentage-based widths for other columns can
produce a layout that has consistently readable line lengths for the main text,
while keeping the whole layout visible in most circumstances.

```
#navigation {
   float: left
   width: 20%
   }

#content {
   float: left
   width: 40em
   }

#advertisements {
   float: left
   width: 20%
   }
```

One more consideration: if you use elastic layouts, it's a very good idea to specify a width on the body or another element that contains the columns so that the layout doesn't break when the text size is zoomed up. See the earlier sections on fixed or fluid layouts for more on this technique.

The Footer

Now that we have that out of the way, let's return to our example page. At present, our footer element will float up alongside the floated columns, but this problem is easily fixed using the `clear` property on the footer to specify that our footer element must not wrap around floated elements above it in the document. So a cleared element is pushed down below the tallest floated element above it, as shown in figure **9.15**. By giving the footer element a `clear` value of `both`, we complete our layout.

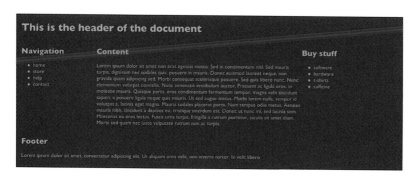

9.15

The **clear** property means an element that will otherwise wrap around floated elements as they float past is pushed below the tallest floated element.

No Easy Way Out

Many of the rules in the CSS specification relating to the height of elements are extremely complex, because they need to specify the calculation of heights in any possible case. Web developers usually don't need to think about the minutiae of these sorts of issues, but sometimes a closer look is necessary if we want to understand the specification's logic. Here are a few pertinent details for those of you who want to understand why height-related CSS problems can be so tricky.

Setting a percentage `height` on an element that is contained inside an element that doesn't have an explicit `height` in pixels, ems, or some other length unit is, in effect, the same as setting the `height` of the containing element to `auto`: the containing element's height is computed based on the size of the element's content.

We could, therefore, wrap all of our floated columns in a container element, and set its `height` to, say, `50em`. But if we do that, the container's height won't adapt to the height of the floated columns it contains—which means that the containing element's height will almost certainly be greater than the height of any of the contained columns (thus leaving a gap beneath the tallest column), or less than the height of the tallest column (thus causing the content in the tallest column to overflow and be clipped to the height of the containing element, or forcing a vertical scrollbar).

So, while this method would allow us to fill each column with a background color, it creates problems that are difficult to fix.

The Color Conundrum

With very little CSS, we've created the desired three-column layout, but one challenge remains: what if we want each column to have a different colored background? Can't we just add a background color with CSS?

Sadly, it's not quite that simple. We know that HTML elements are only as tall as their contents unless we give them an explicit height value. You might think that setting a `height: 100%` for the various columns would make them fill their containing element vertically, but the `height` property doesn't work that way with percentage heights, only with *length-based* height values (that is, height values that use ems, pixels, and other length units). And whereas if all the columns are the same color, it's not really noticeable if they're not all the same height, when each column has a different background color, disparities in height are glaringly obvious. This challenge has long caused developers difficulties. In fact, it's a design pattern you see less frequently now than in the past, perhaps in part due to the difficulty of solving it. Once again, there are several solutions, each with strengths and weaknesses.

The two main approaches to solving this problem are:

- *Faux columns*, developed originally by Dan Cederholm for fixed layouts, has also been adapted for fluid and elastic column layouts.
- The *one true layout* by Alex Robinson (this is a slightly more complex version of the floated column layout we've just explored, which through the ingenious use of negative margins allows the same three columns to be arranged left to right in any order without touching the markup).

Faux Columns

The basic principle of the faux columns technique (*faux*, for those of you non-francophones, means false, or fake) is that we use a background image on the containing element of the columns as a fake background color for the columns. Developed by renowned web developer and author Dan Cederholm, the technique was first described in *A List Apart* (**www.alistapart.com/articles/fauxcolumns**). The technique is, as Cederholm says himself, "embarrassingly simple"—though like many simple things, it's also extremely clever. Suppose we have a page with two columns, floated left, each with a width fixed in pixels:

```
#content {
   float: left;
width: 580px
}
#navigation {
   float: left;
   width: 100px
}
```

Now, on an element which contains both the columns (for example, the `body`), we use a background image that will provide the fake background color for both columns. Figure **9.16** shows an example image we could use. The lighter gray on the left is 580px wide, the darker gray is 100px—the same widths as the two columns, which will then sit on top of these columns of color in the background image. We then tile the background image vertically, and then the content of the columns overlays these background images.

9.16

An image with two solid color backgrounds (top) is vertically tiled as the background image, creating fake column backgrounds. The content of the columns sits on top of this image, creating the effect that the color fills their columns vertically.

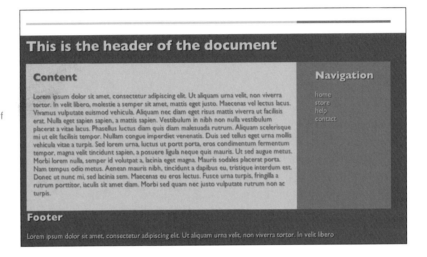

Of course this approach won't work when column widths aren't fixed. Fluid faux columns are possible, though quite a bit more complicated than the fixed-width variety—the core principle of using background images on containing elements to create faux column backgrounds is the same, however. The concept has been explored in detail by Zoe Gillenwater, a well known web development expert and author, at communityMX (**www.communitymx.com/content/article.cfm?cid=afc58**). I recommend her article as a starting point for those who wish to get up to speed with fluid faux columns.

The One True Layout

A different approach to achieving this same outcome is part of the one true layout technique for creating multi-column layouts (**www.positioniseverything.net/articles/onetruelayout**). With this ironically named technique, the column order is completely independent of the source order. This can be beneficial for accessibility and search engine optimization, as it allows us to move content closer to the beginning of our markup, where search engines and assistive devices may give it more attention, but still display this content where we want in a page layout.

One drawback is that the elements which will be our columns *must* be contained within a containing element. One of the principles of design and markup we stress throughout the book is that as much as possible, our markup should not include presentational aspects, be they the obvious presentational elements and attributes, or more subtly, elements there solely for the purposes of presentation. But at times, depending on the needs (and demands) of the job, additional markup may be required. This is one of those cases. Here's our column markup before, with an additional **div** wrapping the column **div**s.

```
<div id="container">
  <div id="navigation">
    . . .
  </div> <!--navigation-->

  <div id="content">
    . . .
  </div> <!--cotent-->

  <div id="advertisements">
    . . .
  </div> <!-- advertisements -->
</div><!-- container -->
```

A big advantage of this technique over the faux columns technique is that the background color or image for the columns is applied directly to the column elements, not to a containing element. The secret to this technique starts with adding the *same* large amount of padding to the bottom of each of our column elements. This value must be large enough so that the shortest column plus the padding is taller than the height of the tallest column (without padding). Now, if you are thinking this will simply make each column taller by the amount of padding added, you are indeed correct. There's still a little more we need to do. Next, we'll add a negative **margin-bottom** of the same amount as the padding we added to each of the column elements. Putting these together, along with the background color for each column element, here's our CSS:

```css
#navigation {
  float: left;
  width: 20%;
  background-color: #6cf625;
  padding-bottom: 500em;
  margin-bottom: -500em
}

#content {
  float: left;
  width: 40em;
  background-color: #e02d12;
  padding-bottom: 500em;
  margin-bottom: -500em
}

#advertisements {
  float: left;
  width: 20%;
  background-color: #0019f9;
  padding-bottom: 500em;
  margin-bottom: -500em
}
```

The negative `margin-bottom` in essence pulls the bottom of the element up the same amount as it has been pushed down by the padding. However, while the footer element is now sitting nice and snug underneath the bottom of the content of the tallest column, the colored background of the columns still extends past the footer and down the page.

The last part of the trick is to add `overflow: hidden` to the containing element of these columns (that's why they must have their own container.) This clips any content (including the padding of the columns) to the actual height of the containing element.

```css
#container {
  overflow: hidden
}
```

And now, in all modern browsers, including Internet Explorer (as far back as IE 5 Windows), we have the holy grail of true columns, with equal heights, regardless of their content height.

Too good to be true? Well, yes. As with many of the more complex web development techniques, there are some challenges. With this approach, when there is a target anchor in any of the columns, if a link is followed to this anchor, then the container of the columns scrolls to bring this anchor to the top. A picture tells a sorry 1,000 words in this case, as figures **9.17** and **9.18** show.

Sadly, there's really not a solution to this problem—well, short of not having internal anchors in columns like this. For long columns of text, this means that a table of contents for the page can't be implemented, which can be a real usability concern. If you have a situation where internal anchors are definitely not required, this is the solution for you. Otherwise, some variations on faux columns is your most likely approach. A recent straw poll conducted on Twitter reveals that as of this writing, Faux Columns continues to be the technique of choice among experienced developers.

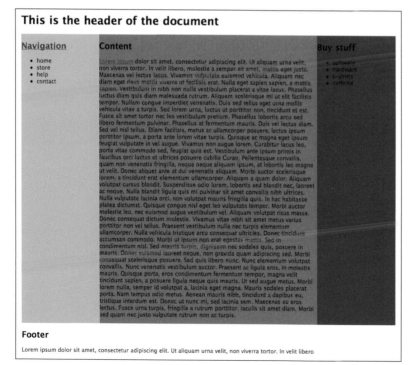

9.17
Before: our three columns.

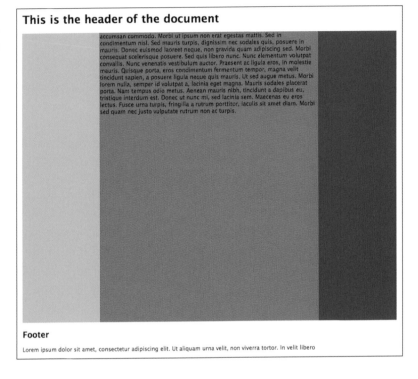

Now that we've explored the most common ways in which page layouts are currently developed, there are two other subjects we should cover at least briefly while dealing with the issue of CSS page layouts. First, we'll talk about the increasingly popular grid layouts, and then we'll turn to a part of the CSS2 standard that is quite widely supported in modern browsers and promises a way out of the complex maze of techniques and workarounds that comprise web page layout with CSS.

Grid Layouts

Despite web design's origins in print design, grid-based layouts—a staple of print design since the 1950s—have only relatively recently begun making inroads into web design, championed by such designers as Mark Boulton and Khoi Vinh. One significant drawback of grid-based designs is that their complexity typically requires that the markup be heavily influenced by the design itself, in contradiction to the widely held principle that markup and presentation should be kept separate as much as possible. (Most of these methods are associated with CSS frameworks, which we'll focus on in Chapter 10.) There are, however, two developments in CSS that promise to help us avoid marking up our content in strange ways just to facilitate grid layouts: CSS2.1 table layout properties, which is almost ready for widespread use, and CSS3's Grid Layout Module, which is still in development. Let's look at the first of these now.

CSS2.1 Table Layout Properties

As was noted at the beginning of this chapter, web design patterns have been heavily influenced by developers' early use of table-based layouts, and as we saw, the CSS page layout model was not designed to work the same way as the HTML table model.

CSS2.1, however, features a table layout model that is supported in all modern browsers, including (for once) IE 8, and which essentially *reproduces* the HTML table model in CSS. Just as we can use CSS to make any element act like a block-level element with the `display` property, with this model, we can now make any element act like a table, a table cell, a table row, and so on. Without using tables in our markup, we can use the table *model* via CSS, thus gaining the benefits of easy vertical alignment, equal width columns, and so on, without touching our markup or making our sites inaccessible.

For example, we can make any element display like a table row with the CSS `display`: `table-row`, or any element display like a `td` element with `display`: `table-cell`. So efficient is this technique that achieving a fluid, unbreakable multi-column layout without any additional containing element and with colors that fill each column can be done with just a handful of CSS properties. For example, to create a fluid, two-column layout in which each column is filled with a background color, we'd need only this HTML, and the attendant CSS.

```
<div id="navigation">
<h2>Navigation</h2>
    <ul>
       <li>home</li>
       <li>store</li>
       <li>help</li>
       <li>contact</li>
    </ul>
</div> <!--navigation-->
<div id="content">
  <h2>Content</h2>
  <p>Lorem ipsum dolor sit amet, consectetur ....</p>
</div> <!--content-->
```

```
#content {
  display: table-cell;
  width: 66%;
  background-color: #e37848
}

#navigation {
  display: table-cell;
  background-color: #3c754c
}
```

We simply give each of the columns a `display` of `table-cell`, and then give the wider column a width (we could also apply a width to the narrower column), along with a background color for each. The browser takes care of the rest. Hard to believe, but try it in any modern browser, including IE 8!

Not Quite Ready for Prime Time

There are however a couple of challenges we need to be aware of.

As was true with old-school, table-based layouts, the order of the elements in the markup determines the order in which elements can be presented using CSS2. So, unlike in the One True Layout, and other float-based layouts, the source order of the HTML will be determined by the layout—which can have implications for search engines and assistive devices. Another drawback is that all versions of Internet Explorer before version 8 do not support CSS table layout properties, which means that as long as older versions of IE are widely used, using these CSS2.1 properties will present significant challenges to developers. The day of simply coded, sophisticated grid-based layouts has not arrived quite yet, but it's coming soon—and we won't have to wait for the CSS3 Grid Layout Module to be developed and supported.

The Wrap

Page layout tends to consume a lot of development time. Fortunately, thanks to the efforts of many developers over many years, there are well documented, robust techniques for implementing many common design patterns—and we now have a far greater understanding of what we can accomplish with existing CSS specifications and common browsers. Additionally, we know that emerging CSS standards will soon add to our armory of techniques.

Still, I sometimes wonder if, when we look back on web development a decade or so from now, we'll have developed entirely new ways of designing for the web—and whether the concerns of this chapter won't look a bit old fashioned. Only time will tell.

CSS Resets & Frameworks

Without a style sheet, your browser displays web pages as a single long paragraph of text, all with the same size and weight. This may come as a surprise, because when you view a page in your browser before adding your CSS, it *isn't* displayed that way. Headings, paragraphs, and other block-level elements are displayed as blocks with margins and padding, and at various text sizes and weights. Links are colored (probably blue) and underlined. This all happens because the browser is using a *default style sheet*—and, of course, each browser's default style sheet is a little bit different.

CSS Resets

Browsers apply the default style sheet first, and then add on any preferences a particular user has set (such as custom default font sizes). Only after the default style sheet and the user preferences are added does the browser use the styles you've defined for the page via inline styles or any embedded and linked style sheets.

Variations between browsers—especially those caused by the browsers' default style sheets—can make it very difficult to maintain design consistency across browsers. In the last few years, developers have begun to use reset style sheets to deal with this problem. Reset style sheets create a consistent, cross-browser baseline for font sizing, element margins, padding, line-heights, and so on, thus providing a smooth foundation for the all the styles called for by a particular project. To use such a style sheet, a developer simply links to it from every page on a site or includes it in one of the site's universally used style sheets.

Benefits of CSS Resets

Most designers and developers tend to work with a single browser during development, switching to other browsers only when it comes time to finish and test the markup and styles. The implicit assumption associated with this approach is that the default styles for the browser we decide to work with will be similar to the default styles of other browsers. Default style sheets, however, can be sufficiently different as to create both subtle and not-so-subtle problems. Using a reset means that we'll never again develop a complex style sheet, only to find problems caused by variation of default styles across browsers that require considerable effort to fix.

The core philosophy of CSS resets is that it's safer and easier to explicitly declare any style you use, rather than relying on (and guessing about) implicit styling. That said, most resets do rely on some core browser default styles. For example, most resets trust the default value of the `display` property rather than explicitly declaring that headings, paragraphs, and other block-level elements use `display: block`; that `strong`, `em`, and other inline elements use `display: inline`; that list items use a `display: list-item`; and so on.

Arguments Against Resets

Critics of the reset technique argue that common features of prominent CSS reset files, such as setting the `margin` and `padding` of every element to `0`, or using the universal selector (`*`) as some resets do, can create considerable performance overhead for the browser. This is why many common reset files no longer use these performance-intensive methods.

Another argument against resets is that they add another server request, which can affect site performance: reducing the number of external resource links in a page is one of the best ways to improve performance. As noted in Chapter 4, there are many simple ways to improve site performance when using CSS, including amalgamating each page's CSS into a single style sheet whenever possible. Increasingly, developers have begun to add their reset styles to the main style sheet for their sites.

Performance problems aside, there are also philosophical reasons to avoid resets—on some projects, at least. Respected web developer Jonathan Snook recently explained why he doesn't use resets:

> The problem I've had with these resets is that I then find myself declaring much more than I ever needed to just to get browsers back to rendering things the way I want. As it turns out, I'm perfectly happy with how a number of elements render by default. I like lists to have bullets and strong elements to have bolded text.
>
> And I'm okay if the various browsers show things slightly differently. I'm okay if one browser displays an H1 a few pixels larger or smaller than other browsers. If one browser defaults to circle bullets and another to squares, that's usually not a problem. If it is, then I create a style that addresses that specific issue. I don't reset it back to zero and then set it again to what I really want.
>
> One of the principles I took away from the Web Standards community was the concept that pixel-perfect precision across the various rendering engines was impractical and a remnant of the table-based layouts of yesteryear. With CSS and progressive enhancement, it was okay that things might look a little different from one browser to the next because of variations in what they supported.
>
> **—www.snook.ca/archives/html_and_css/no_css_reset**

Even if you share these concerns, however, you might choose to use resets in a limited way, explicitly resetting default styles for only those aspects you're particularly concerned with. For example, developers very frequently set `margin` and `padding` to 0 on block elements like paragraphs and headings, while leaving out resets for things like the type of list bullets and the font size of headings.

In the end, the reset approach has both adherents and critics among well respected development experts. As with so many choices in web development, you'll need to consider the practical benefits resets can offer and decide whether or not to use the technique based on the needs of your particular projects.

What Do CSS Resets Look Like?

CSS resets often look something like this one, which is excerpted from a reset developed by leading CSS expert Eric Meyer:

```
html, body, div, span, applet, object, iframe, h1, h2,
h3, h4, h5, h6, p, blockquote, pre, a, abbr, acronym,
address, big, cite, code, del, dfn, em, font, img, ins,
kbd, q, s, samp, small, strike, strong, sub, sup, tt,
var, dl, dt, dd, ol, ul, li, fieldset, form, label, legend,
table, caption, tbody, tfoot, thead, tr, th, td {
  margin: 0;
  padding: 0;
  border: 0;
  outline: 0;
  font-weight: inherit;
  font-style: inherit;
  font-size: 100%;
  font-family: inherit;
  vertical-align: baseline;
}
```

You'll notice that this rule sets the `margin`, `padding`, and `border` for many elements all to 0—which means that after this reset is applied, the width and height of any element will be determined only by its content. The rule doesn't take the once-common approach of using the universal selector (*) to set these values, because as mentioned earlier, this method can harm site performance.

Meyer's rule also removes any default `font-family`, `font-weight`, and type size that the browser style sheets might apply. These are the core elements of most resets.

Common CSS Resets

If you decide to use a reset, get to know it first. Many resets have such subtle effects as removing a browser's default list-item padding, thus making list items flush-left with the rest of the content for a page. If you don't know your reset well, it can be difficult to trace the exact cause of effects like these.

Here are two of the most commonly used resets.

Eric Meyer's Reset Reloaded

meyerweb.com/eric/thoughts/2007/05/01/reset-reloaded

Eric Meyer is perhaps the preeminent expert on CSS development. His reset is based on years of experience and a deep knowledge of the differences between how browsers render pages. Did you know that some browsers indent list-items with `padding`, while others use `margin`? Eric does. He encourages anyone who uses his reset to do so as the basis "for their own resets and for deeper thinking about styling and browsers."

Yahoo Reset CSS

developer.yahoo.com/yui/reset

The Yahoo User Interface Library (YUI), a CSS framework we'll look at shortly, includes a reset file that can be used independently of YUI. Yahoo describes the reset as follows:

> *The foundational YUI Reset CSS file removes and neutralizes the inconsistent default styling of HTML elements, creating a level playing field across A-grade browsers and providing a sound foundation upon which you can explicitly declare your intentions.*

A-grade browsers is a term Yahoo uses to describe the set of browsers that get the full HTML/CSS/JavaScript/DOM experience, and the classification is based on browsers' technology support and market share.

Both of these popular resets set the font size and weight of all elements to the same setting, and both override the browser's default setting of `strong` elements and headings to bold. They also set the `margin` and `padding` of most elements to 0. One important way in which they differ is the `:focus` state. Meyer's reset removes any outline from any element in the focus state, and because this is an important accessibility feature, he recommends setting your own focus styles.

The Do-It-Yourself Reset

This isn't another third-party CSS reset, though there are others. Instead of offering a giant list, I'd like to suggest that you consider developing your own reset based on your specific practices and needs. Building your own reset means that you're necessarily aware of all of its implications, and it also means you can be very specific about which aspects of default browser style sheets you want to trust, and which you want to explicitly override with your reset. Finally, developing your own reset decreases the chance that you'll be hit by some subtle and hard-to-find "gotcha" in a third-party reset.

CSS Frameworks

As we saw in Chapter 5, when it comes to DOM scripting, many developers have begun to use libraries to provide common functionality and gain access to a higher-level and more user-friendly set of tools than that offered by low-level DOM programming. CSS frameworks attempt to provide the same thing for CSS. Whereas CSS resets focus on the specific challenge of creating a baseline style across all browsers, CSS frameworks have the much more ambitious goal of providing reusable core CSS styles for typography, layout, and other design features.

Before looking at popular frameworks in detail, let's consider common arguments in favor of and against CSS frameworks as a whole.

For and Against CSS Frameworks

CSS frameworks offer many real-world benefits, including:

- The ability to reuse code in different projects, rather than crafting layout CSS and HTML individually for each project from scratch
- Shorter development timelines, as a result of code reuse

- Built-in cross-browser layout compatibility—like JavaScript libraries, CSS frameworks are built with browser differences in mind

- Easy implementation of complex, grid-based layouts

Common criticisms of CSS frameworks include the suggestion that because frameworks typically comprise several CSS files, they may harm site performance, as well as the notion that frameworks can lead to a "cookie cutter" approach to page markup and design. The first objection can be addressed by amalgamating and compressing files, but the second is harder to get around. Respected web developer and author Jeremy Keith recently commented on the issue using the example of Blueprint, a popular CSS framework:

> *I don't see myself using Blueprint. It just seems too restrictive for use in a real-world project. Maybe if I'm building a grid-based layout that's precisely 960 pixels wide it could save me some time, but I'm mostly reminded of the quote apocryphally attributed to Henry Ford about the Model T: The customer can have any color he wants so long as it's black.*

> —**www.adactio.com/journal/1332**

There's also quite a bit of debate about using a grid-based approach—a pillar of page layout in print design—in the fluid world of web design. Jason Santa Maria, a highly regarded web and print designer, frames the problem this way:

> *For a long time we've been looking at web design through the lens of print design, and while some of the traditional design practices can make the jump to the screen, some cannot. The screen brings with it different kinds of challenges for visual design, some of which occur exclusively in interactive media. It's unrealistic to think our old methods can fill in all the gaps, but new interaction patterns and visual languages emerge everyday.*

> —**www.jasonsantamaria.com/articles/whats-golden**

All the concerns I've mentioned are worth consideration, but the biggest potential problem with CSS frameworks—especially grid-based frameworks—is that they enforce the use of specific markup to achieve certain layout effects rather than genuinely separating markup from presentation. They also tend to use non-semantic `class` and `id` values such as `grid_18` and `container_12` as part of their markup.

Still, regardless of your position on using CSS frameworks for production code, they are a very popular and highly efficient method of prototyping, so even if you choose not to use them for production code, they're well worth exploring for prototyping alone.

Common Frameworks and Their Uses

Let's take a quick look at some of the most common frameworks and their specific uses.

Blueprint
www.blueprintcss.org

Originally developed by Christian Montoya and now maintained by a strong open-source community, Blueprint is one of the earliest and most well known CSS frameworks. It features a CSS reset, typographic support for font sizing and baselines (helping designers create "vertical rhythms" of text), grid-based layouts, form element styling, and print styles support. It also includes a web-based grid layout builder for WYSIWYG-style grid layout development, which is very useful for prototyping if nothing else. Blueprint is designed for all modern browsers, including IE 6 and higher.

Potential problems with Blueprint include its lack of real support for elastic or fluid style layouts (though there is a plug-in for creating these kinds of layouts), as well as its completely non-semantic naming scheme for classes (it uses names like `push-12` and `prepend-8`).

YAML
www.yaml.de/en

Yet Another Multicolumn Layout (YAML) (which is not to be confused with "YAML Ain't Markup Language," a data serialization language similar to JSON) is another popular mature CSS framework. YAML is widely considered to have better support for elastic and fluid layouts than Blueprint, though it lacks Blueprint's support for sophisticated typographic styling. It also has a visual layout builder, and supports all contemporary browsers from IE 5 up.

YAML has wide support among CMS and blogging systems like WordPress, Joomla, Drupal, and Expression Engine.

YUI Library CSS Tools
developer.yahoo.com/yui

Yahoo's User Interface library, which we touched on briefly in Chapter 5, is much more than a CSS framework—it's really more like the frameworks traditionally used for desktop application development. The library features several CSS tools, including a CSS browser reset, support for sophisticated grid-based layouts (with a visual grid builder), and typographical support. If you are already using YUI for its JavaScript features, it is well worth considering as a CSS framework.

Other Frameworks

There are many other frameworks with their own strengths and weaknesses. Two particularly well-known ones are the 960 Grid System (**www.960.gs**), a framework with visual tools for building grid layouts based on a 960px width, and emastic (**code.google.com/p/emastic**), which provides fluid and fixed layouts, along with typography.

Many organizations also build their own frameworks based on their particular needs; this brief selection is intended to give you an overall a sense of the kinds of frameworks available.

The Wrap

Whether you approve of them wholeheartedly or maintain some reservations, CSS resets have taken root as a common development practice. If you decide that your next project does call for a reset, they're easy to find. If you're using a CSS framework, it will almost certainly come with a reset of its own, and if you're not, there are many popular third-party resets available—not to mention that developing your own is not particularly difficult or time consuming.

CSS frameworks are also extending our notions of what we can easily accomplish with style sheets, promising greater productivity for developers who use them, as well as access to sophisticated typographical styling and grid-based layouts.

They're also controversial, and rightly so. CSS frameworks are based on the idea that markup should be built around an element's position on a page, rather than around the element's content. In that way, the non-semantic, deeply nested markup produced by these frameworks harkens back to the bad old days of table-based layouts. As a consequence, many experienced and thoughtful web developers are less than enamored of frameworks, especially when it comes to grids. Whether or not you should use them depends, as always, on the parameters of your particular projects.

On the other hand, even if you're quite opposed to using frameworks on live sites, they're hugely helpful for rapid prototyping, so you'll probably want to check them out for this purpose alone. All the frameworks mentioned here have strong communities, excellent documentation, and many example files, so you'll find it easy to get a sense of whether a specific framework will solve the problems you face.

And now it's time to move beyond the foundations of web development and begin to explore even newer—and more controversial—techniques and developments, beginning with Chapter 11's in-depth discussion of HTML5.

Part III

Real-World Development

HTML5

What is HTML5?

As we saw in Part I of this book, by around 2000, most major forces in the web development community considered XHTML to be the future of HTML. Much of the first two editions of Jeffrey Zeldman's groundbreaking *Designing with Web Standards*, for example, focus on XHTML and pay little attention to HTML. But even though many developers, myself included, expected XHTML to be *the* future of HTML and accordingly adopted XHTML syntax, browser support for XHTML was slow in coming. In particular, browser support for XHTML 2—the W3C's planned successor to HTML/XHTML—was almost nonexistent, and the W3C has recently ended the development of XHTML 2. As a result, web markup languages stagnated for several years.

In the meantime, revolutionary changes were occurring on the web. The widespread adoption of broadband brought fast connections to many web users, and as a result, streaming audio and video became increasingly commonplace. The rise of blogging brought the concept of user-generated web content to the mainstream. Faster computers and browsers, combined with Microsoft's innovative XMLHttpRequest, made web applications—or "web apps"—a reality.

The web was no longer made up of static pages alone. Applications such as Gmail, Google Maps, and countless others brought sophisticated, desktop-style functionality to the web browser—functionality exemplified by apps such as 280 Slides (**www.280slides.com**), a rich, entirely browser-based presentation application, and Mozilla Lab's Bespin code editor (**bespin.mozilla.com**).

HTML, however, remained rooted in the concept of a web page—which isn't entirely surprising, given that it began life as a document markup language. Meanwhile, the W3C continued its work on XHTML 2, but its work was criticized by many developers and browser-makers as insufficiently attuned to the needs of real-world web development. In 2004, Mozilla and Opera jointly presented the W3C with a more pragmatic proposal for the future of HTML. As the History section of the current HTML5 specification notes, their proposal was "rejected on the grounds that the proposal conflicted with the previously chosen direction for the Web's evolution" (**www.w3.org/TR/HTML5/ introduction.html#history-0**).

In response to this assessment, employees of Apple, Opera, and Mozilla formed an open consortium to address concerns about this "chosen direction" and to develop an alternative specification for the future of HTML. (Microsoft employees declined to participate, citing concerns about the consortium's intellectual property policy.) Thus was born the "Web Hypertext Application Technology Working Group," or WHATWG. WHATWG's specification, originally called "Web Applications 1.0," continued to evolve, and in 2007, the W3C adopted it as the basis for a new version of HTML to be called HTML5.

As of mid 2009, with the formal termination of the W3C's XHTML 2 working group, HTML5 stands as the likeliest future of HTML. However, some concerns about HTML5 remain, including:

- Its lack of extensibility. As was the case with HTML4, HTML5 provides no way to extend its semantics outside of the development of an entirely new version of HTML.

- Its lack of integration with other web technologies, such as RDFa.

- Its perceived over-emphasis on documenting current browser behavior, rather than on the future of the web.

As a result, the current HTML5 specification will almost certainly undergo significant change before it is finalized. However, it also should be noted that there is considerable support for the HTML5 project among web developers, browser makers, and the W3C. In this chapter, we'll focus on aspects of HTML5 that are already supported in browsers—and that are least likely to change.

Key Features of HTML5

HTML5 is designed to be as useful as possible in actual web development practice. It is meant to be evolutionary (rather than revolutionary, like XHTML 2), to be backward compatible with older versions of HTML and older browsers, and to solve real-world problems.

The WHATWG's HTML5 project encompasses much more than the syntax and semantics of a markup language. In this chapter, we'll focus primarily on HTML5's syntax and semantics, but it's worthwhile to take a moment to get a sense of the significance and scope of the HTML5 project. The following are some of the areas the project covers, a few of which have subsequently been spun out into their own specifications:

Error Handling

HTML5 aims to standardize error handling so that all browsers respond to errors in HTML5 markup in the same way. This is a very significant step away from XHTML's XML-based error handling.

The canvas Element

First implemented in Safari, the **canvas** element (which we look at in detail in Chapter 16) is a two-dimensional drawing context that lets developers use JavaScript to render lines, shapes, curves, and other graphical objects in a web page or application.

Local Storage

New in HTML5, this feature lets browsers securely store and access arbitrary amounts of data on the client, which lets web applications run even when a user isn't connected to the web, and improves performance. Essentially, this is like a much more powerful version of cookies.

"Threaded" JavaScript with Web Workers

JavaScript is a single-thread environment, which means that when a computationally intense script is running, a page is essentially unresponsive to user input. There are methods of using timers to simulate the concept of "threads," a feature of most modern programming languages that allows functions to execute in parallel, but these methods can be difficult to use. HTML5 originally introduced the concept of "web workers" (a somewhat confusing name), which is now its own W3C specification. A web worker is a thread or function that can run independently of other functions, allowing for more than one JavaScript function to run at a time or for time-intensive functions to run without disrupting the responsiveness of a page.

Multimedia Support

HTML5 foresees native support of video and audio in the browser, via the new video and audio elements, which we'll take a look at a little later in this chapter.

Location-Aware Web Applications with Geolocation

Now its own specification, and with implementations in Firefox 3.5, betas of Opera 10, and Safari in the iPhone 3.0 version, the W3 Geolocation API, originally part of HTML5, allows developers to query the browser for the user's location. This capability makes possible a huge range of location-aware services that have until now been possible only with native applications on some mobile platforms.

User-Editable Pages

Through its `contenteditable`, `draggable`, and `spellcheck` attributes, HTML5 makes it much easier for users to edit web pages, with far less work by developers.

As you can see, HTML5 is a huge undertaking, and there's a great deal more to it than this brief look reveals. But many of the features discussed here and in the rest of this chapter are usable in one or more current browsers; many commercial developers, including Google, already use aspects of HTML5 today. Perhaps even more importantly, HTML5 has the support of browser developers—something XHTML 2 never received. As a result, it seems likely that many of the false steps of XHTML 2 won't be repeated with HTML5.

Differences from HTML4

To get into the details of HTML5, let's begin by taking a look at how it differs from HTML4.

While HTML5 is designed to be backward compatible with HTML4, it actually has two "flavors" of syntax—an HTML syntax and an XHTML syntax—so you can continue to use HTML5 with whichever syntax you're most comfortable with.

HTML5 also allows developers to use two XML languages—MathML, a markup language for mathematics, and SVG, a markup language for vector graphics we'll cover in the last chapter of this section—directly within HTML markup.

Additionally, HTML5 introduces several new HTML elements, the most useful of which are detailed in the "Headers, Footers, Sections, and other New Structural Elements in HTML5" section of this chapter. Some of the characteristics of current HTML elements have also changed in HTML5. Anchor elements (`<a>`), for example, can now contain any other elements, not just inline elements as is the case with HTML4 and XHTML 1. So it's now possible to link, say, the entire header of a page to a URL simply by putting it within an anchor element. As you might expect, some elements deprecated in earlier versions of HTML, such as `font`, `center`, `u`, and non-`iframe` frames, are not part of HTML5, though other elements that might be considered presentational, such as `<i>`, remain in the language. The specification also includes a number of changes to the DOM, and much more besides.

When it comes to everyday implications for developers, here are some of the most significant changes you'll see in HTML5.

Declaring a *DOCTYPE*

Described in the specification as a "mostly useless, but required" header, a **DOCTYPE** is required in HTML5 documents, mostly to ensure compatibility with older browsers that respond to missing **DOCTYPE**s by rendering such pages in "quirks" or "non-standards" modes. The required **DOCTYPE** is about as simple as it can be. At the top of an HTML5 document we simply use the following:

```
<!DOCTYPE HTML>
```

The **DOCTYPE** is case-insensitive—it can be uppercase, lowercase, or a mix of cases.

Headers, Footers, Sections, and other New Structural Elements in HTML5

As we've mentioned, HTML5 introduces many new elements. In the rest of this chapter, we'll look at several new structural elements of HTML5, along with elements related to embedded content, such as video and audio.

The logic of the new structural elements in HTML5 comes from research into common ways in which current web documents are marked up. Some of the most common `class` and `id` values and most commonly used "patterns" of markup that web developers will instantly recognize include "header," "footer," and "nav" (or some other variation of the term "navigation"). HTML5 uses many of these common patterns and terms for new elements.

header

Many web pages include an area at the top of the page that displays identifying information about the page and site, often including an organization's logo and name, and often also navigation, for example, the different subsections of the site. HTML5 introduces a new element, **header**, for this type of content—though in HTML5, header elements don't have to appear at the top of a page, as we'll see in a moment.

Header elements are governed by a number of syntax rules: They must contain at least one heading (**h1** to **h6**) and must not contain a **section** element, another **header** element, or a **footer** element. Unfortunately, the **nav** element is a kind of section, so the header can't contain **nav** elements. This is a significant challenge in the real world, as many page headers contain navigation systems. Although the most recent editors' draft of the HTML5 specification has relaxed this requirement, as of this writing, the current official draft specification still prevents **nav** elements from being contained within a header. It's to be hoped that the relaxation of this constraint will become a permanent part of the HTML5 specification.

Content Elements

HTML4 and XHTML 1.x offer few ways of grouping together the content of a page. There's the **p** element for paragraphs, but for larger logical chunks of information—chapters, for example—we must use **div**s. And, as we saw in Chapter 4, a **div** is simply a block container with no intrinsic semantic connotations. HTML5 introduces several elements that allow developers to group and semantically identify content.

section

Paragraphs of information are typically grouped together into larger sections, such as a book chapter, a magazine or newspaper article, or a blog post. HTML5 provides the **<section>** element for grouping together content—paragraphs, images, headings, and so on—to form a larger logical unit.

section elements may contain a **header** and a **footer**, and indeed can contain any element that can be contained inside the body of an HTML5 document. They can also include more specific information, or metadata, about a section using the class or id attribute as appropriate. For example, an academic paper often includes an abstract, so we could mark that up as **<section id="abstract">**. A book usually has many chapters, so we'd likely mark up chapters using **<section class="chapter">**.

The **section** element is not designed to be a replacement for the **div** element, which is still part of HTML5; **section** elements should only be used when they're semantically appropriate. For other forms of content groupings, **div** is still the appropriate element to use in HTML5.

article

HTML5 also offers specific types of sections, one of which is the `article`. Articles are sections that can logically exist independently from the page in which they occur. For example, a single page on a newspaper or magazine website might contain several independent articles. By contrast, the chapters of a novel marked up as a single HTML document do not stand independently from the containing page, and so are more appropriately marked up as `section`, rather than `article`, elements. Other forms of content that might be marked up with the `article` element include blog posts, dictionary and encyclopedia entries, and short stories.

Headings in *section* and *article* Elements

HTML4 headings have a significant limitation: there can be, at most, six levels of headings within a given document. There are certainly documents for which this is an unrealistic number: documents such as articles of legislation often require many more levels than six, and heading levels are fundamentally important to the nature of legislation (they are used in legal citation).

HTML5 addresses this deficiency by allowing (and encouraging) each section to begin numbering its headings from level 1 and "strongly encouraging" that each section be associated with a single heading. This single heading should either be an `h1` (that is, each section, no matter how deeply nested within other sections begins with a heading of level 1), or the level of the single heading of each section should match the level of nesting of the section. This is outlined in the specification at **www.whatwg.org/specs/web-apps/current-work/#headings-and-sections**.

As you can see, HTML5 offers a much more sophisticated (and, arguably, overly complex) document structuring model than HTML4. In HTML4, a single parent element—usually the `body` or a `div`—typically contains headings and paragraphs as its direct children. The structure of such documents is revealed only by its numbered headings. In HTML5's sectioning model, it's really the nesting of `section` elements, rather than heading levels, that reveals the structure of the document.

Here's what the structure of this chapter might well look like in HTML4:

```
<body>

<h1>HTML5</h1>

<h2>What is HTML5?</h2>

<h3>Key features of HTML5</h3>

<p>As we saw in Part I of this book, by around 2000, most
major forces in the web development community considered
XHTML to be the future of HTML. Much of the


...
</p>

</body>
```

In HTML5, each heading is associated with a section, and we can explicitly reveal the document's structure via the nesting of these sections. Here's how the same document might be marked up in HTML5:

```
<body>

  <h1>HTML5</h1>

  <section>
    <h1>What is HTML5?</h1>
    <section>
      <h1>Key features of HTML5</h1>

      <p>As we saw in Part I of this book, by around 2000,
      most major forces in the web development community
      considered XHTML to be the future of HTML. Much of
      the ... </p>
    </section>
  </section>

  ...

</body>
```

A Tale of Two Models

What's the difference between the two heading-level models—and more importantly, why have two at all?

First, a significant reason for the new model is to enable more than six levels of headings. It closely matches XHTML 2's model, in which there is only one heading element (h), and in which heading levels are marked solely by the use of the section element, with each nested section increasing the heading level by one.

But why have another model that matches HTML4's heading model? Some browsers—particularly screen readers like JAWS, which are used by people with visual impairments to access the web—use heading levels to create outlines of the content, making pages more easily navigable. Screen readers tend to be developed slowly, and user upgrade rates are correspondingly gradual, so many visually impaired web users will probably lack access to HTML5 support for the foreseeable future. As a result, the widespread adoption of the XHTML 2–style heading-level model could present significant challenges for these users.

Is one of these approaches to be preferred? There's considerable debate about the merits of the first (h1-only) method and about its impact on accessibility. This method tends to make styling with CSS somewhat more complicated, as it requires the use of descendent or child selectors like "`section section section h1`" rather than a simple selector such as h4, and it also makes accessing page elements using JavaScript more difficult. Neither approach is discouraged, so I recommend using the latter model (multiple numbered heading levels) for now provided that the nesting level of sections matches the number of their headings.

Or, we can simply continue to number headings as we would in HTML4, as if the section elements weren't there:

```
<body>

  <h1>HTML5</h1>

  <section>
    <h2>What is HTML5?</h2>
    <section>
      <h3>Key features of HTML5</h3>

      <p>As we saw in Part I of this book, by around 2000,
      most major forces in the web development community
      considered XHTML to be the future of HTML. Much of
      the ... </p>
    </section>
  </section>

  ...

</body>
```

nav

Just as "header" (or some variation of that term) is one of the most commonly used class and id names in HTML, "navigation" (or some variation, such as "nav") is similarly popular. HTML5 introduces the **nav** element, to mark up "a section of a page that links to other pages or to parts within the page." The specification continues, explaining the element is not intended to be used to mark up *all* groups of links on a page: "only sections that consist of primary navigation blocks are appropriate for the **nav** element."

One drawback of the **nav** element is that developers often mark up navigation in HTML4 and XHTML as a list of links—after all, site and page navigation is usually made up of a list of links. Because **nav** is a kind of *section*, however, if we wish to continue using lists for navigation markup, we must wrap our lists in a **nav** element. For example, we may currently use something like the following for our navigation:

```
<ul id="site-navigation">
        <li class="first"><a href=
        "http://www.webdirections.org/" title=
        "Back to the home page">Home</a></li>
        <li><a href="http://www.webdirections.org/resources"
        title="Slides and podcasts from past events">
        Resources</a></li>
        <li><a href="http://www.webdirections.org/events"
        title="Future and past conferences">Events</a></li>
</ul>
```

To continue using this list for our navigation links in HTML5, we'd wrap the whole thing in the **nav** element, like this:

```
<nav>
<ul id="site-navigation">
        <li class="first"><a href=
        "http://www.webdirections.org/" title="Back to the
        home page">Home</a></li>
        <li><a href="http://www.webdirections.org/resources"
        title="Slides and podcasts from past events">
        Resources</a></li>
        <li><a href="http://www.webdirections.org/events"
        title="Future and past conferences">Events</a></li>
</ul>
</nav>
```

aside

Articles and stories often feature sidebars, which contain related secondary content. HTML5 calls these "asides" and provides the **aside** element for marking up this kind of content. We'll see asides, along with other new HTML5 elements, in action in a moment.

figure

HTML4 offers a single way to include images in markup, and CSS provides **background-image** and other ways of adding images as decoration, but not as part of the document itself. In real life, however, images appear in documents in different ways and for different reasons and are often accompanied by captions or descriptions. HTML5 provides the `figure` element for these kinds of images.

A figure in a book or article often includes an image and a caption. Together, the image and caption comprise a `figure` element in HTML5 (though the `caption` element is not technically required.) In HTML4, we'd likely mark up this sort of content as follows:

```
<div class="figure">
<img src="images/src.png" alt="the image itself"/>
<span class="caption">This is the caption for the
image</span>
</div>
```

In HTML5, we can use the `figure` element in place of the `div`, and then go a step further using the `legend` element—which is used in HTML4 to caption form elements—in place of the `span` element in our example. Rather than invent a new element for this purpose, HTML5 reuses an existing element of HTML with similar semantics. Putting these components together, our HTML 4 example could be marked up in HTML5 using the following markup:

```
<figure>
<img src="images/src.png" alt="the image itself"/>
<legend>This is the caption for the image</legend>
</figure>
```

The order of `legend` and `image` can also be reversed.

Somewhat confusingly, the `figure` element can in fact be used for more than just images. The specification states that the element is for content that is "self-contained and is typically referenced as a single unit from the main flow of the document." It can thus be used to mark up illustrations, diagrams, photos, code listings, and so on, that are referred to from the main content of the document but that could, without affecting the flow of the document, be moved away from that primary content, such as to the side of the page, to dedicated pages, or to an appendix.

footer

Another common markup and page design pattern is a page footer, which typically contains fine-print content such as copyright notices, privacy policies, contact details, and so on. As you might guess, HTML5 introduces a **footer** element for this kind of content. Just as **header**s can be used in places other than the top of a document, **footer**s don't appear only at a document's end—they may appear at the end of sections or articles as well. Blog posts often conclude with details such as the author's name, the date and time of publication, tags for the post, and so on, and in HTML can all be sensibly marked up in a **footer** element.

Footers also need not appear at the very end of their containing element—for example, in a blog post or article, they might be followed by comments. For some time, the HTML5 specification stated that **footer** elements could not contain headings, **header** elements, **section**s, or other **footer**s, which was something of a problem, since many web page footers include detailed content structures. Happily, these restrictions have been lifted in the current and (we hope) final draft of HTML5.

An Example HTML5 document

Even if you have not yet used the new elements of HTML5, the concepts behind them will be familiar to you from HTML4 or XHTML. Let's take a look at a fairly standard web page design and see how these new elements might be used.

At the top of figure **11.1** is a **header** element. In figure **11.2**, we see that within the **header** is also a **nav** element for site-level navigation.

11.1
A perfectly ordinary-looking page—but beneath its smooth surface lurks HTML5

11.2
The header of our HTML5 page

The markup for this element looks like this:

```
<header>
  <h1><a href="http://www.webdirections.org/"
  class="logo">Web Directions</a></h1>

  <nav>
    <ul>
      <li id="skip-link"><a href="#content">
      Skip to the content</a></li>
      <li class="first"><a href="http://www.webdirections.
      org/" title="Back to the home page">Home</a></li>
      <li><a href="http://www.webdirections.org/resources"
      title="Slides and podcasts from past events"
      >Resources</a></li>
      <li><a href="http://www.webdirections.org/events"
      title="Future and past conferences">Events</a></li>
      <li><a href="http://jobs.webdirections.org"
      title="Jobs for web professionals">Jobs</a></li>
      <li><a href="http://www.webdirections.org/blog"
      title="Morning coffee for web workers">Blog</a></li>
      <li><a href="http://www.webdirections.org/about"
      title="The people and thoughts behind Web
      Directions">About</a></li>
      <li><a href="http://www.webdirections.org/contact"
      title="Email, phone or write to us">Contact</a></li>
    </ul>
  </nav>

    <div id="upcoming-events">
      <h2>Upcoming events</h2>
      <ul>
        <li><a href="http://south09.webdirections.org/"
        >Sydney: Web Directions Workshops</a> 6-7 Oct</li>
        <li><a href="http://south09.webdirections.org/"
        >Sydney: Web Directions South 2009</a>
        8-9 Oct</li>
      </ul>
    </div> <!-- upcoming events -->

</header>
```

This markup should be nearly self-explanatory. One thing worth noting is that our upcoming events are in a `div`, not a `section`, because headers cannot have sections as descendents. (Remember, too, that we need at least one heading in a `header` element.)

The main content of the page, between the `header` and the `footer`, is made up of two parts: the content of the page, which will be on the left, and a collection of tools and navigation aids, which will be on the right. The content on the left can be sensibly marked up as a `section`, as it is "a thematic grouping of content." The content on the right really doesn't conform to that definition, so it probably should be marked up as a `div` element, as it would be in HTML4.

Turning to the content in figure 11.1, we can see a pie chart with a caption. We know that HTML5 has the `figure` element for this kind of content, which we'd mark up like this:

```
<figure>
  <img src="http://spreadsheets...." alt=
  "markup language use"/>
  <legend>which HTML variant do responders use?</legend>
</figure>
```

The main text of this section [**11.3**] includes two separate sections.

Each section comprises a heading and one or more paragraphs. Although sections can contain headers, the structure of these sections is simple, and the header would only be there to contain a single heading, so in this case we won't wrap the headings in a header.

In more complex sections of a page, such as in the content of a blog post, the `header` element may be appropriate. In figure **11.4**, a specific post at the site has not only a title heading, but also category, author, date, and other information. This would be sensibly marked up inside a `header` element inside the `section` element. What's more, since the section itself is an article that could be meaningfully reproduced elsewhere as a whole, this post would be most appropriately marked up as an `article`. Meanwhile, the sections in our full-page example are part of a larger whole, and as such aren't appropriately marked up as `article`s.

11.3
The main content of our HTML5 page

Markup

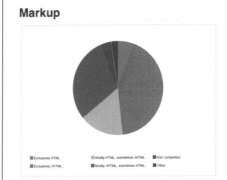

▪ Exclusively HTML.   ▪ Mostly HTML, sometimes XHTML   ▪ Non completed
▪ Exclusively XHTML   ▪ Mostly XHTML, sometimes HTML   ▪ Other

which HTML variant do responders use?

Presentational HTML

In a related question, only 30% of respondents replied that they used no presentational HTML. The width and height attributes at 23% and 19% are still the most widely used presentational HTML – a throwback to the days of slower networks and browsers when adding these attributes to image elements helped browsers layout pages before images had been downloaded and their dimensions could be calculated. The border attribute is also still widely used – most likely for images inside link elements. By default in earlier browsers images inside links were styled with a blue border that was most commonly supressed using the border attribute. 10% of developers still use the center element, reflecting perhaps some ongoing confusion about the ways in which CSS can be used to center text (text–align: center), or blocks inside their parent elements (left and right margins of "auto").

[it's] still a little concerning that nearly 6% of respondents use the font element, and 18% and 15% of respondents respectively still use the b and i elements.

It's both gratifying, but still a little concerning that nearly 6% of respondents use the font element, and 18% and 15% of respondents respectively still use the b and i elements.

So, it's clear that presentational HTML is on the wane, but with up to nearly quarter of respondents using some form of presentational HTML, we'll be seeing it's use for some time yet it would appear.

Extended Semantics

The last two questions in this section aimed to see the extent to which respondents are using "semantic" technologies such as microformats and RDFa in their markup.

Microformats have been around in one form or another since 2003, and build on underlying ideas and practices in markup which go back quite a bit further. RDFa is a much more recent technology. Microformats and RDFa differ in a number of important ways, not least that while RDFa is a W3C "standard", microformats work entirely within the framework of existing HTML standards, and are developed outside the auspices of a recognized organization like the IETF or W3C.

Over a third of respondents answered that they do use microformats in their markup – a surprisingly high number for even such a sample as this. A little under 20% answered "what are microformats", giving around 80% awareness of the technology.

Not surprisingly, only about a tenth as many respondents answered that they use RDFa (3.4%), and nearly half (44%) that they didn't know what RDFa is.

After several years of advocacy and development by a reasonably small but diligent and high profile community, microformats seem to be established among early adopters. While it is early days, RDFa will require it would seem, a similar community and effort to become equally established.

Australia's Government 2.0 taskforce

IN: BLOG | BY: JOHN | JUNE 22, 2009 | EDIT | ☺ LEAVE A RESPONSE

 Via Slattery's Watch, news of the just launched Australian Federal Government's "Government 2.0 Taskforce", which (a wordpress blog no less!). From the site:

Its work falls into two streams. The first relates to increasing the openness of government through making public sector information more widely available to promote transparency, innovation and value adding to government information.

11.4
A section in our HTML5 site

The first of these sections contains a "pull quote," which can be marked up as an **aside** element. So the markup for the first section in our full-page example would look something like this:

```
<section>
<h1 id="presentational-html">Presentational HTML</h1>

<aside>[It's] still a little concerning that nearly
6% of respondents use the font element, while 18% and
15% of respondents respectively still use the b and i
elements.</aside>
<p>In a related question, only 30% of respondents replied
that they used no presentational HTML. The width and
height attributes at 23% and 19% are still the most widely
used presentational ...</p>
</section>
```

We've chosen to mark up the heading as a level 1, but it would equally be appropriate to mark it up as a level 3, since the section is nested inside the body, and then inside the section that contains the main content of the page—in other words, it's nested three levels deep.

On the right of the content section are tools such as the search field, navigational aids such as the tag cloud, and links to related material. As noted earlier, this doesn't really conform to the definition of a section, and so the **div** element remains the most appropriate way of marking it up. However, the tag cloud is primarily a way of navigating through a large amount of information, so it would make sense to mark this up using a **nav** element.

At the bottom of the page, we have what most of us will recognize as a footer [11.1]. But we have a problem. HTML5 footers can't contain sections or headings. Our "footer" contains elements that would be best marked up as headings, and quite possibly sections as well, so rather than marking up the content that *appears* to be a footer using a footer element, we'll reserve that element for the "fine print" content:

```
<footer>
  <p>&copy; 2008-2009 Web Directions....</p>
</footer>
```

As you can see, HTML5 provides these new elements for very commonly used markup patterns, which will for the most part be familiar to developers with experience marking up web documents. Even those with limited experience of markup should find most if not all of these elements conceptually familiar from years if not decades of reading.

The key to good HTML5 markup, just as it is to more traditional HTML markup, is to understand the semantics of the document you are marking up, and using the most appropriate elements (and attributes) for this markup. HTML5 extends the range of semantics developers can use to mark up their content, and these extended offerings are based in part on extensive research on existing common web design and markup patterns.

Video, Audio, and Other Embedded Content in HTML5

Embedded content, including video and audio, has never been one of HTML's strong points. The nonstandard **embed** element has slowly been replaced by the **object** element of HTML4, though it continues to be widely used for embedding all kinds of plug-in–based content. One drawback of the **object** element is its generic nature. It's designed for embedding anything: an image, Flash or Silverlight content, even other HTML documents, and, of course, audio and video. Using a single element for all embedded content makes it difficult for browsers to offer playback controls that are specific to video or audio content, and to provide other media-specific features (such as a placeholder image that makes sense in the case of video, but less so for other kinds of content).

The **embed** and **object** elements are both designed for content rendered by plug-ins such as Flash. In HTML5, video and audio get their own elements: **video** and **audio**, respectively. Unlike **embed** and **object**, these elements allow for:

- Native browser controls, such as play and pause
- Multiple source files, allowing different resources to be fetched depending on browser support for different video or audio formats, or media queries

In addition, like **object** (but unlike **embed**), **video** and **audio** elements make it easy to add "fallback" content for browsers that don't support the element.

So, why have both the **embed** and **object** element been included in HTML5, particularly as **embed** has never been, until now, a standardized part of **any** HTML specification? The authors of the HTML5 specification have decided that since **embed** is almost as widely used as the **object** element, it should be standardized. Regardless of the merits of that argument, I'd suggest using the **object** element for plug-in content that is not strictly video or audio (Flash-based interactive elements, for example), and the **video** and **audio** elements for video and audio content, along with a fallback strategy for browsers that don't support these elements.

Video

The developers of HTML5 initially planned to specify a standard video format, or *codec* ("coder-decoder"), that HTML5–supporting browsers would all support, thus enabling plug-in–free ("native") video playback in these browsers. Unfortunately, due to concerns from browser developers about the patent status of almost every video format, no consensus could be reached regarding such a format or formats. As a result, even though the **video** element is part of HTML5, no specific standard video format is part of the specification. This is a concern for some developers, but historically, the HTML specification has *never* specified which image formats browsers should support. At the time of this writing, Firefox 3.5 has native support for the Ogg Theora codec, but other browsers require the appropriate plug-in to play back video content (while Firefox 3.5 requires a plug-in to play content in formats other than Ogg). All other browsers require plug-ins for playing video.

The Problem with Codecs

A codec is software for compressing and decompressing signals, such as video and audio. Different codecs have different strengths and weaknesses. Most significantly for the web, nearly all modern codecs are "patent encumbered," which means that browser developers would have to pay a royalty fee to one or more patent owners to use them in their code base. This is a significant challenge, particularly for open source browsers. Due to licensing structures associated with these browsers, the use of patented technology may not be legally possible, let alone feasible.

There are older, arguably patent-unencumbered codecs for audio and video, most notably Ogg Vorbis and Ogg Theora, which Firefox 3.5 supports natively. Other browser developers, and some high-profile video sites such as YouTube, are reluctant to embrace these formats for several reasons. These codecs can result in much larger files than other, newer codecs, and some organizations are wary of "submarine" patents that might apply to these formats but that have not yet been asserted by their owners. As a consequence, HTML5 does not presently specify particular codecs for video or audio, nor does it seem likely to do so in the future.

Even though there's no standard video format that we can rely on all browsers to support, the `video` element of HTML5 is still a significant step forward. Let's put it into practice.

There are two ways we can specify the source of the video that the element embeds. A simple way is to use the `src` attribute, with a URL that identifies the video file: `<video src="path/to/src.ogg"></video>`.

Of course, we may well want to provide any number of different video formats to give a browser the best chance of successfully playing the video content. We can do this using `source` elements inside the `video` element. By themselves, `source` elements do nothing, but inside a `video` element, they specify one or more source files for the browser to display. (Note that if the `video` element has a `src` attribute, the `source` elements are ignored.)

source elements also specify their source file using a src attribute. In addition, we can use a mimetype attribute to tell the browser what file format we're using (for example, MP4).

Like link elements, source elements may take a media attribute with a media query value, to specify different sources for different media. For example, we might offer a low-resolution encoding for low-resolution screens, a 16:9 format video for devices with a 16:9 aspect ratio, and so on. But the src attribute of a source element is all that's actually required. (We'll cover media queries in detail in Chapter 14.)

In the following example, we've provided two options: the widely supported mp4 format and the Ogg format:

```
<video>
  <source src="path/to/source.mp4" type="video/mp4">
  <source src="path/to/source.ogg" type="video/ogg">
</video>
```

Where more than one source element is provided, a browser will use the first one whose content type it supports and will ignore the rest.

The video element also includes many attributes that provide the kind of functionality previously available only via plug-ins, such as autoplaying, looping, and the drawing of controls. The element can take the following attributes:

- poster—This attribute provides an image to be used while no video is available (for example, while a video is downloading or pre-buffering). It takes a URL of an image, such as a PNG, which can be used, for example, to display the first frame of the video while that video is still loading.

- autoplay—This attribute tells the browser to begin playing the video as soon as possible.

- loop—The loop attribute tells the browser to play the video repeatedly from the beginning.

- controls—This attribute tells the browser to draw its own controls (such as play, pause, and fast-forward) for the video content.

- width and height—These elements specify the respective width and height of the element. The browser can also use the intrinsic dimensions of the video, but it will only be able to determine these after downloading some of the video file, so specifying width and height is recommended.

If we want our video to display an image while loading, to autoplay when loaded, and to provide the user with browser-drawn controls, we'd add these attributes:

```
<video controls autoplay poster="path/to/poster.png">
  <source src="path/to/source.mp4" type="video/mp4">
  <source src="path/to/source.ogg" type="video/ogg">
</video>
```

The autoplay, controls, and loop attributes are all Boolean attributes. We saw earlier that in HTML4, it's optional to provide values for such attributes—so in HTML4, we can specify an autoplay attribute as either autoplay="autoplay", or simply as autoplay. In HTML5, only the first of these forms is valid. In HTML5, where a Boolean attribute is present in the opening tag of an element, the value of the attribute is true. Otherwise, it is false.

Fallback Content

Unlike the empty embed element, but like the object element, the video element can contain content. source elements make up the primary content of the video element, but we can also provide fallback content for browsers that don't support the video element. The simplest way we can do this is to add some text that displays only when the video element isn't supported:

```
<video controls autoplay poster="path/to/poster.png">
  <source src="path/to/source.mp4" type="video/mp4">
  <source src="path/to/source.ogg" type="video/ogg">
<p>This browser doesn't support HTML5 video</p>
</video>
```

Of course, if possible, we should try and use a complementary method for displaying video on older browsers. As we saw in Chapter 3 of this book, the HTML4 approach is to use the object element, and we also know that the `object` element allows for fallback content. So we could use `object` as fallback content to display video in browsers that support it, and we could also use simple fallback text for all other browsers:

```
<video controls autoplay poster="path/to/poster.png">
  <source src="path/to/source.mp4" type="video/mp4">
  <source src="path/to/source.ogg" type="video/ogg">
  <object data="path/to/source.mov">
    <p>This browser doesn't support HTML5 video</p>
  </object>
</video>
```

Audio

HTML5 also has an `audio` element, which is very much like the `video` element—the only significant difference is that the `audio` element lacks a `poster` attribute. Again, the source of the audio is specified either with the `src` attribute or with one or more `source` elements. Fallbacks to the `object` element of HTML4 or text content are specified in the same way, as are `autoplay`, `loop`, and `controls` attributes:

```
<audio controls>
  <source src="path/to/source.mp3" type="audio/mp3">
  <source src="path/to/source.wav" type="video/wave">
  <object data="path/to/source.swf">
    <p>This browser doesn't support audio</p>
  </object>
</audio>
```

Video and Audio Browser Support

In mid 2009, only Firefox 3.5 and Safari 3.1 and higher had support for the `audio` and `video` elements in final versions of the browsers. Firefox's support is presently limited to two audio formats, Ogg Vorbis and WAVE, and one video format, Ogg Theora. In addition, Firefox *requires* that the `audio` or `source` elements have a `type` attribute. Importantly, even if Firefox 3.5 has a plug-in that enables the playback of another format such as QuickTime, the browser *won't* play this content with the **audio** or **video** element, though it *will* play it with the **object** element. Safari's support is broader than Firefox's. If it has a plug-in to play back the content format, it *will* play **video** or **audio** elements in that format.

One noted problem with **video** or **audio** elements in Safari (at least until version 4) is that the browser begins downloading *all* of the content embedded with these elements at once—a behavior that can soak up a lot of bandwidth and affect browser performance. This could be a problem when a large number of **audio** and **video** elements are on a page.

	Firefox 3.5	Safari 3.1	Opera	Internet Explorer
audio element support	Yes (Ogg Vorbis and WAVE only)	Yes	No	No
Native audio playback	Yes (Ogg Vorbis and WAVE)	No	No	No
video element support	Yes (Ogg Theora only)	Yes	No	No
Native video playback	Yes (Ogg Theora)	No	No	No
object element support	Yes	Yes	Yes	Yes

Video and Audio Accessibility

As we move toward a richer web, we must continue to consider accessibility in our design and development practices. The existence of the fallback feature of audio and video is *not* designed as an accessibility feature but as a mechanism that provides multiple ways to embed content and a means of notifying the user when none of these are supported. This simple fallback mechanism is in no way designed to replace methods of providing accessible audio and video via the use of captioning and transcription. (Audio and video captioning and description are beyond the scope of the book, but they are important to consider whenever you use audio- and video-based content.)

HTML5 Support in Browsers

All these new HTML5 features might sound great in theory, but in practice, can we use them in browsers today? By and large, the answer is yes...but a few challenges remain.

IE7 and Earlier Versions of Internet Explorer

In Safari, Firefox, IE8, and Opera, we can style `section`, `aside`, `nav`, and other new elements using CSS. But in IE7 and older, we can't out of the box. These older versions of Internet Explorer simply ignore CSS like this:

```
section {
  color: red
}
```

Even adding classes to the elements—for example, `<section class="section">`—doesn't let us style them in IE7 and older versions. In essence, the new elements are invisible to CSS in these browsers.

Since these browsers are still used by a majority of web users in 2009, and will likely be used by many for some time to come, does this mean we can't use these new elements? Happily, no. We can in fact use and style these elements, though the method we'll use is imperfect. There is a JavaScript workaround for IE7—and a more aggressive approach for IE6 and older versions of IE—if you must support these browsers.

Workarounds for IE

Remy Sharp has developed a JavaScript-based approach that involves nothing more than linking to a small JavaScript file, HTML5.js, available at **remysharp. com/downloads/html5.js**.

This script tricks IE7 into seeing HTML5 elements, and for IE6, replaces the elements with `div`s or `span`s and classes with values that match the name of the HTML5 element that was converted. This dual approach means that for IE6 compatibility, we'll need to replace CSS rules like this one:

```
section {
  color: red
}
```

...with rules like this:

```
section, .section {
  color: red
}
```

Dean Edwards, the man behind the IE7 JavaScript library, has also created a JavaScript library that enables the use of HTML5 features in browsers that don't support HTML5. It's available here: **code.google.com/u/dean.edwards/updates**.

A Caution

JavaScript-based solutions are far from ideal. Many corporate environments disable JavaScript for security purposes, and for site visitors who use IE6 and IE7 without JavaScript, your HTML5 elements will appear unstyled. The JavaScript methods also create considerable complexity when it comes to styling pages if your project requires backward compatibility with IE6.

Validating and Serving HTML5

HTML5 can be validated using an experimental validator at **validator.nu**. (This is presently the only way in which HTML5 can be validated.) Documents that use the XHTML5 syntax can be checked for "wellformedness" using any XML validator.

Confusingly, the two different syntaxes of HTML5 (HTML and XHTML) must be served in two different ways. HTML5 documents that use the HTML syntax must be served with a mimetype of "`text/html`," whereas XHTML syntax documents must be served as "`application/xml`" or "`application/xhtml+xml`." (If XHTML documents are served as "`text/html`," browsers are to treat them as HTML, not as applications of XML, even if they are valid XHTML documents.) For the most part, the distinction won't have any practical impact on developers; browsers will almost certainly treat XHTML5 documents served as "`text/html`" as HTML5 documents.

Should I Be Using HTML5 Today?

It's certainly possible to use HTML5 markup with today's browsers, though there are significant challenges when it comes to Internet Explorer. HTML5 is also a specification in a state of flux, and doubtless some of what you've read in this chapter will be out of date before HTML5 is finalized, despite our focus on the most stable aspects of the specification. As even the developers of HTML5 have stated, HTML5 should be used with caution. That said, HTML5 will become increasingly well supported over the coming years, and as a practicing web developer, you'll want to know how to use it. As the web becomes an increasingly application-based medium, HTML5 will play an ever-more important role, so developers who focus on web applications should investigate HTML5 sooner rather than later.

Furthermore, although we're unlikely to see HTML5 used as the main markup language for highly trafficked sites in the short term, Google's recently announced Wave communications application uses HTML5 extensively— in particular for its application-focused aspects like offline storage—so the language is far more than simply an experimental plaything, even today.

Finally, it's worth noting that HTML5 is unique in terms of its development at the W3C. Most web standards are developed by a small, closed group of experts. The HTML5 development process, however, is much more open, and its developers actively encourage input. For details on how to participate, see **blog.whatwg.org/help-us-review-html5**.

CSS3 and the Future of CSS

CSS Reloaded

The specifications for CSS1 and CSS2 emerged from the World Wide Web Consortium (W3C) in quick succession in the latter half of the 1990s. By the early years of the following decade—and particularly with the 2001 release of IE6—browser makers and web developers had widely adopted and implemented the entirety of the CSS1 specification, along with the positioning aspects of CSS2. Bad development practices such as the use of presentational HTML elements such as <font> and of tables for page layout have nevertheless persisted, but they continue to decline as the message of web standards permeates the web development profession.

After 2001, the browser landscape largely stayed the same for several years. Internet Explorer 6 for Windows—which when released was considered by most to have first-class support for CSS—came to dominate, while Netscape essentially vanished, and Mozilla, Netscape's open-source successor, seemed to flounder. The Mac platform also languished in the early part of the decade. As a result, IE6 became the de facto standard for many developers. Left untouched by Microsoft for several years, IE6 and its bugs became familiar, and workarounds for those bugs became part of the standard web development toolkit. Many websites, designed to be "best viewed in IE6," broke in browsers that supported standards rather than IE6's idiosyncratic way of doing things. Perhaps most discouraging, browser makers stopped implementing new CSS features, while development of the CSS3 standard stagnated.

Innovation on the web, at least in terms of CSS, appeared to be over.

With the release of Apple's Safari in 2003 and Mozilla's Firefox in 2004, coupled with the resurgence of the Mac platform, web users gained access to options other than Internet Explorer on Windows. Both Safari (which was based on the open source KHTML) and Firefox demonstrated a strong support for web standards, and the makers of both browsers had a vested interest in using innovation to challenge Microsoft's dominant browser.

Enter CSS3

The W3C is currently developing two CSS specifications. The first, CSS2.1, is designed to be a "snapshot" of CSS usage and consists of all CSS features that are implemented in all modern browsers at the date of its final publication. Rather than focusing on innovation, this specification provides a stable baseline of features that are available in all major browsers. The second specification, CSS3, is the hub of innovation in the feature set of CSS. Rather than being a single, monolithic standard like CSS1 and CSS2, CSS3 consists of modules, such as the Selectors module and Fonts module, each of which has different editors and authors as well as varying levels of priority and activity. The modular nature of CSS3 means that the W3C can develop parts of the specification independently from the rest, and that it can easily incorporate new modules, such as the recently added CSS Transitions and CSS Transforms modules.

Although the standards process has been improved, significant challenges remain. How can newer browsers support features of CSS3 not supported in

CSS Support Snapshot

You'll find links to complete, up-to-date CSS support references in the Resources section in the back of this book. In the interim, here's a high-level glance at the support you can expect in current browsers as of this printing.

Internet Explorer

Microsoft claims full compliance with CSS2.1 in Internet Explorer 8. Internet Explorer 7 lacks support for some CSS2.1 selectors and a number of properties, notably generated content and several display properties. Internet Explorer 6 lacks support for some CSS2.1 selectors and many properties. No versions of Internet Explorer support CSS3 properties or selectors. Internet Explorer has long supported embedding of Embedded OpenType fonts but does not currently support linking to TrueType fonts.

WebKit/Safari

Apple claims that Safari 4 supports a large subset of CSS2.1 and some parts of CSS3. Support of CSS3 in Safari 4 includes numerous selectors as well as text and box shadows, opacity, transitions, transforms, RGBA color, the border-radius property, gradients, and linking to TrueType fonts.

Mozilla/Firefox

In Firefox 3.5, Mozilla offers CSS2.1 and CSS3 support similar to that of Safari 4. Apple's proposed gradient and transition extensions are not yet supported, but Firefox 3.5 does support most CSS3 selectors, text and box shadows, opacity, transforms, RGBa color, the border-radius property, and linking to TrueType.

Opera 10

Opera continues its tradition of strong standards support with Opera 10. CSS2.1 support is excellent, and CSS3 support in Opera 10 includes linking to TrueType fonts, RGBa and HSLA colors, text shadows, opacity, and many CSS3 selectors.

other browsers (particularly IE6) without breaking the web all over again? How can they responsibly implement experimental, unfinalized CSS features? Is it possible to have the stability of a standards-based web *and* the innovation that browser competition brings? In the rest of this chapter, we'll explore the ways in which a combination of clever standards development, smart browser implementation, and the judicious use of new CSS features by web developers has put to rest the argument that you can't have innovation within the context of standards—and we'll see how to implement designs like the following navigation menu using CSS alone.

12.1

A navigation bar like Apple's, created with CSS3 and HTML (no images), as rendered in Safari 4 in this unenhanced screenshot

To understand what CSS3 is capable of, consider an implementation of the Apple.com navigation bar [**12.1**] that uses no images and no extraneous markup—just a simple list and CSS. In this chapter and the next, we'll cover all the selectors, properties, and other features of CSS required to implement this navigation bar.

Backward and Forward Compatibility "Solved"?

Backward and forward compatibility pose two related but quite different challenges for web developers who want to use features of CSS3. When developing with these features, we want to ensure that users of browsers that *don't* support them still have access to the information and services our sites offer. But we also want to provide an improved experience for users of more capable browsers. As noted in earlier chapters, the principles of "progressive enhancement" (the practice of adding additional sophistication to the appearance of a page for users of modern browsers) and "graceful degradation" (the idea that when a browser doesn't support a feature, the consequences of that lack of support should have as little impact on the user as possible) will be vitally important to the intelligent use of CSS3 features.

The key to meeting these challenges is to be mindful of the consequences of a lack of browser support for the features we elect to use. Testing with browsers that don't support a particular feature will, of course, be an invaluable tactic. But it's even more important to consider, as early as possible in the design phase, what happens to a page's usefulness if a particular feature is missing. The absence of text shadows, for example, can affect the legibility of information on a page [**12.2**, **12.3**].

Here is a heading of level 2

12.2
A heading that relies on a text shadow to maintain legibility.

12.3
The same heading as displayed by a browser that doesn't support text shadows. Always ensure sufficient contrast between text and background colors.

On a related note, we must ensure that if a browser supports a feature in a buggy or otherwise unsatisfactory way, it won't try to use that feature in its rendering of a page. Since the inception of CSS, buggy and incomplete support has caused more problems than the absence of support for a particular feature. The problem of buggy support was initially worsened by the fact that until recently, developers had to choose between using each feature either in all browsers, or in none of them. As we saw in earlier chapters, a cottage industry of hacks and workarounds has grown up to allow developers to hide CSS from individual browsers. (A classic example of this is the box model hack we examined in Chapter 7.) Fortunately, there is now a standardized, widely supported way of targeting specific browsers: *vendor-specific extensions*.

Vendor-Specific Extensions

Vendor-specific extensions are prefixes added to a property name, selector, or other CSS feature. They specify that only browsers that support a particular extension should use the feature to which they're appended. When you are confident that a feature you want to use is well supported in a particular family of browsers, you can use the feature with the appropriate extension, and rest assured that only the specified browser family will try to use the feature. Once a feature has become part of a published CSS standard and a specific browser developer considers their browser's support to be sufficiently robust, the browser will also recognize the feature without the extension. Until then, in order to use such features, developers must explicitly declare which browsers should use them by adding the appropriate extension.

There are three such extensions in common use:

- `-webkit-` for WebKit-based browsers (for example, `-webkit-box-shadow`)
- `-moz-` for Mozilla-based browsers (for example, `-moz-border-radius`)
- `-o-` for Opera-based browsers (for example, `-o-text-overflow`)

In addition, there are three much less commonly used extensions:

- `-ms-` for Internet Explorer
- `-khtml-` for older versions of WebKit and the Konquerer browser for Linux
- `-wap-` from the WAP Consortium

So how does it work in practice? The `border-radius` property of CSS3 enables you to specify whether the corners of an element should have rounded borders; we'll look at the property in more detail shortly. For some time, `border-radius` was well supported in Safari but not nearly so well supported in Mozilla browsers, and not at all by other browsers. If vendor-specific extensions didn't exist, we'd have had to either use `border-radius` in Safari- *and* Mozilla-based browsers—knowing that this feature would look far from sophisticated in Mozilla browsers—or to not use it at all. Because both Mozilla and WebKit browsers support vendor-specific extensions, however, we can specify the `-webkit-` but not the `-moz-` extension, ensuring that the property is used only by WebKit-based browsers. When using vendor-specific extensions, it's best to *also* specify the standard form—in this case, `border-radius`— as well, when such a form exists. For example, in our `border-radius` case, we'd use something like this:

```
p {
  -webkit-border-radius: 1em;
  border-radius: 1em;
}
```

Providing the standard property name ensures that when future browser versions support a feature fully, we won't need to revisit our code. We can rely on the fact the browsers should only support a feature *without* the browser-specific extension once the feature has become standardized and once that browser supports it fully.

Firefox 3 now fully (and correctly) supports `border-radius`, though still only with the `-moz-` extension, and because Firefox 2 has a rapidly diminishing user base, we might now decide to use `border-radius` in Firefox. So, in addition to the `-webkit-` and standard versions, we might choose to add the `-moz-` version:

```
p {
   -webkit-border-radius: 1em;
   -moz-border-radius: 1em;
   border-radius: 1em;
}
```

This will give rounded borders to all paragraphs in any WebKit- or Mozilla-based browser, and in any browsers that support the property once the CSS3 module specifying `border-radius` is finalized in the future—perhaps in Opera in 2010, in Internet Explorer 8.1, or in an entirely new browser.

For developers who missed out on the browser wars of the 1990s, having a simple, standardized way of targeting specific browsers may not seem all that significant. But I'd argue that one reason for the resurgence in CSS innovation is precisely our ability to pick and choose CSS3 properties based on their support in today's browsers.

Now that we've seen how CSS3 is being designed and implemented in browsers in such a way as to be usable by developers today, let's dive into some of these new features of CSS3. Rather than exhaustively cataloging all new features, we'll focus on a number of selectors and properties in CSS3 that have good support in one or more modern browsers: features that are useful *today*. And throughout, we'll focus on progressively enhancing the experience of users with browsers that support advanced features, while ensuring that users of older or less sophisticated browsers retain access to the information and services our pages provide.

New Selectors

One key to true web development proficiency is the intelligent use of CSS selectors. In Chapter 4 of this book, we looked at selectors such as the descendant and child selectors—selectors often underutilized or ignored by developers but which provide tremendous power when used with care. These selectors can be particularly useful when the HTML for a particular page is off-limits—for example, when the markup is generated by a CMS or other application. CSS3 provides even more powerful and finely tuned selectors that are already widely supported in browsers, even though the CSS3 Selectors module is still a candidate recommendation rather than a final, published standard. All current, popular browsers except for Internet Explorer 8 and its ancestors support most or all CSS3 selectors. We can, therefore, use CSS3 selectors today, though we must take care to ensure that our sites are still useful when viewed in Internet Explorer.

In the following pages, we'll look at a number of CSS3 selectors that can be useful in common development situations and which can be used for progressive enhancement. In the next chapter, we'll follow up by looking at new properties in CSS3.

*There are a number of JavaScript libraries, such as Dean Edward's IE7 (**dean. edwards.name/IE7**) and John Resig's Sizzle (**sizzlejs.com/**), that provide ways in which you can use CSS3 selectors with Internet Explorer 6 and upwards. These libraries do, of course, require users to have JavaScript enabled in their browsers.*

Structural Pseudo Element Selectors

As we saw in earlier chapters, a good understanding of descendant and child selectors can help alleviate the symptoms of "`id`-itis" and "`class`-itis," ailments characterized by specifying `class` and `id` values for elements in an HTML document solely for the purpose of styling those elements. CSS3 provides even more fine-grained selectors for selecting elements based on the structure of a document than its predecessors do. For example, we might want to select every other row of a table, or only the first paragraph inside each parent element, or only the last item in a list. Structural pseudo element selectors in CSS3 give us the ability to do precisely these things.

Document Structure

We saw earlier that we can think of the structure of an HTML document as a tree—a little like a family tree, though with only a single parent per element. Perhaps a better analogy is the classic "tree of life" way of imagining evolution. At the top of the tree is the HTML element: the root element of the document. Every other element:

- Always has exactly one parent element—for example, the body and head elements have the HTML element as their parent.

- May have one or more child elements (elements contained directly within them)—for instance, the body and head elements are children of the HTML element.

- May have one or more sibling elements (elements that share a parent)—the body and head elements, for example, are siblings, as they have the same parent: the HTML element.

- May have descendent elements (child elements of an element's child, or an element's child's child, and so on)—for example, every element in an HTML document is a descendent element of the HTML element, and all headings, paragraphs, links, and so on, are descendants of the body element.

first-child

In print design, the first paragraph is often styled differently from subsequent paragraphs in a chapter. It's not hard to style a web page using CSS in this way by applying a class value to such paragraphs. For example, using a little of the HTML5 we picked up in the last chapter, we might do the following:

```
<section class="chapter">
<p class="first-paragraph">It is a truth universally
acknowledged, that a single man in possession of a good
fortune must be in want of a wife.</p>
<p>However little known the feelings or views of such a
man...</p>
</section>
```

Now, in the example of a classic such as *Pride and Prejudice* it is rather unlikely that the first paragraph of a chapter might need moving elsewhere, but many other kinds of documents are far more dynamic—articles in the process of being edited, for example, or blog posts, or developing news stories. As a consequence, during the development or maintenance of a site, a paragraph might easily be copied elsewhere with the **first-paragraph** class intact, which would mean that the new "first" paragraph wouldn't be styled correctly. In cases like this, it would make a lot more sense to apply a style based on an element's place in the structure of the document. This is a far less *fragile* solution than marking up the document with classes, and the **first-child** selector is designed for precisely this kind of situation.

Syntax

Using the **first-child** selector is very straightforward. We simply append **first-child** to a selector that identifies the element we wish to select. For example, **p:first-child** selects any paragraph that is the first child of its parent element. We might use this selector to, for example, make the text of first paragraphs bigger than following paragraphs, using a rule that looks like this:

```
p:first-child {
    font-size: 1.1em;
}
```

Note that this example selects all paragraphs that are the first child of their parent elements, *not* the first child of all **p** elements. (You can think of the **first-child** selector as being similar to a dynamic selector like **a:hover**, except that instead of selecting an element when it is in the hover state, it selects an element when it is the first child of its parent element.) Note also that if we hadn't specified any element before the first colon in this example, this rule would have selected *all* elements that are the first child of an element. We're unlikely to want to indiscriminately select all first child elements, but if we needed to do so, that's how we'd do it.

We can also append **first-child** to other selectors. For example, we can select any element with a class of "chapter" that is *also* the first child of its parent element, like so: **.chapter:first-child**. We can also combine **first-child** selectors with, for example, descendant selectors, thus selecting only paragraphs that are the first child of section elements with the class "**chapter**." Here's what that looks like:

```
section.chapter p:first-child {
   font-size: 1.1em;
}
```

first-of-type

Now, the preceding example may seem a little artificial, because you'd probably expect a section element to contain a heading that comes before the chapter's contents. A more realistic example might look like this:

```
<section class="chapter">
<h1>Chapter 1</h1>
<p class="first-paragraph">It is a truth universally
acknowledged, that a single man in possession of a good
fortune must be in want of a wife.</p>
<p>However little known the feelings or views of such a
man...</p>
</section>
```

In this case, there is no element that matches the selector **p:first-child**, because the first paragraph in the section is preceded by a heading. If we want to style the first paragraph element of every section that has chapter as its class, we'll have to turn elsewhere. CSS3 does offer a more general selector than **first-child**: the **nth-child** selector works in a similar way, but although we'll examine this selector in detail shortly, it's still not the best match for this situation. If, for example, we used **nth-child** to select paragraphs that were the second child of their parent elements, we would still have to rely on a stable document structure. If one or more chapter sections had a different structure, or if we changed the whole document's structure during development, our solution would need to be changed once more.

Less fragile is another CSS3 structural selector, **first-of-type**. This selector allows us to select an element when it is *the first instance of the specified type of element* within its parent element. In this case, **first-of-type** is the selector we want, as it will allow us to select only the first paragraph inside an element, whether that paragraph is preceded by other elements (like headers) or not. Our rule will look something like this:

```
section.chapter>p:first-of-type {
  font-size: 1.1em;
}
```

This is a much more robust solution than adding class to the markup or relying on a specific document structure. If we move a paragraph elsewhere in a section or document, or if the structure of the parent element's content changes, our solution will still work. And unlike `class`- and `id`-based solutions, the **first-of-type** selector won't require us to touch the document's HTML at all. Looking for the least fragile selector pays long-term dividends in the form of easier code maintenance and greater reliability.

How can we decide whether a solution is fragile or robust? It's more an art than a science, but fragile solutions will tend to be inflexible, to rely on a specific document structure, or to require that we change the document's markup to accommodate styles, usually by adding `class` or `id` values. Robust solutions often allow us to select elements based on characteristics that don't require a specific, rigid document structure. CSS3 provides sophisticated selectors, and it pays to consider them before falling back on methods like using `class` and `id` for styling. Anytime you find yourself changing the markup of a document to accommodate CSS, alarm bells should ring. We have more appropriate tools than the hammer for adding to our markup, and if you do alter markup, it should be as a last resort.

As is the case with all CSS3 features, we should use these selectors to progressively enhance a page's presentation. In the preceding example, there's no great loss for the users of browsers that don't support these selectors—the only thing those users will miss is a slight change in type size for the first paragraph of each chapter.

last-child

The selectors we've seen so far select elements based on their order beginning with the first child of the parent element and counting forward, but we
can also select elements based on their order beginning with the last child and
counting backward. Just as **first-child** selects an element when it is the first
child of its parent, **last-child** selects an element when it is the last child of
its parent element. Similarly, **last-of-type** selects an element when it is, for
example, the last paragraph inside its parent element.

Such selectors are useful for selecting, say, the last paragraph within a chapter
section, perhaps in order to add additional margin space, or a border. The following example applies the solid thin black border to paragraphs that are the
last child of a section with the class **chapter**:

```
section.chapter p:last-child {
  border-bottom: solid thin black;
}
```

More robust, however, is the **last-of-type** selector. If the structure of our
section changes such that an element other than a paragraph becomes the last
element, the last paragraph of the chapter will still be selected—and thus still
have a border—if we use **last-of-type** in our CSS rule:

```
section.chapter p:last-of-type {
  border-bottom: solid thin black;
}
```

So far, we've been selecting specific, individual children of an element, but we
can also select groups of elements that meet specific structural criteria within
an element. We'll turn to these selectors next.

nth-child

One of the most common ways of styling data tables, both in print and on the
web, is to alternate the background colors of rows of data—a technique sometimes referred to as *zebra striping*. Typically, zebra stripes are implemented in

HTML and CSS by applying a class such as odd or even to every other row in the HTML markup, then using a class selector to apply a background color to odd, even, or both classes of row. This method violates our rule of changing markup as little as possible for the purposes of styling, but until CSS3, there was no other way—short of using JavaScript—to implement zebra stripes without markup changes. As you might guess, CSS3 provides a selector that solves our problem.

CSS3 introduces the **nth-child** selector, which selects an element when it is the 3rd, 17th, or any other specified child of an element. We need a selector that will allow us to select *every other row* in a table, and luckily, we can use **nth-child** to do this in several ways.

In addition to using **nth-child** with numbers such as 1 or 27, we can use two keywords: odd and even. As you might guess **tr:nth-child(odd)** selects every odd-numbered table row, and **tr:nth-child(even)** selects every even-numbered row. We might use the following rule:

```
tr:nth-child(odd) {
   background-color: #ededed;
}
```

...which would produce a table that looks something like this:

12.4
Zebra striping a table
with **nth-child**

number of rows	6
Number of columns	2
number of cells	12
Number of colors	3
number of elements	18
Number of self referential statements	1

We could also specify two alternating background colors by using both odd and even **nth-child** selectors:

```
tr:nth-child(odd) {
    background-color: #d4f128;
}
tr:nth-child(even) {
    background-color: #e0f64c;
}
```

…which would produce a table that looks something like this:

number of rows	6
Number of columns	2
number of cells	12
Number of colors	3
number of elements	18
Number of self referential statements	1

12.5
Two-color zebra striping in a table using **nth-child**

But what if we wanted to use three different background colors? This is where another feature of CSS3 structural selectors becomes useful. We can use a formulation like `2n`, `3n+1`, or `5n+2` to select groups of child elements, based on their position within their parent element. For example, **tr:nth-child(2n)** selects all the even children of an element, and **tr:nth-child(2n+1)** selects every odd table row. You can think of n as a variable that is replaced with every integer from 0 on. So **tr:nth-child(2n)** will select these rows:

- **tr:nth-child(0)** — (2*0)
- **tr:nth-child(2)** — (2*1)
- **tr:nth-child(4)** — (2*2)
- **tr:nth-child(6)** — (2*3)

…and so on. If a table had 1,000 rows, the 1000th row would be selected by this selector, because 1,000=2*500.

The selector `tr:nth-child(2n+1)`, on the other hand, selects all the *odd* children of an element:

- `tr:nth-child(1)` — ($2*0+1$)
- `tr:nth-child(3)` — ($2*1+1$)
- `tr:nth-child(5)` — ($2*2+1$)
- `tr:nth-child(7)` — ($2*3+1$)

The 999th row of a thousand-row table would be selected by this selector, because $999=2*499+1$.

We can also use `nth-child` selectors to select, for example, every third element (`tr:nth-child(3n)`), the element that comes *before* every fifth element (`tr:nth-child(5n-1)`), and so on. Let's see how can we use these selectors to give three different background colors to a table's rows.

We'll create one selector to select every third element, one to select every third element *plus one*, and one to select every third element *plus two*. The following three selectors will do the trick:

- `tr:nth-child(3n)` — selects every third element
- `tr:nth-child(3n+1)` — selects the first element after every third element
- `tr:nth-child(3n+2)` — selects the second element after every third element

We can now apply three different background colors, repeated indefinitely, with the following CSS:

```css
tr:nth-child(3n) {
  background-color: #94239f;
}
tr:nth-child(3n+1) {
  background-color: #bb46c9;
}
tr:nth-child(3n+2) {
  background-color: #bf69cc;
}
```

number of rows	6
Number of columns	2
number of cells	12
Number of colors	3
number of elements	18
Number of self referential statements	1

12.6
Alternating three-color stripes in a table with `nth-child`

To get a sense of just how sophisticated these selectors can be, let's take a look at a real-world example [**12.7**].

10:15AM - 10:45AM	Morning tea		
10:45AM - 11:40AM	Font embedding and typography Mark Boulton	Getting bang for your SEO buck Cheryl Gledhill & Scott Gledhill	Best practices for speeding up your site Mark Stanton
11:40AM - 11:45AM	Changeover		
11:45AM - 12:40AM	Using Ajax to enhance UX Tania Laing	Accessibility means business Damien McCormack	The state of developer tools Ben Galbraith
12:40AM - 1:40PM	Lunch		
1:40PM - 2:35PM	Designing for suits Pete Ottery	TBA	Canvas Dmitry Baranovskiy
2:35PM - 2:40PM	Changeover		
2:40PM - 3:35PM	Information seeking behaviours Donna Spencer	The state of the web as platform Nick Galvin	jQuery Earle Castledine
3:35PM - 4:05PM	Afternoon tea		

12.7
Styling a table with `first-of-type` and `nth-of-type`, as displayed in Safari 4

As with zebra-striped table rows, before CSS3 selectors became available, we'd have had to use classes to style the various td elements in figure 12.7 with different background colors. Using CSS3 selectors, we can simply select the first td element in a row and give it a reddish background, select the second td element in a row and give it a blue background, and select the third td element and give it a grey background. Our CSS rules would look like this:

```
td:first-of-type{
   background-color: rgb(255,0,0);
}
td:nth-of-type(2){
   background-color: rgb(0,64,128);
}
td:nth-of-type(3){
   background-color: rgb(76,76,76);
}
td:[colspan]{
   background-color: rgb(200,200,200);
}
```

Because the td elements that span three columns (such as the registration row)
are the first of their type in their row, unless we specify a different background
color for these rows, they'll also be red. So, the fourth rule, which has an attribute selector, selects td elements that have a colspan value and gives these
elements a lighter grey background. (If you need a quick refresher, check out
the discussion of CSS2 attribute selectors in Chapter 4.)

As always, we need to consider what happens if a selector is not supported by
a user's browser. In this case, the text color of the session names could be very
similar to the background color of td elements, which would compromise legibility. We can rely on specificity (which we discussed in Chapter 4) to help
us avoid this problem. A suffix such as **nth-child** *increases* the specificity of a
selector, which means that **td:nth-of-type** will override any plain **td** selector.
So, we can safely use something like the following CSS rule to allow for graceful degradation:

```
td {
   background-color: rgb(0,64,128);
}
```

This rule ensures that browsers that don't support our CSS3 selectors will give
all our td elements a blue background, and browsers that do support the structural CSS3 selectors will override this rule and apply the more sophisticated
styles illustrated in figure 12.7.

It's a little-known but useful fact that the keywords odd and even, as well as formulations like 3n+1, also work for other structural pseudo element selectors, such as **nth-of-type**.

The structural selectors of CSS3 are among the most significant enhancements to CSS in this version of the language. We've touched on many of them here, and on some of CSS3's extensions to the CSS2 attribute selector that we looked at in Chapter 4. We've also covered the most important concepts for understanding how these selectors work. You can find more resources for investigating CSS3 selectors in the resources section at the end of this book.

target

For a completely different new selector in CSS3, we turn to the **target** selector. Any web developer will be familiar with selectors such as **link** and **hover**, which along with **focus**, **active**, and **visited** are referred to as "dynamic"—or, to be exact, *dynamic pseudo-class*—selectors. The **target** selector is an additional dynamic selector in CSS3. It selects an element when it is the element currently being pointed to by the document's URL. For example, if the current URL in a browser's address bar is **http://westciv.com/index.html#resources**, the element **<p id="resources">** is the current target. (Of course, documents frequently lack a current target—for example, if the current URL is **http://westciv.com/index.html**, there is no target element.) When the current URL is **http://westciv.com/index.html#resources**, the target selector **p:target** will select the paragraph with an **id** of resources. Similarly, if we use **target** by itself, we can select whatever element is the target of its document (if there is a target). We can also chain selectors to make the target selector more specific. In the preceding case, if we want to select only the paragraph with an **id** of resources when it is the target, but *not* to select any other targeted element, we can use this rule:

```
p#resources:target.
```

So, what good is this selector exactly? When we jump to a location inside a page, either from within that page or from another page, it's often not immediately clear what (or where) the linked element is. We can use the **target** selector and a visual cue, such as a particular background color, to draw attention to the target of the link and help the users orient themselves within the page. We might use a rule that looks like this:

```
p:target {
    border-bottom: background-color: yellow;
}
```

In this example, whenever the user follows a link—from within or from outside a document—to any specific paragraph on our page, that paragraph will be styled with a yellow background until the target URL for the page changes.

The target selector is an example of the new features in CSS3 that are more focused on web applications than traditional web pages. In fact, there are a number of new properties specifically designed for working with web applications, some of which we'll see in the next chapter.

The Wrap

In this chapter, we've taken a look at many of the new selectors in CSS3, along with examples showing they can be used to progressively enhance sites for users of browsers that support them. These selectors give us more power and finesse in selecting elements based on a document's structure and help us continue to separate a document's markup from its presentation. Thanks to these selectors and their increasingly broad support in contemporary browsers, we are approaching the day when `class` and `id` values applied solely for styling purposes will be a thing of the past. The benefits of this "cleaner" markup aren't only theoretical: as more teams work with shared resources on version control systems, fewer markup changes mean more efficient collaboration—and when structural changes to the markup no longer affect our CSS, our sites become much easier to maintain.

Just as the intelligent use of descendent and child selectors is one of the hallmarks of the adept CSS developer, the understanding and use of new CSS selectors—especially structural selectors—will be vital skills for CSS developers for years to come.

But of course, selectors aren't much use without properties. In the next chapter, we'll take look at the really fun part of CSS3—the new CSS properties we can begin to use now.

New Properties in CSS3

For all the power and precision of the new selectors we've just seen, it's CSS3's properties that get most developers' hearts racing. Imagine never again having to break open an image editor to style text with shadows, or to use any font other than the standard web fonts. Imagine never again using image replacement techniques for text. Imagine drop shadows and rounded corners *without* extraneous markup. All these scenarios and more are a reality with CSS3, and all are supported in one or more widely available browsers in ways that let them degrade gracefully. As long as you don't believe all web pages must look exactly the same in every browser, the future of web development has already begun.

Shadow Effects

Shadow effects—on text and more recently on page elements—have been a staple of web design for many years. But until recently, with the exception of text shadows in Safari (supported in 2003's version 1.1), it has been difficult to add shadows to elements or text, and the process has come with serious drawbacks.

Until now, developers have been forced to use images to achieve such effects as text with a drop shadow. For years, the only way to produce this effect was simply to use an image in place of the text—a technique with many attendant accessibility and usability issues. The advent of image replacement techniques such as FIR (Fahrner Image Replacement), sIFR (Scalable Inman Flash Replacement), and Cufón have addressed some of these problems, but even these techniques (which are discussed in Chapter 4, if you'd like a refresher) are plagued by accessibility, usablity, and workflow problems.

Adding a box shadow to an element has traditionally been even more complicated, typically requiring extraneous HTML elements to contain the box-shadowed element, with background images on these containing elements providing the desired effect. (If this description sounds complicated, you should see the markup.)

Thankfully, CSS3 offers properties like `text-shadow` and `box-shadow`, which will in time make these painful workarounds unnecessary.

text-shadow

The `text-shadow` property allows you to add one or more shadows to the text of any element. Each shadow is specified with a horizontal offset, a vertical offset, a blur, and a color. Consider the following rule:

```
h1 {
    text-shadow: 2px 2px 2px #888
}
```

This rule adds to the text of all `h1` elements a shadow which is offset 2px to the right and 2px below the position of the text itself [13.1]. The shadow will be blurred by `2px` (the higher the blur value, the more blurred the shadow will be), and it will be a pale gray. The color value may be placed either before the three length values or after them, but the three length values always follow the same order: horizontal offset, vertical offset, blur.

13.1
A simple `text-shadow`

With a negative horizontal offset, the shadow begins to the left of the text, and with a negative vertical offset, the shadow begins above the text:

```
h1 {
   text-shadow: -2px -2px 4px #888
}
```

Text shadows don't just take pixel value offsets and blurs, they can also take relative values like ems. This can have a surprisingly significant effect. For example, figure **13.2** shows our first shadow example, with `2px` offset and blur, zoomed up to a very large text size:

13.2
A zoomed, pixel-based `text-shadow`

Here's the same text, using a text shadow with `.1em` offsets and blur [**13.3**]. As with other properties we've seen in the book, relative length values like em often make for much more scalable or adaptable designs.

13.3
A zoomed, em-based `text-shadow`

Multiple Shadows

Individual drop shadows are nice, but `text-shadow` can produce more sophisticated effects via multiple shadows on the same element. We can add any
number of text shadows to an element (Opera has a limit of about six shadows,
which in practice is enough for just about any effect) by adding a comma-
separated list of shadow values to the `text-shadow` property. For example,
an etched effect is simple to achieve using just two shadow values:

```
h2 {
    text-shadow: 1px 1px white, -1px -1px #333;
    color: #cccccc;
    font-family: Helvetica, Arial, sans-serif;
    font-weight: normal;
    background-color: #b3b3b3;
}
```

The above statement gives us the effect shown in figure **13.4**.

13.4

An etching effect created
using two text shadows

This example also demonstrates why we must be careful with features supported in some, but not all, browsers. Figure **13.5** shows how the same heading
would be rendered by a browser that doesn't support `text-shadow`.

13.5

`text-shadow` may cause
backward-compatibility
problems when its
shadow effects mask
insufficient contrast
between the underlying
text color and back-
ground color.

Astute readers will note that these shadows only have two length values, not
three. In the case where a length value is omitted, the value is treated as zero.
So here we have a blur of `0`—which is, in effect, no blur at all.

We can also emboss using just two `text-shadow` values, like this:

```
text-shadow: -1px -1px white, 1px 1px #333
```

This CSS rule produces an effect like that seen in figure **13.6**:

13.6
An embossed effect created with two text shadows

More, and more elaborate, effects can be achieved using additional shadow values. Consider this commonly used example from the website **CSS3.info** [13.7]:

13.7
Complex effects created using multiple text shadows

You can achieve this effect using the following CSS:

```
text-shadow: white 0px 0px 4px,
rgb(255, 255, 51) 0px -5px 4px,
rgb(255, 221, 51) 2px -10px 6px,
rgb(255, 136, 0) -2px -15px 11px,
rgb(255, 34, 0) 2px -25px 18px;
```

In this example, there are five shadows, but how do we indicate which order they should be drawn in? Because `text-shadow` is not part of any definitive CSS standard (it was in CSS2 which never became a final W3 recommendation, is not in CSS2.1, and is now in CSS3's text module), there is no definitive answer. Safari renders the last specified shadow first, and then so on until it renders the first shadow last. Opera and Firefox render in the opposite direction. There is often little practical difference.

Compatibility

`text-shadow` is supported in Safari (version 1 and higher), Opera (version 9.5 and higher), and Firefox 3.5 and higher. Internet Explorer doesn't support the `text-shadow` property, but it does have a proprietary filter mechanism that enables various shadow and other effects. With the release of Internet Explorer 8, use of these filters becomes quite a complicated matter, because filters can't be used with the browser's "standards" mode, only with "Quirks" mode. Since they will almost certainly never be supported in browsers other than Internet Explorer, the use of these filters in new projects is something that should be carefully considered. (We'll touch on IE filters again when we look at the `opacity` property.)

box-shadow

The `text-shadow` property was part of the draft CSS2 recommendations and was implemented in Safari 1.1 back in 2003, but the ability to add shadows to an element's box hasn't been implemented in Safari and Firefox until recently, and is still not supported in Internet Explorer 8 and Opera 10.

Like `text-shadow`, the `box-shadow` property specifies one or more shadow values that are applied to the element's box outside its border, but inside its margin. No matter the size or offset of the shadow, it has no effect on the flow of the document, meaning that it won't affect a page layout in any way. This greatly aids its use for progressive enhancement, as there is no need to take into account a shadow's size when laying out a page (this is true of text shadows as well).

To add a shadow around a block of text, we'd use a CSS rule like this one:

```
p{
  box-shadow: .2em .2em .3em #888;
  padding: .5em;
}
```

...which will give us a shadow like the one in figure **13.8**:

However little known the feelings
or views of such a man may be on
his first entering a neighbourhood,
this truth is so well fixed in the
minds of the surrounding families,
that he is considered the rightful
property of some one or other of
their daughters.

13.8
A simple `box-shadow`

Or at least, such a rule will work in theory. In practice, because the CSS3
Borders and Backgrounds Module is not final at the time of writing, browsers
that support this feature do so only with their vendor-specific extensions:
`-moz-` and `-webkit-`. To make this work in WebKit- and Mozilla-based
browsers like Firefox 3.5, we'll need to use a rule like this one:

```
p{
    -moz-box-shadow: .2em .2em .3em #888;
    -webkit-box-shadow: .2em .2em .3em #888;
    box-shadow: .2em .2em .3em #888;
    padding: .5em;
```

As with `text-shadow`, we can add multiple shadows to etch or emboss a box,
using, for example:

```
box-shadow: -.1em -.1em .15em #ffffff,
.1em .1em .15em #001199;
```

This rule produces an effect like the one shown in figure **13.9**:

However little known the feelings or
views of such a man may be on his first
entering a neighbourhood, this truth is
so well fixed in the minds of the
surrounding families, that he is
considered the rightful property of some
one or other of their daughters.

13.9
An embossed
`box-shadow`

Shadows in CSS3 are easy to implement and increasingly well supported. They are also backward-compatible, provided you maintain high contrast between text color and background color to ensure good legibility without text shadows. Otherwise they are an almost perfect candidate for progressively enhancing your sites.

Compatibility

box-shadow is supported in Safari (version 3.1 and higher) and Firefox 3.5 and higher. Internet Explorer doesn't support the **box-shadow** property, but it does have its own proprietary filter mechanism that can enable various shadow and other effects. With the release of Internet Explorer 8, use of these filters becomes quite a complicated matter, and as they will almost certainly never be supported in other browsers, using these filters in new projects is something that should be very carefully considered. We'll touch on the issue of IE filters again when we look at the **opacity** property.

border-radius

Rounded corners on box elements, although visually appealing, have long been difficult to implement with HTML and CSS. Generally, developers must add several elements with background images to produce the effect, and the CSS to make it all work can be complicated. Fortunately, CSS3 comes to the rescue in the shape of the **border-radius** property, supported in Safari (versions 3 and up) and Firefox (poorly in version 2, but well in versions 3 and higher). The old-school hacks will still be required to support rounded corners in Internet Explorer (and possibly Opera) for some time, but this design effect is a good candidate for progressive enhancement.

border-radius is very simple to use. The property takes one or two positive length values, which specify how "rounded" the corners of an element's box are. (You can also specify different radii, if you wish.) Let's begin with the simplest case of a single length value for **border-radius**.

```
p{
   border-radius: 1em;
}
```

If we add a **border-radius** to the element we've just "etched" using **box-shadow**, figure 13.10 shows how Safari will render it.

> However little known the feelings or views of such a man may be on his first entering a neighbourhood, this truth is so well fixed in the minds of the surrounding families, that he is considered the rightful property of some one or other of their daughters.

13.10
A paragraph with rounded corners, created using **border-radius**

The Math of Rounded Corners

How exactly does the value `1em` translate into a rounded corner? For those who need to know the gruesome details, **border-radius** defines an ellipse for the corner. When there is a single value, the ellipse has a vertical and horizontal radius of `1em`. And an ellipse with equal radii is a circle. Now, imagine the circumference of the circle aligned so that a quarter of the circle aligns with the corner of the element, as in figure 13.11.

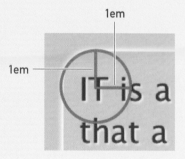

13.11
A **border-radius** with horizontal and vertical radii of `1em`

As with many other properties, we'll use relative em units, rather than a unit like pixels, and figure **13.12** shows why.

> However little known the feelings or views of such a man may be on his first entering a neighbourhood, this truth is so well fixed in the minds of the surrounding families, that he is considered the rightful property of some one or other of their daughters.

13.12
A **border-radius** of `10px` at normal zoom

When we specify a `border-radius` of `10px`, as in figure 13.12, it appears fine at a normal zoom. But what happens when we increase the font size?

13.13
A `border-radius` of
`10px`, zoomed by several
font sizes

However little known the feelings or views of such a man may be on his first entering a neighbourhood, this truth is so well fixed in the minds of the surrounding families, that he is considered the rightful property of some one or other of their daughters.

As we see in figure **13.13**, the radius remains the same size (`10px`), but the proportions change markedly. However, if we specify with ems, the border radius scales up and down with the text, maintaining the proportions we see in figure **13.14**.

13.14
A `border-radius` of
`1em`, zoomed by several
font sizes

IT is a truth universa
that a single man in
good fortune, must |
However little knowr
views of such a man

Relative length values like ems—whether used for `font-size`, `shadow`, `margin`, `padding`, `line-height`, or many other CSS properties—give your designs a flexibility that absolute units like pixels don't. An understanding of the power and appropriate use of relative units is a much-overlooked aspect of CSS, and one all professional developers should have as part of their toolkit.

Compatibility

`border-radius` is supported in Safari (version 3 and higher), Firefox 2 (with aliased corners, producing an unattractive effect), and Firefox 3 (good support) and higher. The browser specific extensions `-moz-` and `-webkit-` are still required, at least in Safari 4 and Firefox 3.5.

transparency

With many CSS3 properties like `shadow`, `border-radius`, and others, you may notice a pattern: many of these features provide a straightforward, standards-based approach to techniques used by developers for years, but which have typically required complicated hacks, and very messy HTML and CSS (sometimes even requiring JavaScript).

Another very common design effect is the use of apparently overlapping semi-transparent elements.

There are several ways of achieving transparency in web pages, some from CSS2, and some involving image formats like PNG or GIF. CSS3 provides new ways of achieving transparency.

background-color: transparent

You've long been able to set the background color of an element to `transparent`. Then, anything "behind" an element with such a background is visible. However, text is still fully opaque, and there's no way to make semi-transparent backgrounds—there's no `color`: `transparent` equivalent of `background-color`: `transparent`.

Semi-Transparent Background Images

The still-common GIF format allows for single-color transparency. You specify which color in the image should be transparent, and the browser renders any pixels in the image that are that color transparent. However, GIF transparency is either off or on, which limits its usefulness.

The PNG format has long since brought variable or "alpha-channel" transparency to the web... almost. Although PNG has been supported in Internet Explorer since version 4, alpha channel transparency support only came with version 7. There are numerous workarounds for this problem, which we also explored earlier. The problem remains that this form of transparency applies only to the background of an element. There are cases in which we'll want the whole element (including its children) to be semi-transparent. We can accomplish this with CSS3 in a couple of ways.

opacity

The CSS3 property `opacity` has been supported in all contemporary browsers (other than Internet Explorer) for some time, and there's no need to use a browser-specific extension. `opacity` takes a single value between `0` (completely transparent) and `1` (completely opaque). So, a value of `.5` is 50% transparent.

For example, this rule produces the effect seen in figure **13.15**:

```
p{
    -webkit-border-radius: 1em;
    -moz-border-radius: 1em;
    border-radius: 1em;
    border-style: solid;
    padding: 1em;
    opacity: 0.3;
    background-color: #ffffff;
}
```

13.15

A semi-transparent element created using `opacity`

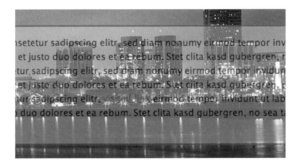

Note that the background, text, and any descendent elements are also semi-transparent. This cannot be overruled by setting an `opacity` of `1` to child elements within a semi-transparent element, which can decrease the legibility of text—semi-transparent text over a semi-transparent background can be very difficult to read. Fortunately there's a related CSS3 feature to help us address this.

RGBa Colors

Now supported in Firefox, Opera, and Safari, RGBa color values specify an alpha-channel transparency value of `0` to `1`, in addition to red, green, and blue color values. This allows us to make semi-transparent backgrounds using an RGBa color value. Figure 13.16 shows the preceding example, but with an RGBa background color instead of `opacity`.

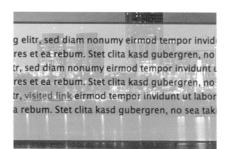

13.16
A semi-transparent element created using RGBa colors

The text is more legible because it is completely opaque, while the background is semi-transparent [**13.15**].

We can set an RGBa color anywhere we can use a color value. So, we can make the border semi-transparent by using a property value like **border-color**: `rgba(0,0,0,0.5);` giving us a border with 50% opacity. And we can create semi-transparent text using an RGBa value for the **color** property.

To a developer with a hammer, everything looks like a nail: we often learn one skill, then use it any time it might work, without considering potentially superior alternatives. In this case, CSS provides several alternatives for creating transparent elements. Understanding the strengths and weaknesses of each (**opacity** is inherited by all its descendents and can't be overridden; RGBa applies to individual properties; the transparent color value only applies to backgrounds; PNGs can be difficult to use with older versions of Internet Explorer) we can use the simplest and most appropriate solution to a particular problem.

Compatibility

RGBa is supported in Safari (version 3 and higher), Firefox 3, and Opera 9.5 and higher. **opacity** is supported in Safari version 3 and higher, Firefox 3 and higher, and Opera 9 and higher, without the need for a vendor-specific extension. Opacity can be created in Internet Explorer 5 and higher using the IE-only filter "opacity."

Multi-Column Text

We devoted an earlier section to multi-column page layouts. CSS3 has a multi-column feature, but rather than applying to page layouts, it applies to the flow of text inside an element. With CSS, it has so far only been possible to have a single column of text inside a given element, such as a paragraph. With CSS3's multi-column properties, it's now easy to make the text inside an element flow into two or more columns.

At present, the multi-column properties are part of the as-yet-unfinalized Multi-column Layout module. It's supported in Safari 3 and higher and Firefox 3 and higher, in both cases with their vendor-specific extensions: `-webkit-` and `-moz-` respectively.

The multi-column properties allow you to specify:

- `column-count`: Number of columns to display.
- `column-width`: A length value that specifies how wide each column should be (columns must all be the same width). If no width is specified, the browser calculates the width based on the number of columns, padding, the gap between the columns and so on. If the `column-width` is too wide to allow the number of columns specified by `column-count` into the width of the element, a smaller number of columns will be used. In essence, `column-width` is more important than `column-count` for calculating how many columns are displayed.
- `column-gap`: A length value that specifies the space between each column.
- `column-rule`: A value similar to `border` that specifies the style, width, and color of a vertical line or rule between columns.

The `columns` shorthand takes two space-separated values, specifying the number of columns and their width, in that order.

The `column-count` property can be used without the other properties—but of course, without a `column-count` value, the other properties won't have any effect.

Here we'll specify that each paragraph is to have three columns of text, each `15em` wide. The gap between each column is `5em`, with a medium dotted gray rule between the columns.

```
p{
  column-count: 3;
  column-width: 17em;
  column-gap: 5em;
  column-rule: .1em #d2d2d2 solid;
}
```

At present, you'll need to add **-moz-** and **-webkit-** to the properties for these browsers to display the multiple columns, but I've left off these properties here as the CSS can get quite unwieldy when replicated for each browser extension. The effect is shown in figure **13.17**.

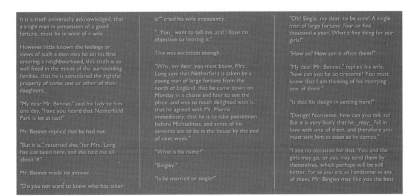

13.17
Three text columns created using **column-count.** Note that the browser balances the length of the text in each column as much as possible.

Multi-column text can usually be used to progressively enhance our pages safely; when browsers don't support the properties, a single block of text will be displayed. This may decrease legibility when an element is particularly wide, but these properties should not cause problems for readers whose browsers don't support them, as seen in figure **13.18**, which shows the same page as rendered by Opera 10.

13.18

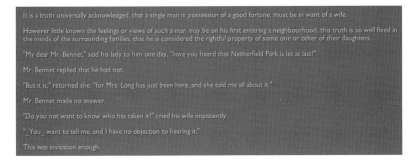

Transitions

Rounded corners, semi-transparency, shadows—these are all staples of the "Web 2.0 aesthetic." Another of the most commonly used effects among websites—and particularly web applications—are transition effects such as fading, zooming, and the smooth scrolling and panning of elements.

These effects are currently achieved using JavaScript, increasingly as part of JavaScript libraries like **script.aculo.us** and **mootools**, which take a lot of the effort out of implementing effects and help ensure cross-browser consistency. However, Apple has proposed as part of CSS3 (and implemented in Safari) several properties that make transition effects as simple as specifying any other CSS property. While it is still only a draft standard—and only implemented in Safari—it does point the way toward ever more sophisticated capabilities of CSS.

The Transitions Controversy

There's some controversy over transitions in CSS and whether this sort of functionality is more appropriately implemented with JavaScript. The argument for JavaScript is that these properties are more closely associated with behavior than with presentation. As we saw earlier, the separation of markup, presentation, and behavior is a key concept in modern web standards-based development. The counterargument is that the change of background color from one color to another is simply a more sophisticated form of presentation.

Conceptually, a transition allows a smooth change to the value of a property like an element's position, size, or color. We can specify the property for which we want the transition to occur (it's possible to specify all properties at once), the time the transition should take (in seconds), and optionally, a "timing function" and a delay.

But what causes a property value to change? One way in which a property value might change is via CSS rules with dynamic selectors, like **hover**, **focus**, or the new **target** selector we saw in the previous chapter. The second way that properties might change is via scripting. They might even change when users change their preferences—by changing the page zoom, for example. Transition properties apply regardless of how a property changes.

Specifying a Transition

Transitions are specified by a number of properties. The required properties are:

- `transition-property`: The property that the transition should apply to. Use the property name, a comma-separated list of property names, or the keyword `all`.

- `transition-duration`: The length of time in seconds the transition should take. If multiple properties are being transitioned, then this is a comma-separated list of durations in seconds, corresponding to the comma-separated list of property names, respectively.

There are also two optional properties:

- `transition-timing-function`: Specifies how intermediate values are calculated during the transition. This takes one of several keywords which specify ways in which the animation will occur. For example, an `ease-in` timing begins the animation slowly and accelerates it, and `ease-out` has the opposite effect.

- `transition-delay`: A time value that specifies how long the browser should delay before performing the animation.

It's rather difficult to give an example of an animated property in print, so you'll have to jump online to see it in effect at **www.devwws.com/examples/ transitions**. A very common technique is to change the background color of a link when it is in the hover state. But instead of an abrupt transition, what if it faded more smoothly, as seen in the fade effect pioneered by sites like 37 Signals' Basecamp (**www.basecamphq.com**)? Here's how we can accomplish this with CSS transitions:

```css
a:hover {
   background-color: red;
}

a {
   background-color: white;
   -webkit-transition: background-color;
   -webkit-transition-duration: 1s;
}
```

As with most of the other properties we've seen in this chapter, you'll need a browser-specific prefix (in this case `-webkit-`) to see this in action at present—and of course Safari 3.1 or higher.

Now, when the user hovers over a link, the background color will smoothly transition from white to red (and then back again when the mouse no longer hovers over the link), taking one second to do so.

If `transition-duration`: `1s` draws a big "huh?"…well-spotted.

Seconds are a valid CSS3 value (typically used with aural style sheets). The format is a number followed by the letter s. Fractions of a second like `2.5s` and `.2s` are permitted.

As we mentioned, transitions are still a WebKit-only proposed addition to CSS, and they were first available in Safari 3.1. They point in the direction we are likely to see CSS head. But should you use them today? In most cases, adding a transition to a property value should have no impact on the usability or legibility of a page. So, along with the other properties discussed in this section, transitions are great for progressively enhancing your pages. If you are looking for effects that work across as many browsers as possible, you can always investigate the various JavaScript libraries which provide these kinds of effects. With luck, we'll be using CSS for these kinds of effects before too long. Only time will tell whether we'll come to regret these innovations as much as we do the `blink` element.

Other Properties

In a sense we've only scraped the surface of many of the new properties available in CSS3, and proposed and implemented in browsers like Firefox, Safari, and Opera today. Some of the other new CSS properties you might be interested in include the following:

Border Images

You can specify an image to be used as the border of an element. Presently supported in Opera, Safari, and Firefox, border images can be tricky to use, because they require slicing a single image into components to be used as the borders and corners of an element. And in some ways, RGBa colors, `box-shadow`, and `border-radius` reduce the need for border images, as these are the kinds of decorations developers and designers usually add to the borders of an element.

A widely-seen example of `border-image` in use is in IUI-based applications tailored to mobile Safari. IUI is an HTML, CSS, and JavaScript framework that helps give web-based applications and sites a "native" iPhone appearance and behavior.

IUI uses `border-image` to create buttons. Figure **13.19** shows a source image and some examples of buttons created from it. This single image and the `border-image` property can create a button of varying widths:

13.19
Buttons styled with
`border-image`

Multiple Background Images

CSS3 allows you to add multiple background images to a single element, though this is presently only supported in Safari, where it has been since version 1.3.

As such, its usefulness is limited, as high contrast between foreground text and background colors is essential for good legibility, and when using multiple background images, the contrast between the foreground and various background colors will vary. You'll need to carefully ensure that text is still legible when only a single background image is showing.

CSS Transforms

Like CSS transitions, CSS transforms are a feature of CSS3 proposed by Apple, and are now a working draft, the first stage in the process of becoming a W3C standard. Unlike transitions, transforms are supported by Firefox 3.5 as well as Safari. Transforms allow you to scale and rotate an HTML element (for example, you could rotate a page by 90 degrees) while keeping the element's text still selectable, the links still clickable, and so on.

Transforms are a bit complicated, but anyone with a good grasp of CSS will be able to understand them readily. We won't go into them in detail here because they are difficult to use in ways that degrade gracefully for older browsers. An example of what can be achieved with transforms is the remarkable cube effect (**www.fofronline.com/2009-04/3d-cube-using-css-transformations**) by Paul Hayes [**13.20**].

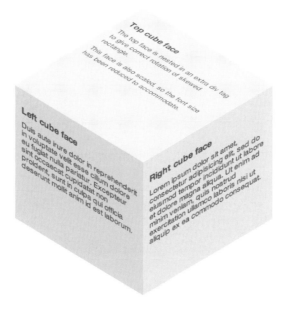

More on CSS Transforms

While transforms are too detailed to explore in depth here, you'll find a full explanation and tools to play with them at this book's companion website (**www.devwws.com**).

Gradients

The gradient background is another increasingly common design effect on the web. Gradients are typically created as images, then added as backgrounds to an element using the `background-image` property. It's also possible to create gradients in SVG. But WebKit once more has proposed an extension to CSS for CSS3, the gradient function. `-webkit-gradient` (implemented in Safari 4 and higher) generates an image which may be used in CSS anywhere an image is— for example, as a `background-image`, a `border-image`, a `list-style-image`, or with generated content. One example is the Apple navigation bar we saw in Chapter 12 [**13.21**].

13.21
Apple's navigation bar, implemented using CSS gradient backgrounds

We create the gradient `background-image` using this CSS rule:

```
background-image: -webkit-gradient(linear, left top,
left bottom, from(#c9c9c9), to(#848484),
color-stop(0.6, #a1a1a1));
```

More on Gradients

While gradients are too detailed to go into in any depth here, you'll find a full explanation and online tools for play with gradients at the book's companion website (**www.devwws.com**).

More, More, More!

There are yet more CSS3 properties in various stages of development—both as standards and in browsers—including features that focus on web application functionality (like editable text, control appearance, and drag and drop) as well as vastly improved typography (which we'll look at in Chapter 15). The properties we've covered in this chapter are on track to be CSS3 standards, and to be widely supported in contemporary browsers. Most importantly, they are relatively easy to implement in backward-compatible ways, so you can safely start using them today to add extra sophistication for users whose browsers support them, without negatively affecting the experience of the users whose browsers don't.

I hope you're now intrigued enough to go and investigate some more CSS3 features, and to start using these in your projects right now... but we aren't finished with CSS3 quite yet. In the next chapter, we'll turn to the question of how, given an increasing variety of web-enabled devices, we can tailor our style sheets to devices based on such characteristics as their resolution, color depth, and more.

Targeting Media with CSS

For many years, developers could safely assume that the platforms their readers were using would be similar to one another: they would have a certain screen size (640px × 480px, 800px × 600px, and so on), screen resolution, color depth, and so on. So developers built sites with a core set of platform characteristics in mind. We assumed everyone had color devices—when was the last time someone used a monochrome device to surf the web... ah yes, the Kindle—rather large minimum screen dimensions (1024px × 768px or higher), a relatively low resolution (72 or 96dpi), and so on. Essentially we assumed users would view our sites using something like a desktop computer or laptop.

But something has happened to the web landscape in the last few years. The diversity of devices that people are using to browse the web has increased significantly, and this is a trend that will only accelerate over time. It's no longer far-fetched to suggest that PCs and laptops will be the minority of devices used for browsing the web sometime in the next five years. There has been an explosion of first-class web experiences on mobile devices like the iPhone, the Palm Pre, Nokia's S60 platform, the Nintendo DSi, and other handheld devices; game machines like the Nintendo Wii, which supports a version of Opera optimized for TV use; internet-enabled televisions like the Panasonic Viera, some versions of which also feature an Opera browser; the high-resolution but monochrome Kindle; and many other devices, all of which are bringing the web to users in a much wider range of formats and locations than we're used to.

The traditional "one size fits all" approach of web development—one that assumes relatively large-screened, low-resolution, full-color devices—will soon make little sense.

Traditionally, we've had a number of options for targeting various devices using CSS:

- The delightfully named user-agent sniffing, in which we use JavaScript to detect the version of the browser and serve a style sheet based on this information. User-agent sniffing can also be done on the server.

- Hacks that rely on browser bugs to hide or show a style sheet to a browser (we covered this in some detail in Chapter 7).

- CSS **@media** rules and links to different style sheets based on media types in HTML 4.01.

Let's take a closer look at these approaches.

User-Agent Sniffing

User-agent sniffing is something to avoid, for a number of reasons.

- Client-side browser detection relies on JavaScript being enabled, and a surprising percentage of web users (five percent or more, according to **www.w3schools.com/browsers/browsers_stats.asp**) have JavaScript disabled, particularly in larger organizations and in the financial sector.

- Browsers lie. Because so many developers have used this technique badly in the past, thus effectively excluding or downgrading the experience of users of unsupported browsers (even if their browsers could cope perfectly well with the site), many browsers spoof their identity, typically pretending to be Internet Explorer. As a consequence, determining the actual identity of a browser can be very tricky.

- Browsers improve. Just because a version of a browser did not support a feature, or otherwise failed to display your site well, this does not mean that it always will. Using browser detection means keeping track of an ever more complicated matrix of browsers and versions over time. And that's without beginning to worry about mobile devices, gaming machines, TVs, eBook readers, web-ready refrigerators, and so on.

Hacks

Using browser hacks might occasionally be worth the effort and risk for *very* specific situations such as working around a particular browser bug, but for serving different style sheets to different browsers based on their media types, it's really not a solution.

So, is there a solution? Yes. You guessed it: CSS3 media queries.

Media Queries

As we saw in Chapter 4, HTML has supported the ability to link to different style sheets based on the media type of the display (Screen, Print, Handheld, Projector, TV, and so on) since version 4. It was a good idea in theory, but not widely used in practice, largely because with the exception of the Print media type, the Projection media type in Opera, and a small number of mobile browsers with the Handheld media type, browsers haven't really supported the technology.

CSS3 introduces a much more sophisticated, flexible mechanism for targeting different media according to such features of a device as its width, height, orientation (portrait or landscape), and resolution. The media query mechanism is based on the same concepts and syntax as HTML 4 media types, and has been cleverly designed so as to be backward compatible with today's browsers.

It's important to understand how this differs from browser-focused approaches to compatibility we've seen in earlier chapters. With media queries, we don't target specific browsers. Rather, we tailor visual designs for a given media type, regardless of the browser being used to display the page. With this method, we can take into account small screen sizes in some devices, high-resolution screens in others, low-resolution screens in still others, and so on. We can even design for combinations of these features—for example, we might tailor a style sheet specifically for small, high-resolution, monochrome screens.

How Yahoo Grades Browsers

Yahoo Developer Network, home to some of the industry's most thoughtful and influential web developers and many valuable open source projects like the Yahoo User Interface Library (YUI), has a "graded browser" approach, detailed at their development site: **developer.yahoo.com/yui/articles/gbs**.

They have three levels of support:

- C Grade: Browsers to which they deliver only semantic HTML—with no CSS or JavaScript delivered. About 3% of their visitors receive "C Grade" pages.
- A Grade: These receive the full features of the site, delivered via HTML, CSS, and JavaScript. They claim 96% of site visitors receive this level of support.
- X Grade: About 1% of browsers are not known to be either A or C Grade, due to their rarity. They are treated as A Grade.

Here's how media queries work: rather than simply specifying a targeted type of media from a limited predefined set (as in HTML 4 and CSS2), CSS3 media queries allow you to specify the *characteristics* of the device you are targeting. For example, you might want a specific style sheet for devices with a maximum screen width of 800px × 600px, that aren't handheld devices, or one style sheet for printing to color printers, and another for printing to black-and-white printers.

In addition to the familiar HTML 4 media types, such as Print, Screen, Handheld, and so on, CSS3 media queries introduce a number of media features including:

- **width:** the width of the *viewport*—the viewport is typically the window, but for some devices, such as the iPhone (which has no windows), it's the device width

- **height:** the height of the viewport (see above)
- **device-width:** the width of the entire screen—or in the case of print, the page); for devices like the iPhone, this will be the same as the width
- **device-height:** the height of the device or page
- **resolution:** the pixel density of the device—for example, the typical resolution for common operating systems is 72dpi for the Mac OS, 96dpi for Windows, 160dpi for the iPhone, and 163dpi for the iPod touch
- **color:** the number of bits per color component (the value will be 0 for monochrome devices)
- **monochrome:** the number of grayscale bits for the device (the value will be 0 for color devices)

CSS3 media queries also include logical operators like `and`, `not`, and `or`, and the prefixes `min-` and `max-`. The media features, along with these operators, let us form *expressions* that narrow the scope of the HTML 4 media types. An example media query might be:

```
(max-width: 600px) and (max-height: 800px)
```

An expression is contained in brackets, and each expression is either true or false. A device with a `width` of 600px and a `height` of 900px won't be targeted by the media query in the example above, because while it matches the first expression, it doesn't match the second.

Using Media Queries

Like media types in HTML 4 and CSS2, media queries are used with either `@media` statements, or as the value of a `media` attribute of a `link` element in the `head` of an HTML document. In the `media` attribute or `@media` statement, we specify the criteria we want the media to meet in order for the `@media` statement or linked style sheet to be used.

For example, we might want a style sheet to be served only when a page is to be printed in color. For this example, we'd use a statement like this:

```
@media print and (color) {
  . . .
}
```

The preceding example tells a device to use only the `@media` statement for printed media, and only for color devices.

Similarly, if we want a linked style sheet to be used only when the window is greater than 800px wide, we can use the following:

```
<link rel="stylesheet" media="all and (min-width:800px)" />
```

And if you wanted to use a linked style sheet only when the device window is less than 800px wide, you could use this:

```
<link rel="stylesheet" media="all and (max-width:799px)" />
```

Media queries are cleverly designed so that older browsers can still use them to an extent. A browser which only recognizes the older keywords like *"print"* and *"all"* will recognize the first word it sees—for example, *"screen"*—but once it sees a keyword like *"and,"* it will ignore the rest of the statement. This allows us to use media queries for newer devices that recognize them, and older ones that don't. Browsers that don't support CSS3 media queries, but do support older style media statements will see `@media print and (color)`, and treat it like a standard print style sheet.

We can even use media queries to specifically target a device, such as the iPhone, by targeting its particular features. For example, this statement:

```
@media only (device-width: 480px) {
  . . .
}
```

targets the iPhone in landscape mode—and other devices with a device width of *exactly* 480px—while this:

```
@media only (device-width: 320px) {
...
}
```

targets devices with a width of 320px, like the iPhone in portrait mode.

Why the `only`, you ask? Well, `all` is the default value for a media type, so if we simply use this statement:

```
@media (device-width: 320px) {
...
}
```

then older browsers might use this statement, seeing it as:

```
@media all and (device-width: 320px) {
...
}
```

Similarly, we can hide a style sheet from a device with a maximum `device-width` of more than 480px (including, of course, the iPhone) using this code:

```
@media only (device-width: 481px) {
...
}
```

We can also make our media queries even more specific. For example, if we wanted to specify only devices with a device width of exactly 480px in portrait mode, we could use:

```
@media only (device-width: 480px) and
(orientation: landscape) {

...
}
```

To bring all these examples together, media queries take the format of a comma-separated list of entries. Entries may be media types (like Print and TV, and so on, specified in CSS2 and HTML 4) or *expressions* comprising an optional media type (such as `screen`) plus a logical statement about the features the device must support to use this style sheet or `@media` rule (such as `max-width: 480px`). These logical expressions are contained within brackets, as in the preceding example:

```
(device-width: 480px) and (orientation: landscape)
```

`@media` rules are widely supported, and CSS3 media queries are currently supported by Safari 3 and higher (including Mobile Safari in the iPod touch and iPhone), Opera 9.5, and Firefox 3.5 or higher.

Many of these features, like `device-width`, `resolution`, or `color depth` might seem to be fixed for each device, but that's not necessarily true. Rotate a device like the Palm Pre or iPhone, and it changes page orientation from landscape to portrait—or vice versa—and takes on a new `device-width` at the same time. Similarly, although it's more uncommon for users to change the resolution on a device, such as an external monitor, doing so will still change the `device-width`, even while a page is displaying. Even moving a browser window from one screen to another in a multi-monitor setup will almost certainly change the resolution, and quite possibly other features as well. And, of course, the `width` of a page can be changed on a desktop browser by resizing the window.

Given this inherent instability in device characteristics, the question arises: if features change while a page is displaying, when will the browser redraw the page using the new value for the media queries? The specification is silent on this issue, so it's up to the browser implementers to make a decision. Firefox 3.5 and Opera 10 beta generally redraw a page when the window is resized, regardless of which features are associated with a media query. Safari seems to redraw a page after the window is resized *only* when width is part of the media query—if other features (like resolution or device width) are part of a media query but width is not, Safari only redraws the page on reload. So we can't rely on the browser to redraw the page based on a media query if features of the device change after the page is loaded. The sole exception seems to be `device-width`, which prompts Safari, Firefox, and Opera to redraw the page based on the media query when the window is resized.

What Are Media Queries Good For?

CSS3 media queries are intended to let developers tailor the presentation of content to the device presenting that content, rather than serving different content to different devices. Still not convinced of their usefulness? Read on.

Even as monitor (and laptop) screen sizes and resolutions get larger, a new breed of small-screened netbooks has evolved, and mobile devices like smart phones offer yet smaller screens. Optimizing page layout across this broad range of widths is becoming increasingly challenging. Many developers use a JavaScript-based technique Cameron Adams calls "resolution dependent layout" (**www. themaninblue.com/writing/perspective/2004/09/21**), which involves changing the number of columns in a layout based on the width of a browser window. With media queries, you can achieve this effect *without* JavaScript.

Here's how: as the length of a line of text increases, the text eventually becomes harder to read, so we need a way of serving shorter line-lengths for users with big screens, without neglecting users of smaller screens. Using a CSS3 media query with `max-width`, we can specify, for example, that:

- window widths of more than 1280px will get three columns of text,
- window widths of between 800 and 1280px will get two columns of text, and
- even narrower window sizes will get a single column of text.

This approach will keep the line length from getting too long for readability, and yet ensures lines don't become too short, which can also reduce readability. To accomplish this, we'll use two **@media** statements (or two links to different style sheets): one for widths of at least 1280px, and another for widths of at least 800px. Let's revisit the multi-column text example from Chapter 13, and force it to adapt to different window widths:

```
@media (min-width: 1024px){
  .section {
    column-count: 2;
    column-gap: 5em;
  }


}
@media (min-width: 1280px){
  .section {
    column-count: 3;
}
```

We will also have a base rule for the aspects of the layout that we want to serve to all devices:

```
.section {
  margin: 2em .5em;
  column-gap: 5em;
  column-rule: .1em #d2d2d2 solid;
}
```

Depending on the user's window width, they'd see one, two, or three columns, as figures **14.1**, **14.2**, and **14.3** show.

14.1

Our content will display with three columns at widths greater than or equal to 1280px.

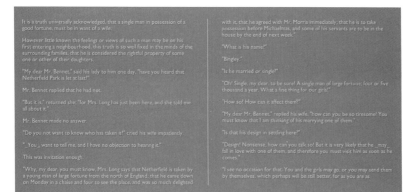

14.2
Two columns at widths between 800px and 1280px

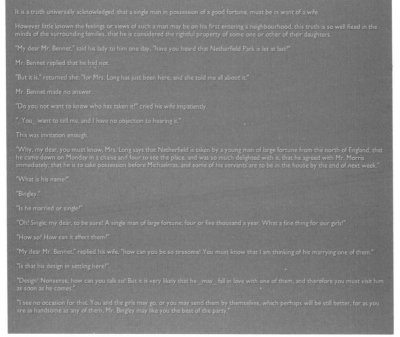

14.3
And a single column at widths less than 800px

As we saw a moment ago, in browsers that support media queries and multi-column text features, the number of columns will change as the width of the window changes.

An even more obvious reason to use media queries is to target mobile devices. This can come in handy not simply for different layouts, but also for developing lighter pages that download faster and use less bandwidth.

As we saw, CSS2 and HTML 4 introduced a number of media types, including Handheld. So, why not simply use that? For a variety of reasons, mobile WebKit-based browsers (which include, of course, Mobile Safari on the iPhone and iPod touch) don't identify themselves as handheld devices, and so don't use linked style sheets or `@media` statements that have a media type of Handheld. Since there's no specific media type to which all mobile devices definitely belong, how else might we use one or more media features to specify a mobile device?

In this case, we are going to have to make an assumption—for example, that mobile devices will have screens of less than 500px in width. We'll also want to ensure that older browsers that don't support media queries won't use this style sheet. To do that, we'll use the `only` keyword as one of the media features, and a `max-width` of 500px.

```
<link rel="stylesheet" media="only and (max-width: 500px)"
href="path/to/stylesheet">
```

In fact, this example demonstrates why media types like Mobile aren't necessarily a sensible way of specifying a style sheet to be used with a given device. That approach is built on the assumption that all devices of a particular type—mobile, projection, print, TV, and so on—will share common characteristics with other devices of the same media type. But of course, devices within a particular media type may vary dramatically in terms of width, resolution, and other features. It's far better to focus on the particular *characteristics* of the device, using features that let us tailor a design to the user's current browsing setup, regardless of the actual device being used.

As the web becomes accessible on an ever-increasing array of devices with different characteristics, media queries can provide a stable, backward- and forward-compatible mechanism for targeting these devices.

Compatibility

CSS3 media queries are widely supported in Safari 3.1 and higher, Opera 9 and higher, and Firefox 3.5 and higher. Not every media feature of CSS3 media queries is supported in each of these browsers.

But Is This Really Any Better Than User-Agent Sniffing?

You may be wondering, Just how are these complicated-looking media queries any better than user-agent sniffing? Happily, the answer is simple. Whereas user-agent sniffing targets specific browsers or browser versions, media queries target specific media and—more importantly—device characteristics, regardless of what browser displays the page. After all, even today, Opera might be running on a laptop, a mobile device, the Wii, or a television. A WebKit-based browser might be running on a mobile device or laptop, as might Internet Explorer and Firefox. All other problems aside, user-agent sniffing just isn't up to coping with the huge variety of user agents on the web.

Furthermore, whereas user-agent sniffing is often used to work around buggy CSS support in specific browsers, media queries are used to deliver the appropriate style sheet to *any* browser based on the medium in use. This means that any browser that supports media queries will be able to use a style sheet specified for, say, color printing on US Letter pages, or for windows wider than 1024px, where the minimum resolution is 72dpi. There's no need to continually update your matrix of browser support, since you're not targeting browsers. As new browsers and browser versions are released, there'll be no need to change anything to support them—your media queries will just…work. And, as we've seen, we can use media queries now with browsers that already support HTML 4 media-based linking and CSS2 `@media` rules, even if they don't yet support features in media queries.

The Wrap

The web's ties to the PC and laptop are fast disappearing. It's time to make sure your designs work in devices like high-resolution handhelds, low-resolution TVs, and other increasingly common browsing platforms. Media queries are a key tool in achieving this.

Web Fonts

For most of its history, the web has been a text-based medium. Despite this, the range of fonts available to web designers and developers has been severely limited. Unless a font is installed on a user's system, a designer can't use it, so we've been forced to rely on a small palette of fonts installed on both major web browsing platforms, Mac OS X and Windows. Despite the fact that both OS X and Windows come with dozens of installed fonts, the overlap between the two platforms is small. As we've seen, CSS does provide a mechanism for specifying a group of fonts so the browser has fallback options if a specific font isn't installed. Unless we specify a group of fonts that have roughly the same default size, the legibility and appearance of the page can be markedly different depending on which font is available.

As a consequence, designers have several techniques that use images or Flash for text, while still attempting to maintain the accessibility of their sites. Such techniques, which we saw in Part I, fall short of really solving the problem. They produce complicated markup and—in the case of image-replacement schemes—greatly increase the complexity of production workflows, as each piece of image-replacement text must be rendered as an image before that image can be embedded or added via CSS. Every time the text needs to be changed, the image must be edited and re-uploaded—not to mention that linking to so many images can harm site performance. Flash-based image replacement techniques come with their own problems, not least of which is that Flash's text-rendering engine is different from the browser's text-rendering engine.

Even after text-replacement effects are achieved, they're far from ideal. For image-based text, the text can't be found by the user with the browser's "find" functionality, and when text or the page is zoomed, the image either doesn't zoom at all (with text zooming), or becomes pixelated (with page zooming). These techniques can also produce design problems: The replaced text, having been rendered by a tool such as Photoshop, or Flash, is necessarily rendered differently from all other text in the document, which has been rendered by the operating system. All in all, these methods aren't really *solutions* at all, but their popularity speaks volumes about designers' need for a wider variety of fonts.

The irony is that for the last decade or more—since long before the invention of techniques like FIR (Fahrner Image Replacement) and sIFR (Scalable Inman Flash Replacement)—most people have been using a browser that actually supports real font embedding, the ability to download fonts from a web server, and render pages with these fonts. So, why haven't we seen this technology in use? Therein lies a tale.

Linking vs. Embedding

What's the difference between "linking" and "embedding" a font? In truth, the distinction is largely artificial, and the terms are often used interchangeably.

Linking technically refers to the use of a downloadable external font file that has not been altered to be associated with the page or domain it is being used to render. With this method, the same font file could be linked to from any page regardless of its domain.

Embedding typically refers to using a font file somehow altered so that it is tied to a specific page or domain. Embedded font files can't be used on any page on any domain, only in association with the page or domain they're associated with.

A Brief History of Font Linking and Embedding

The release of version 4 of both Netscape Navigator and Internet Explorer marked a watershed in web development history. Both browsers introduced real-world (rather than experimental) support for CSS and support for something approaching what we know as the modern DOM—the two standards that have defined modern web design and development.

Both browsers also supported font linking. That's right—in both IE4 and Netscape 4, it was possible for designers to use fonts that lived on a web server, rather than on each user's machine. The catch? The two browsers used incompatible methods to do so.

Netscape 4 used TrueDoc, a format created by a font technology company called Bitstream. Internet Explorer 4 (and every subsequent version of IE) used the proprietary Embedded OpenType (EOT) format. Web developers, on the other hand, didn't really use either. They never fully adopted TrueDoc, in part because when Netscape became an open source project as of version 6, it lost access to TrueDoc due to licensing complications. And although Internet Explorer still supports EOT, the format never caught on with developers, even at the height of IE's popularity. Precisely why is difficult to say. EOT was and is a Microsoft proprietary format, a fact that may have made early-adopter web

developers less likely to embrace the technology (it has subsequently been proposed as a W3 standard format, though it currently seems doubtful that it will
become one). Perhaps more importantly, EOT files are complex and difficult to
create, a fact that has discouraged developers from experimenting with them.

Whatever the particular reason—and despite a clear demand for more sophisticated typography on the web—font embedding has simply not taken off. However, due to recent technical, legal, and business developments, this may be
about to change.

The Current Legal Situation

Before we delve into the technical aspects of using fonts served on the web, it's
important to understand the legal implications of such use.

Fonts, like a great many other creative works, are protected by copyright. In
the absence of an express license to do so, fonts can't be copied or distributed.
Which almost certainly means that placing a font on a server and allowing
browsers to use it to render web pages—without express permission to do so—is
a breach of copyright. Remember that phrase, "express permission," because
it's going to come up a lot.

What About Image Replacement?

You might be wondering why then it is permissible to use a rendered image
of a font, as with FIR and other image replacement techniques. Just as a copy
of a piece of music is still subject to copyright, why isn't a copy of an image
rendered with the font? (We're copying the fonts' letterforms after all.) The
difference is that the copyright in fonts lies not in the letterforms themselves,
but in the hinting information that smoothly renders the font onto a screen.

When you purchase a font, you typically agree to an End User License Agreement (EULA). The terms of these licenses vary; commercial fonts are rarely
licensed in a way that allows them to be used via font linking. Furthermore,
although there are many "free" fonts available online, at least for alphabets
used in Western European languages, in the absence of an *express license to
do so*, you can't legally upload these fonts to your server and use them for font

linking. You can read an overview of the legal problems with free font licensing at TypeKit (**blog.typekit.com/2009/06/11/when-free-fonts-arent-free**), a service we'll discuss in detail shortly.

The Current Technical Situation

Although IE has supported font embedding using the EOT format for over a decade, until Safari 3.1, no other modern browser supported font linking or embedding. With 3.1, Safari introduced support for font linking, for the True-Type and OpenType formats—the formats that operating systems use for fonts—but not the EOT format. Firefox 3.5 and Opera 10 beta also support font linking to TrueType and OpenType fonts, but again, not the embedding of EOT fonts.

So, are we back where we were in 1997, when each major browser offered competing, incompatible formats? Luckily, no. We can use a CSS mechanism that links to fonts in such a way that Internet Explorer will use EOT and other browsers will use TrueType or OpenType. Nevertheless, we must keep in mind that we can only legally use fonts when we have express permission to link.

@font-face and Embedding Fonts

The process of linking or embedding a font is *nearly* identical for all modern browsers. We do have to take into account the different formats those browsers support, but we can do so in a standards-based, efficient way.

The first step in the process is to specify a font name and source using the CSS statement **@font-face**. We can then use this newly named font in our CSS just as we would any other font. **@font-face** was introduced in CSS2 and is modified in CSS3. An **@font-face** statement defines the name of a font to be used in a style sheet, and the source of the font (a URL locating the font file on a server). Here's how we'd define a font called "Blackout":

```
@font-face {
    font-family: Blackout;
    src: url(http://server.com/fonts/blackout.eot)
}
```

We would then use this font for headings of level 1 in our pages like this:

```
h1 {
   font-family: Blackout, san-serif;
   }
```

You can think of the name in the `@font-face` statement as a variable—it doesn't have to match the font's file name on the server, but it's the name we must use in our style sheet.

That's it. Simple isn't it? If you're wondering why font linking has been used so sparingly, though, you're about to find out the answer.

Embedding Fonts with Internet Explorer

Before we can embed a font with Internet Explorer, we must convert it to the EOT format. Because EOT files are "tied" to specific web pages, we can't simply create an EOT file once and be done with it. Every time we create a new site—and depending on various factors, even when we add new pages to our site—we will probably need to create a new EOT file. Furthermore, there's really only one way to create such files, and it's not an especially pleasant experience.

Firstly, you'll need Windows.

Yep. Well, technically, there's a UNIX command-line utility called TT2EOT, which you can also use on Mac OS X, for those who are comfortable with such things. Otherwise, you'll need to download the Web Embedding Font Tool (WEFT) from Microsoft, which runs only on Windows.

The WEFT tool takes a font file in a format like TrueType, and a web page, and creates the EOT file from that combination. By default, the EOT file won't contain the entire font—it will contain a *subset* of the font's characters, based on the contents of the web page you feed it. You can force the WEFT tool to make EOT files that contain the entire character set, which will result in larger but more maintainable files. WEFT requires that you give it a list of "allowed roots" or access URLs for the font. In other words, you must encode into the EOT file all the root URLs you want to use the font with. So, for example, you might need to use **http://webdirections.org**, **http://www.webdirections.org**—and, for good measure, **file://c:** so you can test your pages locally—as well as the addresses of internal test servers, and so on.

Once the EOT font has been created, you can upload it to your server and then use `@font-face` and CSS as described earlier, setting the `src` URL value to the location of the font file on the server.

Linking Fonts with Other Browsers

Because other (non-IE) browsers support linking to TrueType and OpenType fonts, the formats that operating systems also use, there's no need to process these font formats in any way before using them with `@font-face`. We simply upload the fonts to a server, and create an `@font-face` rule that assigns the font a name and specifies the URL where the font is located.

We can then define two different `@font-face` rules defining two different fonts: one for Internet Explorer, and one for other browsers that support True-Type and OpenType formats:

```
@font-face {
   font-family: Product;
   src: url(./fonts/Know-Your-Product/know_your_product.ttf)
}

@font-face {
   font-family: Fenwick;
   src: url(./fonts/Fenwick/fenwick-2.eot)
}
```

and then our CSS looks like this:

```
h1 {font-family: Product, Fenwick, san-serif}
```

We've defined a TrueType font, "Product", and an EOT font, "Fenwick". But we still have a challenge. Font files tend to be quite large—they may be several hundred KB per file (or more). If a browser downloads all the fonts defined by `@font-face` statements, it will download twice as many as it requires. (Safari 4 won't download files with names ending with .eot defined in `@font-face` rules, but Firefox 3.5 will, and Internet Explorer will download TrueType and Open-Type fonts even though it can't use them.)

We can do two things to ensure that browsers download only the formats they support, and so improve the performance of our site. First, with our `@font-face` rule for non-IE browsers, we add a format hint (which is part of CSS3) after the `src`, like this:

```
@font-face {
  font-family: Product;
  src: url(./fonts/Know-Your-Product/know_your_product.ttf)
  format("truetype")
}
```

Internet Explorer ignores any `@font-face` statement with a hint like this.

Hiding statements from Firefox and other browsers, however, requires falling back on trusty conditional comments, which we met in Part II. Because conditional comments work only in HTML, we can only hide the `@font-face` statement for IE from other browsers by putting it into a separate CSS file and then hiding the link to this file using comments, like this:

```
<!--[if IE]>
<link rel="stylesheet" type="text/css" media=
"screen, projection" href="style/iefonts.css" />
<[end if]-->
```

If the `@font-face` statement is in the head of a document—though, as we've seen, embedding CSS instead of linking to a separate style sheet is not generally recommended; instead, use something like this:

```
<!--[if IE]>
@font-face {
  font-family: Fenwick;
  src: url(./fonts/Fenwick/fenwick-2.eot)
}
<[end if]-->
```

Challenges

Using these techniques with properly licensed fonts, we can design our pages using a much broader range of fonts than we have previously relied on. We can also avoid the hacks and attendant downsides of font-replacement techniques. Once a user's browser has downloaded a font linked using the methods just discussed, text set in that font can be cut and pasted, zoomed without text pixelation, and so on—all things you can't do with font replacement.

Still, as noted earlier, font files can be quite large, and each is an individual file. So unless they are cached locally, it will take some time for fonts to be downloaded and used to render a page. This raises a question: While a font is downloading, what should a browser do? Not display the text in those fonts on a page at all? Display it with substitute fonts? Both solutions can cause problems for the end user. If a large section of a page remains blank for seconds while a font downloads, readers may conclude the page is broken. The alternative— styling with one font, then switching to a second once it is downloaded— is potentially disorienting, since the text may shift around on the page to accommodate the size metrics of the new font.

Safari chooses the former approach and leaves large gaps where text will be when the font is downloaded. Firefox, Opera, and Internet Explorer all use the second approach, using a generic font, then swapping in the specified font once it downloads. Neither is ideal, but until connection speeds increase significantly, one or the other of these approaches will be required. (And with some effort, you can simulate either approach using JavaScript, thus forcing Safari to adopt the default-font-then-switch behavior, or making IE, Opera, and Firefox leave blank space until the font is downloaded.)

It's not clear whether viewers will be too concerned about a change in font once the font is downloaded, though anecdotally, Safari's approach of not rendering text until the font is downloaded does seem to confuse or disturb readers. In a year or two, we'll have a much clearer picture of what behavior web users find acceptable.

@*font-face* Support in Contemporary Browsers

	IE 4	Safari 3.1	Firefox 3.5	Opera 10
Formats	EOT	TrueType/ OpenType	TrueType/ OpenType	TrueType/ OpenType
Preload behavior	Generic font	Invisible text	Generic font	Generic font
Downloads unsupported formats?	Yes (use format hint)	No (ignores .eot extension)	Yes (use conditional comments)	No

Mitigating the Problems

Given the usability challenges associated with font linking, it may make sense to restrict the use of downloaded fonts to headings and other non-body text. That way, the user—who is likely to be focusing on the main page content anyway—can begin reading immediately and won't be overly distracted once the linked fonts download, since the text they are reading is likely to remain largely unaffected by the loading-in of the linked fonts.

Due to the performance problems we've noted, you'll probably want to use as few fonts as possible—and, where possible, to use fonts with smaller file sizes. And, of course, make sure each browser downloads only the font formats it needs. (Sadly, you can't simply zip your fonts.)

Fonts as a Service

Once `@font-face` began to be supported in Safari, Firefox, and Opera instead of only in IE, several groups spotted a business opportunity as a provider of "fonts as a service"—that is, of inexpensive, hosted, and fully licensed fonts that web developers can easily use. As of mid 2009, three such services have been announced: TypeKit, Kernest, and FontDeck. Full disclosure: I'm an advisor for TypeKit, and my blog posts on web fonts motivated the service's founding. It's impossible to know which of these services will succeed, it seems likely that services such as these will help developers surmount the legal and technical obstacles preventing them from linking to fonts and will thus hasten the arrival of widespread downloadable fonts on the web.

The Wrap

Now supported in all contemporary browsers, the use of downloadable fonts in web development is both technically feasible and practical. Legal challenges remain, but several new "fonts as a service" projects are poised to address this hurdle—plus, it's increasingly likely that at least some foundries will see the revenue potential in font embedding and linking and will license their fonts for use in this way without the need to go via an intermediary .

Used judiciously, font embedding will offer a new sophistication long lacking in web typography. As with the `blink` element back in the 1990s, new typo-graphical options will doubtless produce some dreadful sites, but despite that, the web will be the better for embedded fonts. Use them well, and your sites will delight your visitors—who have, after all, been wandering a typographical wasteland since the web was born.

SVG and the Canvas: Rich Graphics in the Browser

For over a decade, browsers have supported a range of bitmap image formats (such as GIF, PNG, and JPG) natively, but the search for a standard, widely supported, native vector image format for the web continues to this day. Though not widely used for this purpose, Flash has provided vector web graphics since the mid 1990s in every browser that supports the Flash plug-in.

In 1998, Microsoft and Macromedia proposed VML (Vector Markup Language) as a W3C standard for vector graphics. Around the same time, Adobe, Sun Microsystems, and others proposed the competing PGML (Precision Graphics Markup Language) format. In the end, neither PGML nor VML were adopted. Instead, in 1999, the W3 began working on the Scalable Vector Graphics (SVG) format, and in 2001, they finalized SVG 1.0.

Vector vs. Bitmap

Vector images treat each of the lines, curves, and other aspects of an image as individual *objects*. PNG, GIF, and JPG, while all "bitmap" formats, differ considerably from one another, as we saw in Chapter 3. Bitmap formats divide an image into a two-dimensional matrix of pixels and store information (such as color) about each pixel. (You can think of a checkerboard as an 8 x 8 two-dimensional matrix.)

The most significant difference between the two formats is that vector graphics are resolution independent—that is, they can be scaled indefinitely up or down in size, and maintain the smoothness of their lines, curves, and so on.

Vector and bitmap images have different uses. Bitmaps are typically best for photographic images, while vectors are best for artwork and illustrations comprising lines and curves. Despite this, bitmaps are still widely used on the web where vector images would be more appropriate, due to the lack of native support for a single standard vector format across all major browsers.

SVG has been widely adopted: the format is now supported natively by all modern browsers except for Internet Explorer, which continues to support VML natively and SVG via plug-ins. Despite this, in 2004 Apple introduced another vector solution—the HTML **canvas** element. Unlike SVG, the **canvas** element is not actually a format: it's an HTML element with a programmatic interface that allows images to be generated "on the fly" using JavaScript. The **canvas** element, initially controversial among standards-focused developers, has become part of the HTML5 standard and is now supported in all modern browsers other than Internet Explorer. There are also workarounds that enable the use of **canvas** with Internet Explorer, and we'll look them later on in this chapter.

In this chapter, I'll focus on SVG and the canvas: how they work, what they are designed for, the challenges of using them in the real world today, and some of their core concepts and syntax. Each of them is worthy of a book themselves, so I won't be able to do much more than touch on their many uses and features. Still, I hope you'll get a sense of their uses and get interested in exploring them more. As always, you'll find resources for learning more at the end of this book.

SVG

SVG is a vector graphics format; it's also an application of XML. This means that every line, curve, path, and other component of an image in SVG format is marked up in XML—and that, in theory, you can author SVG with nothing more than a text editor. In practice, complex images quickly become very complex XML documents, so text-based editing of SVG files is not usually practical. Here's some simple SVG code for drawing a red rectangle 100px tall and 200px wide:

```
<svg xmlns="http://www.w3.org/2000/svg">
    <rect x="100" y="100" height="100" width="200"
    fill="#0000ff"/>
</svg>
```

SVG is capable of all sorts of effects you might be familiar with from vector drawing applications like Illustrator or Freehand, including support for:

- Basic shapes like circles and polygons
- Including other graphics formats like PNGs
- Bézier paths and curves
- Text, including text on complex paths
- Opacity
- Transformations, like rotate, skew, and scale (we saw in Chapter 13 how CSS3 has proposed support for transformations, which closely mirrors SVG transformations)
- Gradients
- Animations

and much more.

Core SVG Concepts and Syntax

As an application of XML, the basic SVG syntax should be reasonably familiar to web developers who are comfortable hand-coding their HTML. Mostly, SVG documents are composed of SVG elements (like `circle` and `rect`), attributes (like `height` and `width`), and CSS.

Whether your SVG is inline (that is, part of your XHTML document itself), or embedded (that is, in a stand-alone SVG file, linked to from an HTML or XHTML document using the **object** or **img** element), the root of all SVG is an **svg** element:

```
<svg   xmlns="http://www.w3.org/2000/svg"></svg>
```

Namespaces

You may be wondering about **xmlns**. It's an XML namespace attribute. Namespaces are a mechanism in XML that allow the use of more than one variation of XML (for example, SVG and XHTML) in a single document. They're needed because two XML-based languages might share the same name for an element. If that were the case, when a parser encountered such an element, there'd be no way of knowing which language the element was part of without some kind of labeling. Web developers can, on the whole, ignore namespaces—they play no part at all in HTML, and are only relevant if you use XHTML or the XHTML version of HTML5.

Within the **svg** element, there can be one or more elements, such as lines, shapes, and text. We can group these elements using the **g** element, and once elements are grouped, transformations and other effects applied to the group apply to all its descendants.

Some of the most common SVG elements are:

Rectangles—the **rect** element. These have a top-left position, specified by the attributes x and y, respectively, a width and height, and optional horizontal and vertical corner radii. Here's an example:

```
<rect x="20" y="20" rx="0" ry="0" width="160" height="160"
fill="#444" />
```

This is an *empty* element—it has no content, and so closes with **/>**, like empty elements such as **br** in XHTML. You might also notice that the numeric attributes (like height) have no units of measurement—in SVG, length values with no units are assumed to be in pixels.

Circles—specified using the `circle` element. Circles have a horizontal and vertical center, and a radius.

```
<circle cx="100" cy="100" r="90" stroke="#666"
fill="#fff" />
```

The default fill color of an object like `rect` or `circle` is black.

Ellipses—specified with the `ellipse` element. Ellipses have a horizontal and vertical center, and horizontal and vertical radii.

```
<ellipse cx="100" cy="100" rx="120" ry="80" fill="blue" />
```

Figure **16.1** shows each of these shapes as rendered in Safari, which has native SVG support.

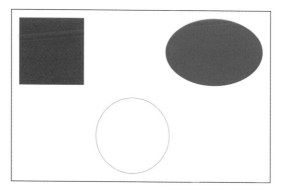

16.1
The rectangle, circle, and ellipse rendered by Safari

The SVG Coordinate System

Unlike the Cartesian coordinate system we are all familiar with from high school mathematics, in which y values increase on the plane from 0, in the SVG coordinate system, a **y** value of 0 is at the top of the page or containing element. The higher the value for **y**, the further down the page or containing element we are. Figure **16.2** shows this in action. This shouldn't cause web developers familiar with CSS any trouble, as this is how CSS also uses vertical values.

16.2

The Cartesian (left) and
SVG (right) coordinate
systems

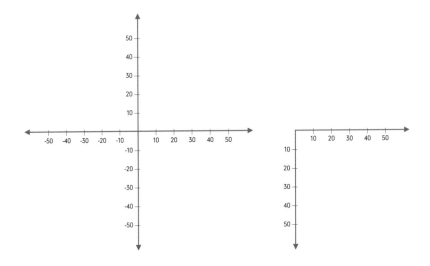

There's obviously a great deal more to SVG than these basic shapes and attributes, but this should provide a taste of how SVG works. As mentioned earlier, most SVG is likely to be generated using tools, or by software, and most web developers are unlikely to need a detailed knowledge of the features of SVG in their day-to-day work.

Benefits of SVG

As you'll see in the sections that follow, the process of using SVG in our work can be a little bit complicated. So before we go any further, you may be wondering, "Is there really any point in going to all this trouble to use SVG?"

Well…yes.

SVG has several benefits that make it well worth considering when choosing an image format for your web content. Before examining those benefits in more detail, though, I should note that there are uses for which SVG is an inappropriate format: photographs and other images that are *fundamentally bitmaps* are better formatted as JPG (photographs) and PNG (non-photo bitmaps) images. For almost everything else, though, SVG is at the very least a strong candidate.

Now let's take a look at what makes SVG so special.

Accessibility

SVG is designed to make images accessible as a matter of course.

When a user magnifies an SVG image, as people with visual disabilities often need to do, the image remains essentially unaltered. Bitmap images, on the other hand, often become less comprehensible as they are scaled up. Figure **16.3** shows what happens when the image shown in figure 16.1 is zoomed as a bitmap image.

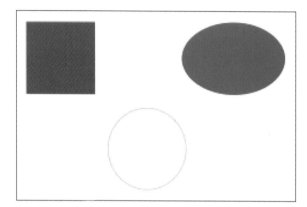

16.3
Bitmap images scale poorly compared with SVG images.

Additionally, in SVG, text is rendered *as text*, and developers can easily build in textual equivalents for objects. A bar graph, for example, could have built-in textual equivalents for each bar, while an illustration of an engine could have a built-in text equivalent for each component.

File sizes

In most circumstances, the file size of an SVG image will be much smaller than the same image rendered as a bitmap image. Bandwidth savings alone can make SVG worth serious consideration.

Scalability

Increasingly, web browsers are offering users full-page zoom capabilities that scale images along with text. SVG images scale much more smoothly than bitmap images, and this feature will only become more important as small, higher-resolution devices like the Palm Pre and the iPhone make zooming a common aspect of web use. The same features that make SVG images more accessible for people with visual disabilities also make them a better fit for a broad range of screen sizes and resolutions.

Scriptability

Every aspect of an SVG image can be manipulated via JavaScript and the DOM. This means you can change SVG image elements' size, fill color, opacity, and so on, just as you can alter these properties of (X)HTML elements.

Animation

While we haven't had the chance to look at this aspect of SVG, it supports animation as a core part of the language. Any SVG element, or group of elements, can be animated in SVG, with no need for scripting.

For example, we might fade the rectangle mentioned earlier using the **animate** element as a child of the **rect** element (in this case, **rect** is now a non-empty element; this is one way in which SVG differs from XHTML: elements can be both empty and non-empty):

```
<rect x="20" y="20" rx="0" ry="0" width="160" height="160"
fill="#444">
<animate attributeType="CSS" attributeName="opacity"
        from="1" to="0" dur="5s" repeatCount="indefinite" />
</rect>
```

We don't have the space to go into SVG animations in detail, but there are links for more information at the end of the book.

SVG Use Cases

Here are just a few of the situations in which SVG is much more appropriate than non-vector formats.

Geographical Information Systems

SVG is being widely used in GIS (for example, in Google Maps—for all browsers other than Internet Explorer, in which VML is used).

Graphs and Data Visualization

Graphs and other data visualizations are ideal candidates for SVG. Data visualization projects typically have a direct relationship between each aspect of an image (the objects, their size, their color, and so on) and the underlying data. With SVG, each of those data points and relationships can be made explicit, by adding textual equivalents for each of the visual representations of data.

SVG graphs and visualizations are also much more accessible than those made with bitmap images, and they can be scaled by both browsers and users. SVG also makes it much easier to create interactive graphs in which users can, for example, click a bar in the graph to see more information. With image formats like PNG, this would be far more difficult to implement. Figure **16.4** shows an interactive SVG traffic graph.

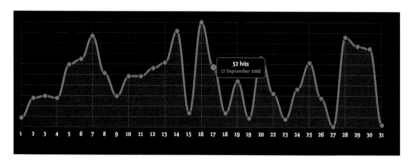

16.4
An interactive SVG traffic graph, developed using Raphaël

Logos

Logos are usually created as vector images, and are often displayed at many different sizes on a site. Rather than creating numerous bitmap versions of a logo, you can simply use a single SVG image.

Including SVG in Web Pages

There are two ways to include SVG in a page: by embedding the SVG file (that is, by linking to it through an `img` or `object` element), or by including the actual SVG within the web page itself. This is referred to as inline SVG.

Embedded SVG

Embedding your SVG is by far the less complicated of the two methods—though "embedding" is a bit of a confusing term, because like all "embedded" HTML content, the SVG file is linked to from the page, rather than being more literally "embedded" in the page. There are two standards-based ways to include an external SVG image in a web page.

The first way to include an SVG image is the most obvious: via the HTML `img` element that we'd use for other image formats such as PNG. But although it's an obvious approach, this has only recently come to be supported by browsers that support SVG natively. Safari 3.1, Opera 9.5, and Firefox 3.5 and higher all support native rendering of SVG files linked from an `img` element:

```
<img src="../images/image.svg"
alt="a description of the image "/>
```

For older versions of these browsers—and browsers such as Internet Explorer that don't support SVG embedding via the `img` element—the `object` element, which we saw in Chapter 3, is designed for embedding just about any kind of content. Here's how we'd link to the SVG image using an `object` element:

```
<object type="image/svg+xml" data="../images/image.svg"
        width="500px" height="500px">
        <p>Unfortunately your browser can't display this
        image. You might try installing an
<a href="http://www.adobe.com/svg/viewer/install/main.html"
>SVG plug-in</a></p>
</object>
```

So is there a difference between these two approaches, except that the latter is more widely supported in browsers? Well, yes. SVG included via the `object` element is included in the HTML document's DOM, allowing it to be scripted. SVG included via an `img` element is *not* included in the DOM—well, the `img` element is, but the SVG itself isn't.

Inline SVG

The second, more challenging way of including SVG in a page is putting the actual SVG into the code of the page itself. The challenge is that this is only possible with XHTML, not with HTML. This is one of the few cases in which the distinction between HTML and XHTML has real impact. For the most part, developers consider HTML and XHTML to be identical except for some very minor syntactic differences, and this distinction is usually accurate enough. Indeed, as we saw in Chapter 3, almost all XHTML is served as text/html for reasons of compatibility and practicality, which means that even browsers that have an XML parser treat documents served as text/html with XHTML syntax and `DOCTYPE` as HTML.

But, inline SVG can't be contained within an HTML 4 document, only in an XHTML document. Real XML parsers, like those found in Safari and Firefox, take into account the MIME type of a document (as sent by the sever), not just its DOCTYPE and syntax, when determining its real nature. So, unless the document containing our inline SVG is being served as application/xml or application/xml+xhtml and has an XHTML DOCTYPE—and is syntactically correct—the SVG won't be displayed.

But, there's yet another complicating factor. Remember, if we serve XHTML as application/xml, Internet Explorer will simply display the markup, rather than rendering the document. So if we serve the XHTML correctly for browsers that have real XML support, we'll not only stop Internet Explorer from displaying the SVG, but from displaying the document at all.

There are ways to specify a MIME type of text/html for Internet Explorer and application/xml for other browsers, but these methods depend on the server being used to serve your documents, and are beyond the scope of the book, but we do have links to resources for this at the end of the book. It is possible, but it's much more complicated than embedding SVG, and so linking to SVG files is typically the preferable option.

Inline vs. Embedded SVG

Given all these complications, is there an advantage in using inline over embedded SVG? If you want to expose the SVG elements via the DOM for scripting purposes, as long as you use the object element, embedding is little different from using inline SVG. There are one or two complications: when you use embedding, the SVG element is the child of an object element, whereas when the SVG is inline, it is the child of the element in the HTML it's contained by.

There's also some suggestion that embedding uses more memory, because with an embedded SVG document via the object element, browsers create a whole SVG document in the DOM, and this produces much more memory overhead than if the SVG element is simply part of the HTML document. This would be something to consider carefully if you are embedding several SVG documents in a single page—or in the context of mobile browsers, which even at the best of times tend to run on devices with relatively little memory.

SVG Browser Support

There are many factors to consider when it comes to SVG support in browsers. First, does a browser support SVG natively or require a plug-in? Firefox 3.5,

Safari 3.1, and Opera 9.5 all natively render SVG, and do not require a plug-in. Older versions of these browsers, and all versions of Internet Explorer up to at least version 8, require a plug-in to render SVG.

The second factor to consider is how the SVG is included—is it embedded or inline? Browsers that support native rendering also support embedding SVG via the `img` element. All browsers support embedding via the `object` element, though those without native support require a plug-in to do so. Inline SVG is only supported by browsers with native SVG rendering and when a document is true XHTML—valid markup, with an XHTML `DOCTYPE`, and served as XML.

With a bit of effort, it's possible to use SVG content in all common browsers. Let's summarize all these different aspects of SVG support.

Browser Support for SVG

Browser	Plug-in required	Embed via `img`	Embed via `object`	Inline
Internet Explorer	Yes	No	Yes	No
Safari 3.1+	No	Yes	Yes	Yes
Firefox 3.5+	No	Yes	Yes	Yes
Opera 9.5+	No	Yes	Yes	Yes

SVG and Internet Explorer

While SVG is not, as we've seen, supported natively in Internet Explorer (even version 8), it will be rendered by that browser when a plug-in is available for rendering SVG content. There is however, another way of using SVG while working around this limitation of Internet Explorer. Internet Explorer supports its own vector graphics format, VML, and the two languages are sufficiently similar that it's possible to deliver VML-formatted content for Internet Explorer and SVG content for browsers that support SVG. (There are also tools that can convert from one format to another or save as either format.)

A second option is to use one of several JavaScript vector graphics libraries that use SVG when it is supported in a browser and VML when a page is viewed in Internet Explorer, or use Flash, or Silverlight in Internet Explorer when these are available.

SVG Support Libraries

Raphaël by Dmitry Baranovskiy (**raphaeljs.com**) provides a JavaScript API for rendering objects and other features of SVG.

Drawbacks of this approach are that it requires JavaScript to be enabled, and that it uses a programmatic interface via JavaScript, rather than SVG markup. So instead of markup like this:

```
<circle cx="50" cy="40" r="10" stroke="#666" fill="#fff" />
```

we'd have JavaScript that looked like this:

```
var paper = Raphael(10, 50, 320, 200);

// Creates circle at x = 50, y = 40, with radius 10

var circle = paper.circle(50, 40, 10);
```

Despite being written with JavaScript, Raphaël in fact creates SVG—or VML, for IE, even when a plug-in for SVG is available—so the objects it creates are in the DOM and can be accessed via JavaScript. You can think of it as an alternate, JavaScript-based syntax for creating SVG.

SVG Web

A different, and very promising (though still alpha-stage) project from Brad Neuberg at Google, SVG Web (**code.google.com/p/svgweb**), uses a different approach. You simply link to a JavaScript library, and in browsers that support SVG, the native engine is used to render inline or embedded SVG; in those that don't have native support (and in particular Internet Explorer), Flash is used to render the SVG.

Serving SVG

Most browsers that support SVG will not render SVG files served as anything other than with a MIME type of "image/svg+xml." The most common cause of embedded SVG files failing to render is that they're being served with incorrect types, usually as text.

Beyond SVG

As we've seen, we now have several optimized bitmap formats to choose from, along with SVG for vector illustrations. So are there any needs that these existing formats can't meet? Once again, the answer is "yes"—or at least, "maybe."

Websites and web applications sometimes need to generate images "on the fly." None of the commonly supported bitmap formats are suitable for this—the best we can do with bitmap images is to generate new images on the back-end and update the images in the browser using JavaScript. SVG *does* allow us to manipulate the SVG DOM, changing properties of SVG elements or even adding and removing SVG elements with JavaScript, but DOM manipulation is memory intensive and can result in performance problems.

Although we can use SVG for dynamically generated images, HTML5's **canvas** element was developed specifically to allow for dynamically created images via JavaScript.

The HTML5 canvas Element

Originally developed by Apple as part of their Dashboard widget platform for Mac OS X, the **canvas** element is now supported in WebKit-based browsers, Firefox 1.5 and higher, and Opera 9 and higher, as well as being part of the HTML5 draft specification. Although the element is not supported in Internet Explorer 8, there are JavaScript libraries that allow you to write the same JavaScript for all these browsers to generate images dynamically. These libraries serve **canvas** to browsers that support it, and VML or Flash to Internet Explorer. We cover these libraries later in the chapter.

Using canvas

The key to the **canvas** element is a unique DOM interface that lets developers use JavaScript to draw shapes, fill regions, and perform other graphics operations on a resolution-dependent bitmap canvas. We'll look at some of this API in detail in a moment.

There are two distinct aspects to using the **canvas** elements:

- Add a **canvas** element to an HTML document.
- Use JavaScript with the canvas DOM interface to draw the graphics we want.

Let's tackle these in order.

Immediate Mode Graphics

The **canvas** element provides what is called *immediate mode* rendering. This means that each time a line, curve, shape, and so on needs to be drawn, JavaScript must explicitly perform the operation.

SVG, on the other hand, uses *retained mode rendering*. In this mode, once a model has been defined—say, a red square of a certain size—then the browser "knows" about the red square and can draw it as required.

Immediate mode rendering is typically faster, and less memory intensive, but often more work for the developer, as we'll see later in the chapter when we compare SVG and the canvas in detail.

Adding the *canvas* Element

We can add a **canvas** element to a document by including the element as part of the HTML markup, or by programmatically adding it when required using JavaScript.

If we insert it directly in the markup, the **canvas** element looks like this:

```
<canvas id="prices-graph" width="150" height="150">
  <img src="images/latest-prices-graph.png" width="150"
  height="150" alt="Latest pork belly futures prices"/>
</canvas>
```

We've used a fallback image for browsers that don't support **canvas** (much like the fallback for **object**, **video**, and **audio**), but there is a complicating factor to consider. In versions of Safari prior to 4, **canvas** was an empty element (like **img**). So in older versions of Safari, the fallback content will be rendered *in addition to*, rather than instead of the **canvas** element. Safari users tend to upgrade quickly, so this may not be a problem for very long, but it's worth considering how many of your visitors use Safari 3 or older. If lots of your users are still rocking old versions of Safari, you should probably add the **canvas** element using JavaScript, rather than putting it in the document markup. (Since JavaScript is already required for using **canvas**, the usual downside of JavaScript—excluding users—doesn't apply, since non-JavaScript users are excluded to begin with.)

In the preceding example, we've set a `width` and `height` for the **canvas** element. If we don't explicitly set these, the default height of a **canvas** element is 150px and the default width 300px. These properties can be changed using CSS, but if you do so, the graphics drawn into the canvas will be scaled accordingly. For example, if the original height and width are 150px, and we use CSS to set these to 300px, if we draw a line from 0,0 to 150,150, our line will be a diagonal not from the top-left corner to the midpoint of the canvas, but from the top left to the bottom right. In essence, coordinates of a **canvas** element scaled with CSS are also scaled by the same amount as the element. The easiest way to manage this complex situation is to use JavaScript, rather than CSS, to set the `height` and `width` of a canvas explicitly. If we use JavaScript instead of CSS to set the `height` and `width` of a canvas whose original height and width are 150px to 300px, drawing a line from 0,0 to 150,150 will now draw a diagonal from the top-left corner to the midpoint of the canvas.

If we were to view our page so far in a browser that supports **canvas**, we'd see... well, nothing. By default, the canvas is completely transparent. Now we need to use JavaScript and the canvas DOM interface to draw our graphics.

Getting a Drawing Context

To draw graphics with the canvas, we need to get a *drawing context* from the **canvas** element. At present, there is only one type of context, 2D rendering, though there are experimental 3D rendering contexts in some browsers, and the HTML5 specification suggests that an Open 3GL–based 3D context will be part of the specification at some stage.

We get a drawing context like this:

```
var theCanvas = document.getElementById('prices-graph');
var theContext = theCanvas.getContext('2d');
```

The preceding code creates a variable called **theCanvas** by calling the DOM method **getElementById** on the **document** object of the DOM, which should be familiar from Chapter 5. We then simply ask **theCanvas** for its drawing context called **2d**. (The method **getContext** on the **canvas** element is part of the HTML5 DOM specification for **canvas**.)

Don't Fear the JavaScript

We haven't covered much JavaScript in this book so far, but this is one place where it is absolutely required—to use the canvas, you must use at least some JavaScript. But, even if you've never used JavaScript before, don't be put off. You can do a good deal with the canvas without having to be a hardcore JavaScript programmer.

In Chapter 5, we also introduced the concept of unobtrusive JavaScript. One aspect of this practice is testing for the availability of a feature of the DOM before trying to use it. (Using an unsupported feature will cause an error that different browsers handle in different ways, some of which can be confusing to users. We want to avoid this.) In this case, we can detect support for the **canvas** element by testing to see whether the **getContext** method is supported:

```
var theCanvas = document.getElementById('prices-graph');
if (theCanvas.getContext) {
  var theContext = theCanvas.getContext('2d');
}

else {
//if the canvas element isn't supported we handle that
here
}
```

Drawing with the Context

Now we get to the fun part—doing the actual drawing. We don't have the luxury of being able to go into great detail about all of the functionality provided by the canvas when it comes to drawing, but we'll look at the core concepts and then take an overview of what can be done.

The Canvas Coordinate Space

The canvas has a *coordinate space* or *grid*, that starts in the top-left corner of the element and extends right and down [**16.5**]. In the top left, the coordinates are x=0 (horizontal coordinates) and y=0 (vertical coordinates). As you go to the right, the x coordinate values increase in value; as you go left, they decrease.

Similarly, as you go down the element, the y coordinate values increase, and as you go up the element, the values decrease.

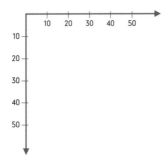

16.5

The canvas coordinate space

Shapes and Paths

It's trickier to draw shapes in the canvas than in SVG, because unlike SVG, which offers a number of *primitive* shapes such as circles and ellipses, the canvas offers only the rectangle. But we can draw other shapes in the canvas by combining paths.

Rectangles

With rectangles, we can:

- Clear a rectangle, which erases a rectangular part of the canvas, and anything already drawn there, but not anything "behind" the canvas, such as text in a paragraph that the canvas overlays
- Fill a rectangle with a color, pattern, or gradient
- *Stroke* the rectangle (draw the edges of a rectangle)

We'll do this with three functions of the 2D context—**clearRect**, **fillRect**, and **strokeRect**.

For example, to outline a rectangle that is 50px on each edge, and centered at 75px, 75px, we'd use:

```
theContext.strokeRect(75,75,50,50)
```

A context has a *fill* and a *stroke style*, each of which specifies a color, gradient, or pattern to be used for stroking or filling a path or rectangle. Although gradients and patterns are too involved to examine in detail here, we would set the color of the current **strokeStyle** for the context like this:

```
theContext.strokeStyle="rgba(255,0,0,.5)"
```

We can use any color we would use with CSS as a string value for the **strokeStyle** (and **fillStyle**). If we want to draw a red outlined rectangle and then a blue outlined rectangle, we'd set the context's stroke color to red, draw the first rectangle, then set the color to blue, then draw the second rectangle.

Paths

As noted earlier, any shape other than a rectangle has to be drawn using paths. Here's how to draw a path:

1. Begin the path with the **context.beginPath** method.
2. Draw one or more subpaths using one of a number of possible methods, including **lineTo**, **arc**, **quadraticCurveTo**, and **bezierCurveTo**.
3. Fill or stroke the area bounded by the path with **context.fill** or **context.stroke**.
4. Close the path with **context.closePath**. A path must be closed before a new one can be started.

Once again, we won't go into these various methods in detail, but here's a quick overview of the various path-drawing methods you can use in the canvas. Imagine that there's an imaginary "pen" that draws on the canvas. We can use the following canvas methods to draw with the pen:

- **moveTo**—Moves the pen to a given x and y position on the canvas
- **lineTo**—Draws a line from the current pen location to a specified x and y position on the canvas, which becomes the pen's new location
- **arc** and **arcTo**—Allow us to draw paths along the arc of a circle
- **quadraticCurveTo**—Draws a path from the current pen location to a specified location along a quadratic curve
- **bezierCurveTo**—Draws a path from the current pen location to a specified location along a Bézier curve

Lines

We draw lines using the **moveTo**, **lineTo**, and other methods we've just seen, but there are a number of context properties we can use to change *how* our lines are drawn. Among others, we can set:

- **lineWidth**—Specifies how wide the lines will be
- **lineCap**—Specifies how the end of a line should be drawn; has a value of butt, square, or round
- **lineJoin**—Specifies how two joining lines should be joined; has a value of round, bevel, or miter

Text

The original implementation of the canvas in Safari did not allow for the drawing of text, but this feature is part of the HTML5 specification and is supported by Safari from version 4 and in Firefox 3.5 and higher. This means that for some time, visitors to a site may be using a browser with the canvas enabled but without support for text rendering by the **canvas** element. The intelligent use of images—as we'll see in a moment, you can in addition to shapes and paths draw images into a canvas—with unobtrusive JavaScript techniques may allow for a simple approach that uses the **canvas** element, with images in place of the strings where text in the canvas is not supported.

Where text is supported, in the same way we can draw paths and shapes we can *draw* (or *render*) a string of text on the canvas using the **fillText** and **strokeText** methods of the context. For example:

```
theContext.fillText("this is the text to fill", 50, 50)
```

draws the string "this is the text to fill" starting from the point 50px, 50px. You can also set the font, text alignment, color, and other text styles using properties of the context.

Text rendered by a **canvas** element is far less accessible than text marked up in an HTML document. **canvas**-rendered text is not part of the DOM, and it is mostly or entirely invisible to search engines. One way of exposing the text to the DOM, assistive devices, and search engines is to include structured text inside the **canvas** element. This text would be accessible to search engines and via the DOM, but not displayed by browsers that support the canvas. Well, almost. There's a complicating factor with Safari 3, which, as we saw treats **canvas** as an empty element, and so it will display this additional text. The best solution to this is to use JavaScript to add the canvas element to the DOM, and in Safari 3 (yes, here we are browser sniffing, on rare occasions it may be unavoidable!), don't add the additional content.

Transparency

You can use transparency with the canvas in two ways. You can either:

- Use RGBa colors for fill and stroke colors and set the **globalAlpha** property of the context to a value from 0 to 1 (this alpha channel value will apply to any operations you perform while the value is set).

- Change the **globalAlpha** value between operations to have different alpha values for different fills, strokes, and so on.

Transformations

We saw briefly in Chapter 13 that CSS3 now features "transform" properties that can scale, rotate, skew, and otherwise transform HTML elements. The canvas contexts can also be transformed in similar ways—for example, to rotate or move horizontally and vertically the drawn contents of the canvas.

Images

We can use images directly in the canvas—that is, we can draw an image into the canvas. To do so, we'll need to use an **img** from the DOM, rather than just a URL. So we'll first need to use a DOM method like **document.getElementById** to get the image element. Then we can draw the image like this:

```
theImage=document.getElementById('logo');
theContext.drawImage(theImage, 50, 50)
```

This draws the image of the element with an **id** of logo at 50px, 50px. There are more sophisticated ways to use **drawImage**, including scaling the image up or down and putting only part of the source image onto the canvas. You'll find resources for these methods at the end of this book.

Shadows

Anything we can draw (paths, rectangles, text, and so on) with the canvas, we can draw with a *shadow property*. This looks similar to the method for setting fill and stroke colors. We give the context one or more of the following values:

- **shadowOffsetX**—A pixel value for how far to the right (positive values) or left (negative values) of the object the shadow should be drawn
- **shadowOffsetY**—A pixel value for how far below (positive values) or above (negative values) the object the shadow should be drawn
- **shadowBlur**—A pixel value that specifies, like with CSS, how blurred the shadow should be—the higher the value, the more blurred the shadow
- **shadowColor**—A color for the shadow

When these properties are set for a context, everything drawn on the canvas will have these shadow values. (You'll recognize this shadow model from CSS text and box shadows.)

And More…

There's even more to the canvas than we've discussed. Here are just a few of the additional possibilities:

- We can directly manipulate the image data of a **canvas** element, pixel-by-pixel.
- We can create linear and radial gradients and use them as the fill and stroke styles in place of colors.
- We can create patterns based on images to be used as fill and stroke style.
- We can use the **canvas** element's many compositing styles to specify how new content is drawn onto existing content in the canvas.
- We can use *clipping paths*, which determine where new content is drawn; for example, you can create a circular clipping path, thus mandating that content be drawn only into this circle.

The canvas provides very powerful drawing primitives, though it's likely that most developers will prefer to use a JavaScript library that provides features such as more complex shapes, or specialized functions for tasks like graphing.

Libraries also help target Internet Explorer, which as of version 8 does not support **canvas**. These libraries include:

- **Processing.js (www.processingjs.org)**—An implementation of the processing language designed for data visualization. Processing.js is also supported in Internet Explorer, using VML rather than the **canvas** element.

- **LiquidCanvas (www.ruzee.com/content/liquid-canvas)** is a plug-in for JQuery, which provides a higher-level (and so easier to use) programming interface to the canvas API.

- **ExplorerCanvas (ExCanvas) (code.google.com/p/explorercanvas)**— A simple way to get **canvas** support in Internet Explorer, developed by Google, and used widely by them.

- **RGraph (www.rgraph.net)**—A library that uses the canvas to create sophisticated charts and graphs.

Browser Support for *canvas*

Browser	IE (all versions)	Safari 3	Safari 4	Firefox 1.5+	Firefox 3.5	Opera 9
Basic canvas support	No (yes with ExCanvas)	Yes	Yes	Yes	Yes	Yes
Canvas can contain fallback content	Yes	No	Yes	Yes	Yes	Yes
Canvas text rendering	No (yes with ExCanvas)	No	Yes	No	Yes	No

canvas Use Cases

Anytime we need to use dynamically generated images, we should consider using **canvas**. Common examples include:

- **Graphs and charts**—With **canvas**, these can easily be generated from content found, for example, in a data table.

- **Games**—Game graphics in the canvas can be animated using JavaScript, making **canvas** useful for the kind of games usually developed using Flash.

- **Applications**—Mozilla Labs' browser-based coding tool Bespin uses **canvas** to render its UI and the text you edit. (Mozilla chose **canvas** over HTML/CSS for text rendering due to performance issues with large text files.) Some developers are concerned by the accessibility problems associated with this approach—as we saw, text in the canvas is not accessible via the DOM. There are potential workarounds for this challenge being explored, and there is work by the developers of HTML5 to address this accessibility difficulty. Ben Galbraith, one of the lead developers of Bespin, discusses some of these issues here: **benzilla.galbraiths. org/2009/02/18/bespin-and-canvas-part-2.**

We've made reference to various aspects of browser support for `canvas` throughout this section. The preceding table brings together the information we've discussed and covers browser support in all major browsers and versions that are currently in widespread use.

Workarounds for IE

Several JavaScript libraries provide support for `canvas` in Internet Explorer. The best-known is ExplorerCanvas (commonly known as ExCanvas). Developed at Google, it's widely used, well maintained, and used extensively in Google web applications.

Using ExCanvas is straightforward: just include a link to an excanvas.js file when the browser is IE, like this:

```
<!—[if IE]><script src="excanvas.js"></script><![endif]—>
```

Your `canvas` code should now work in Internet Explorer as well as browsers that support `canvas`, though you shouldn't expect full compatibility with all the features of `canvas` in Internet Explorer. Dynamically generated `canvas` elements (`canvas` elements created with JavaScript) need some extra steps to be usable, and as of the time of writing, ExCanvas didn't allow for text rendering, though this feature is slated for inclusion in the future. You'll also notice subtle and not-so-subtle differences in IE, because ExCanvas uses VML to emulate the `canvas` element.

All these differences and more are documented at the ExplorerCanvas Google Code site: **code.google.com/p/explorercanvas/wiki/Instructions.**

The Canvas vs. SVG

Though they produce similar effects, the Canvas and SVG are designed for quite different tasks. Some of the key differences:

- As mentioned earlier, SVG uses retained mode rendering, meaning that the browser takes care of rendering SVG objects, while the canvas uses immediate mode, meaning that your code needs to do all the drawing. If, for example, you need to rotate a rectangle in front of other graphics on the canvas, each step of this animation must be redrawn, not just for the rectangle, but for the graphics that the rectangle overlays as well.

- SVG elements are part of the DOM unless the SVG is embedded in an `img` element. The canvas itself is part of the DOM, but none of the graphics drawn on the canvas are.

- It is much easier to create accessible content with SVG than with `canvas`.

- SVG provides more primitives, shapes, and built-in animation, whereas `canvas` is a low-level toolset in which complex shapes and animation must be implemented with JavaScript.

- The `canvas` element is part of the HTML5 specification, whereas SVG is a stand-alone markup language derived from XML. SVG can, however, be used inline with XHTML, and HTML5.

The Wrap

Web developers have long been restricted to using HTML, CSS, and a handful of bitmap image formats, along with plug-in technologies like Flash, to develop sites. Rapidly maturing support for SVG and the canvas, as well as the development of libraries that enable their use in Internet Explorer, gives us access to much more sophisticated standards-based tools for both graphic design and the visual representation of data. And unlike in the "bad old days" of the browser wars, these innovations—like those we are seeing in HTML5 and CSS3—are taking place within the framework of web standards, ensuring greater interoperability between browsers and less uncertainty for developers. We don't have to "pick winners" like we did during the browser wars—standards are the winner.

This is an enormous change in just a few short years, and it's due to several factors: the diligence of browser developers, the advocacy of the many web designers and developers who've worked to make this standards-based approach the cornerstone of professional web design and development, and the ongoing custodianship of the web by the W3C.

In the 16 or so years I've been developing websites, I genuinely believe that this is the most positive period yet for the web's underlying technologies. We learned a lot from the browser wars, and this time around, there's considerable goodwill on all sides to ensure we don't repeat our old mistakes. As a result, we're finally seeing the maturity and widespread adoption of technologies that have been in development for many years.

We are also seeing the rise of the web beyond the desktop—on mobile devices, televisions, game consoles, and elsewhere—the promise of which I believe will far outstrip the value of the web we've seen to date. I also believe that the technologies we've covered in this book—HTML, CSS, JavaScript, SVG, and more—will be the way we develop not just for the web, but almost all user interfaces in the coming years, whether they're for ATMs, inflight entertainment devices, microwave ovens, or even devices that may never even be connected to the Internet.

Having come to grips with these technologies in this book, I hope you feel equipped for this coming revolution. I'm sure we'll look back on the end of the first decade of the 21st century as the end of the infancy of the web. We'll doubtless smile at the naivety of what we then called Web 2.0, but I think we'll also realize that this is where the seeds for our future web were sown: powerful standards with widespread cross-browser, cross-device support, and all the developments they will enable.

Resources

Chapter 1 Before You Begin

Web Development Resources

- https://developer.mozilla.org/en/Web_Development
- http://westciv.com
- http://www.sitepoint.com
- http://code.google.com/doctype

Chapter 2 Philosophies and Techniques

A Dao of Web Design

- http://www.westciv.com/style_master/house/good_oil/dao/index.html
- http://www.alistapart.com/articles/dao

Progressive Enhancement

- http://www.alistapart.com/articles/
  understandingprogressiveenhancement

- http://www.sitepoint.com/blogs/2009/09/22/
  progressive-enhancement-graceful-degradation-basics

Separation of Markup, Presentation, and Behavior

- http://www.alistapart.com/articles/behavioralseparation

Chapter 3   Markup

Specifications

- HTML 4.01—**http://www.w3.org/TR/html4**
- XHTML 1.0—**http://www.w3.org/TR/xhtml1**
- XHTML 1.1—**http://www.w3.org/TR/xhtml11**
- HTML5—**http://www.w3.org/TR/html5**

XHTML

- **https://developer.mozilla.org/en/XHTML**

Video for Everyone

- **http://camendesign.com/code/video_for_everybody**

SWFObject, JavaScript Object Embedding

- **http://code.google.com/p/swfobject/wiki/documentation**

Macromedia Flash Objects

- **http://kb2.adobe.com/cps/415/tn_4150.html**

Iframes

- **https://developer.mozilla.org/en/HTML/Element/iframe**
- **http://softwareas.com/cross-domain-communication-with-iframes**

Website Performance

- **http://developer.yahoo.com/performance/rules.html**
- **http://stevesouders.com**

Image Compression

- http://www.stubbornella.org/content/2008/09/30/new-tool-easy-image-optimization-with-smush-it

Chapter 4   Presentation

Specifications

- CSS1—http://www.w3.org/TR/CSS1
- CSS2.1—http://www.w3.org/TR/CSS21
- CSS3—http://www.w3.org/Style/CSS/current-work

CSS 3 Info

- http://www.css3.info

CSS Guide

- http://westciv.com/wiki/CSS_Guide

Quick CSS Tutorials

- http://westciv.com/style_master/house/tutorials/quick/index.html

CSS Compatibility

- Yahoo Graded Browser Support—http://developer.yahoo.com/yui/articles/gbs
- Methods for Testing in Multiple Versions of IE—http://www.communitymx.com/content/article.cfm?page=1&cid=8897D
- Litmus Testing Software—http://litmusapp.com
- Multiple IEs in Windows—http://labs.insert-title.com/Multiple-IEs-in-Windows_article795.aspx
- Microsoft Virtual PC—http://www.microsoft.com/windows/virtual-pc/default.aspx
- http://msdn.microsoft.com/en-us/library/cc351024(VS.85).aspx
- http://westciv.com/wiki

Chapter 5   The DOM

Introductory DOM concepts

- **http://www.digital-web.com/articles/the_document_object_model**

JavaScript Statements

- **http://quirksmode.org/js/state.html**

DOM References and Specifications

- **https://developer.mozilla.org/en/DOM**
- **http://www.w3.org/DOM**

JavaScript and DOM Security

- **http://www.howtocreate.co.uk/tutorials/javascript/security**
- **http://yuiblog.com/blog/2007/04/10/json-and-browser-security**
- **http://www.webdirections.org/resources/wdn08-douglas-crockford**

JavaScript Libraries

- Dojo Toolkit—**http://www.dojotoolkit.org**
- jQuery—**http://jquery.com**
- MooTools—**http://mootools.net**
- Prototype—**http://prototypejs.org**
- Scriptaculous—**http://script.aculo.us**
- Others—**http://www.w3avenue.com/2009/05/25/list-of-really-useful-javascript-libraries**

Advanced DOM Scripting

- **http://jspro.org/toc**
- **http://ejohn.org/apps/learn**

Chapter 6   Accessibility

Accessibility and the Law (United Kingdom)

- http://www.webcredible.co.uk/user-friendly-resources/web-accessibility/uk-website-legal-requirements.shtml

Accessibility and the Law (United States)

- http://jimthatcher.com/law-target.htm
- http://joeclark.org/book/sashay/serialization/AppendixA.html
- http://www.w3.org/WAI/Policy
- http://www.caslon.com.au/accessibilityguide2.htm

Accessibility and the Law (Australia)

- http://www.hreoc.gov.au/disability_rights/webaccess/index.htm

Audio and Video Captioning

- http://www.webaim.org/techniques/captions
- http://www.sloan-c.org/cannect/projectone/advice/video-audio.php

WCAG 2

- http://www.w3.org/TR/WCAG
- http://www.webaim.org/standards/wcag/checklist
- http://boagworld.com/accessibility/video-introduction-to-wcag-2

Accessibility

- http://juicystudio.com
- http://jimthatcher.com
- http://www.paciellogroup.com

Chapter 7   Working With, Around, and Against Browsers

IE 8 Compatibility Modes

- http://blogs.msdn.com/ie/archive/2008/08/27/introducing-compatibility-view.aspx

- http://farukat.es/journal/2009/05/245-ie8-and-the-x-ua-compatible-situation
- http://msdn.microsoft.com/en-us/ie/cc405106.aspx

Bugs and Bug Fixing

- http://www.communitymx.com/content/article.cfm?cid=C37E0
- http://www.webcredible.co.uk/user-friendly-resources/css/internet-explorer.shtml
- http://www.virtuosimedia.com/tutorials/ultimate-ie6-cheatsheet-how-to-fix-25-internet-explorer-6-bugs

Position is Everything

- http://www.positioniseverything.net

Westciv Wiki

- http://westciv.com/wiki

Chapter 8   Best Practices for Modern Markup

Improving Code Readability

- http://www.smashingmagazine.com/2008/05/02/improving-code-readability-with-css-styleguides
- http://www.graphicrating.com/2009/02/23/css-code-readability-tips

ECML

- http://xml.coverpages.org/IETF-RFC-4112-ECMLv2.txt
- http://xml.coverpages.org/ecml.html

Microformats

- http://microformats.org/get-started
- http://microformatique.com/book
- http://erincaton.ca/media/cheatsheetHandout.pdf
- http://suda.co.uk/projects/microformats/cheatsheet

Oomph JavaScript Library

- http://visitmix.com/lab/oomph

Optimus Microformats Transformer/Validator

- http://microformatique.com/optimus

Browser Extensions

- https://addons.mozilla.org/en-US/firefox/addon/4106

Site Performance Improvement

- http://developer.yahoo.com/performance/rules.html
- http://stevesouders.com
- http://stubbornella.org/content

Chapter 9   CSS-Based Page Layouts

Vertical Centering

- http://www.jakpsatweb.cz/css/css-vertical-center-solution.html
- http://hicksdesign.co.uk/journal/how-to-vertical-centering-with-css

One True Layout

- http://www.positioniseverything.net/articles/onetruelayout

Faux Columns

- http://www.alistapart.com/articles/fauxcolumns

Faux Fluid Columns

- http://www.communitymx.com/content/article.cfm?cid=afc58

Position is Everything

- http://www.positioniseverything.net

Chapter 10   CSS Resets and Frameworks

CSS Resets

- http://meyerweb.com/eric/thoughts/2007/05/01/reset-reloaded
- http://developer.yahoo.com/yui/3/cssreset

CSS Frameworks

- 960 Grid System—http://960.gs
- Blueprint—http://www.blueprintcss.org
- Typogridphy—http://csswizardry.com/typogridphy
- http://speckyboy.com/2008/03/28/top-12-css-frameworks-and-how-to-understand-them
- http://www.smashingmagazine.com/2007/09/21/css-frameworks-css-reset-design-from-scratch

Chapter 11   HTML5

HTML5 Specification

- http://dev.w3.org/html5/spec/Overview.html

HTML5 Controversy

- http://www.brucelawson.co.uk/2009/this-millenium-in-html-5-politics

Video & Audio

- http://www.brucelawson.co.uk/2009/accessibility-of-html5-video-and-audio-elements
- http://blog.gingertech.net/2008/12/12/attaching-subtitles-to-html5-video

Further Reading

- http://html5doctor.com

Chapter 12   CSS3 and the Future of CSS

CSS Compatibility

- http://westciv.com/wiki

Further Reading

- http://hacks.mozilla.org/2009/06/css3-of-type
- http://www.456bereastreet.com/archive/200601/
  css_3_selectors_explained
- http://CSS3.info
- http://designshack.co.uk/tutorials/introduction-to-css3-
  part-1-what-is-it

Chapter 13   New Properties in CSS3

- http://westciv.com/tools
- http://CSS3.info

Chapter 14   Targeting Media with CSS

- http://www.w3.org/TR/css3-mediaqueries
- https://developer.mozilla.org/En/CSS/Media_queries

Chapter 15   Web Fonts

Converting Fonts to EOT

- http://www.kirsle.net/wizards/ttf2eot.cgi
- http://www.microsoft.com/typography/web/embedding/weft3/
  overview.aspx
- http://edward.oconnor.cx/2009/07/how-to-create-eot-files-without-
  microsoft-weft

EOT Fonts

- http://fontembedding.com

Further Reading

- http://www.fontsquirrel.com
- http://openfontlibrary.org
- http://lists.w3.org/Archives/Public/www-font/2009AprJun/0000.html
- http://blog.fontembedding.com
- http://www.theleagueofmoveabletype.com

Chapter 16   SVG and the Canvas

SVG Basics

- http://articles.techrepublic.com.com/5100-10878_11-5246919.html
- http://www.w3.org/TR/SVG
- http://www.w3.org/Graphics/SVG

Canvas Basics

- https://developer.mozilla.org/en/Canvas_tutorial
- http://www.whatwg.org/specs/web-apps/current-work/multipage/the-canvas-element.html

SVG Animations

- http://www.w3.org/TR/SVG/animate.html

Configuring Servers

- https://developer.mozilla.org/En/Properly_Configuring_Server_MIME_Types
- http://devedge-temp.mozilla.org/viewsource/2003/mime-types/index_en.html

Images in the Canvas

- https://developer.mozilla.org/En/Canvas_tutorial/Using_images

Index